Transpersonal Books

JAMES FADIMAN, *General Editor*

Transpersonal Books explore the psychology of consciousness, and possibilities for transcendence through altered states of consciousness, paranormal phenomena, spiritual disciplines, and other modes of extended awareness.

C. WILLIAM HENDERSON, an architect and former head of lunar base planning for NASA, delved into the realm of transpersonal psychology long before it had that name. This interest culminated in his returning to college to study psychology and pursue a new career in psycho-spiritual growth.

AWAKENING

Ways to
Psychospiritual Growth

C. WILLIAM HENDERSON

A SPECTRUM BOOK

PRENTICE-HALL, INC., Englewood Cliffs, New Jersey

Library of Congress Cataloging in Publication Data

Henderson, C William.
  Awakening.

  (A Spectrum book) (Transpersonal books)
  1. Self-realization—Societies, etc. 2. Sects. 3. Religions. I. Title.
BP603.H46   291.4   75-11596
ISBN 0-13-055467-7
ISBN 0-13-055459-6

© 1975 by C. William Henderson

A SPECTRUM BOOK

All rights reserved.
No part of this book may be reproduced
in any form or by any means
without permission in writing from the publisher.

10 9 8 7 6 5 4 3 2 1

Printed in the United States of America

PRENTICE-HALL INTERNATIONAL, INC., *London*
PRENTICE-HALL OF AUSTRALIA PTY., LTD., *Sydney*
PRENTICE-HALL OF CANADA, LTD., *Toronto*
PRENTICE-HALL OF INDIA PRIVATE LIMITED, *New Delhi*
PRENTICE-HALL OF JAPAN, INC., *Tokyo*
PRENTICE-HALL OF SOUTHEAST ASIA (PTE.) LTD., *Singapore*

CONTENTS

FOREWORD

American history is basically a saga of people concerned with external voyages. At first, the exploration, exploitation, and settlement of a new continent occupied their attention. This was followed by the development of industrial empires at home and the assertion of diplomatic power overseas. Then came the most distant ventures of all—the probes into outer space.

However, in recent years, a small but growing number of Americans have placed higher priority on internal events and inner growth. Some individuals view this in terms of a spiritual quest whereas others consider it a voyage of self-discovery or a search for personal fulfillment.

The roads taken to attain these goals vary. But of special appeal are those paths written about in this book—the quick and hazardous openings offered by LSD, the explosive encounters found in sensitivity training, the deep probes provided in Jungian types of therapy, and the metaphysical routes implicit in religious movements. Awareness of Eastern wisdom has helped facilitate the process of many seekers. Yoga, Zen, and other Oriental disciplines are all alternatives to consider, either in their original form or in the synthesis offered by many contemporary scholars.

In this book, C. William Henderson does not claim that one way is best for all pilgrims. Each person progresses along lines that are consistent with his or her motivation and interest. And the charm of this book is that it reflects not only the spectrum of inner growth processes, but also the kaleidoscopic world we live in. Indeed, there often seems to be chaos as traditional standards break down and disappear. At the same time, however, this confusion offers something for everyone.

So, a Reformation of Consciousness may well evolve as, for the first time in its history, the entire gamut of human hopes, aspirations, and teachings become available for us to grasp and to incorporate. C. William Henderson's book is a part of this Reformation and should shed light upon the roads being taken by so many curious travelers.

STANLEY KRIPPNER, Ph.D.
Humanistic Psychology Institute
San Francisco

PREFACE

This book is intended as a practical guide to modern growth methods in the United States and Canada. It defines many different ways and levels of self discovery which are presented to the reader by means of detailed descriptions of specific organizations representative of one or more growth or spiritual approaches to self-inquiry. The descriptions include each organization's background, what it teaches, what it costs, where the training is given, which groups provide instruction by correspondence. And they define the results that many participants, though not all, might reasonably expect to achieve. In addition to specific organization descriptions, a little theory, philosophy, religion and history is thrown in to fill out the big-picture. Hopefully this information is sufficiently well arranged that you will not only learn what each school specifically offers, but how each school compares with others and how each fits into the over-all spectrum of psycho-spiritual growth.

Methods and depths of self-understanding throughout North America are nearly limitless. Yet they cover a continuous spectrum. Some practitioners of self-inquiry prefer that their specific methods be considered as therapeutic or as geared toward growth. Those at the other end of the spectrum like to think of themselves as being involved with spiritual enlightenment or religious practices. Yet any practice that leads to inner personal or spiritual discovery, if pursued to its ultimate end, must eventually lead to observations of deeper realms that transcend your personal self. And these transcendental discoveries fall into that area of science now being called Transpersonal Psychology. But for centuries these same occurrences

and the practices that bring them about have been known as
mysticism.

The word "mysticism" scares some people. They associate it
with the dark and ominous practices of sorcery, black magic and
voodoo. They see it as inseparable from crystal-ball gazing,
demonology and spirit communication. Yet these and other practices more properly belong in the realm of the occult. They aren't
mysticism. Mysticism, in its purest form, is a profound science of
spirit. It's also a science of mind. It's an ancient practice of
awakening in all individuals the universal man that resides within
their psyches. And its ultimate goal is to fully experience that
universality.

There are over eight-thousand ways to awaken in North
America. Of that large number of growth, self-realization and
mystical organizations, only a fraction can be detailed in a single
book. Fortunately, of those eight-thousand, a well chosen few can
reasonably represent the spectrum of philosophies, methods and
prices in the field. Therefore, this book describes a limited number
of groups in depth while including many others in the appendix as
brief entries. Some organizations were excluded by their own
request or because they were noncommunicative. The Gurdjieff
groups are an example of both. Those selected for extensive
description are not necessarily superior to those getting lesser
attention, but they are probably better examples since they meet
one of the following three criteria. They may be large and well
known, thus making them accessible to great numbers of readers.
Or they might have exceptional merit due to some special
technique or philosophy. Lastly, a few spiritual centers, though
small and remotely located, still are so unique that the book would
be incomplete if they were not included. Other criteria for selection
were my own perversities and whims, though I hope to no great
extent. Then there is that ever present possibility that some groups
were just plain overlooked. If so, hopefully, they appear among the
150-plus entries in the appendix. My apologies to any group that
feels it has been slighted.

Many organizations in this book have overlapping goals and
practices. That made them difficult to classify. Since many organizations teach and explore the same realms, their inclusion in a
specific chapter is not necessarily based on what is *taught*, but more
on what is emphasized and the depth of psychic development

stressed. Actually, nearly every organization in the book covers a much broader range of mental and spiritual development than the chapter category might initially indicate.

Despite this time of inflation, the prices charged or expected as donations by the organizations have been included. Though the prices will change in the future, those indicated here will still be useful as indicators of relative cost. Mailing addresses and brief descriptions of all organizations discussed in the main text can be found in Appendix A along with similar data for many other groups. Correspondence course offerings are repeated in Appendix B for convenient comparison.

Every organization covered in depth in this book has considerable merit for someone. Yet we all differ in what appeals to us. If you already know what you want to achieve through self-realization, and are now seeking that special pathway just for you, while reading about the different ways available, you may recognize the ideal one. Or you may be intrigued by several organizations and try a few different approaches. But even if you have no deep longing to know yourself, perhaps now you will become inspired, or at least fascinated enough, to devote a little time to exploring and awakening to your inner being.

C.W.H.

Chapter 1

MEETING YOUR SUBCONSCIOUS

People who have explored their inner selves will tell you that to really understand your buried psyche, you have to experience it. You can't just read books about it or attend lectures. You have to feel it yourself with your conscious mind, with your awareness. How could a Polynesian islander, by reading a book, possibly know the crunch of boots on crusted snow; or the exhilaration of skis racing down a steep slope of hardpack; or the chill wind in his face; or the ignominious thump and icy sprawl when he catches a ski edge on a mogul? Nor can you understand your inner self unless you meet it face to face.

Sigmund Freud postulated that all people have three different levels of consciousness. Everyone is acquainted with what he called the "conscious." This is the part of your mind that reasons. It plans, it deducts, it is where the decisions are made. Then there is another part of your mind that controls all automatic functions of your body. It increases or reduces your heart beat, respiration and other functions, along with secreting juices when you need them. It wakes you up and puts you to sleep. This Freud called the "unconscious." But in between these two minds lies a strange form of mentation that seems to reason, but in an unusual way. And it is also the seat of emotion and is semi-independent. This Freud called the "preconscious," and it is the least understood of all your thinking equipment.

All three levels of mind blend like colors of the rainbow, one into the others. This is especially true of the little-understood unconscious and preconscious minds. For this reason and because there is seldom any reason to distinguish between them, many people for simplicity lump the two terms into a single one—"subconscious mind."

As with most strangers, it takes time to get acquainted with your subconscious. You will find it has its own motivations, its intimate secrets, and its separate will. It can even be stubborn at times. In fact, it often acts as an independent entity.

Lots of people have learned ways of communicating with their inner selves. A simple way is with a pendulum. You may already know about the technique, and may have used it to get answers to questions. But since you have probably neglected to follow through with the method, a little reminding doesn't hurt. If you have never done this before, you will be amazed at how your subconscious controls your body without your being aware of it.

Get yourself a weight like a ring and suspend it from a string eight inches long. Now hold the free end of the string between your thumb and forefinger. You will notice it is impossible to keep the pendulum from moving at least a little. Now if you imagine the pendulum swinging from side to side, you will be amazed to discover that within minutes it is doing just that. The same holds true if you imagine the pendulum moving in a circle, or to and from you. This is ideomotor response, subconscious control of your body. It doesn't take much imagination to see how you can follow up on this and work out a "yes" and "no" code with your subconscious to get back its answers to your questions. Sometimes you will be amazed by what it tells you.

Centuries ago the pendulum technique was refined by holding a pendulum over a circular design with letters around the perimeter. Appropriate pendulum swings could then spell out messages. In 1892 William Feld improved even this. He marked "yes" and "no" along with the alphabet on a slick, hard surface over which a sliding pointer could be moved by subconscious hand movements. He named this board after the French and German words for "yes"—_oui_ and _ja_. With experience, operators of the ouija board can get startling and sometimes extremely sage messages, often with amazing speed. More often the messages are just plain good common sense. The original manufacturers of the ouija board once queried their device on how to increase sales. The board answered simply "Make more ouija boards." They did.

Many people who use ouija boards believe the responses are due to spirit possession by deceased beings or guardian angels and demons. Scientists say no. It's all in your mind. But they do make concessions about what in your mind it is. Freud and other analysts discovered in the early 1900's that everyone has deeply hidden impulses and secretive *mental* demons that are itching to be heard and create mischief. Coupled to this they discovered an incredible inner wisdom that often appears like Divine inspiration.

Then there is automatic writing. This is the ability to touch pencil to paper with your mind completely blank while your hand briskly writes an intriguing message unknown to your conscious mind. Some adept automatic writers can do this while reading a book or conversing with other people, completely oblivious to what their hands are putting on paper until they read the message. Some people type their automatic messages. What is amazing about automatic writing is that the messages often come out entirely alien to the writer's way of expression . . . as if someone else did the writing. This, like the ouija board, leads some people to believe they are possessed, or at least guided by a spirit. The noted occult writer Ruth Montgomery thinks so. She claims her book *The World Beyond* was written this way when the deceased psychic Arthur Ford temporarily inhabited her body for brief periods every day to type the manuscript.

Again most scientists say "not so." Yet they find automatic writing is an impressive psychological tool. Los Angeles psychiatrist Anita Mühl encourages it for her patients. She probes their repressed memories this way. Dr. Mühl says that any normal person can learn to do automatic writing. But it takes perseverence.

That's not the only way your subconscious can communicate. It's not even the best way. It certainly isn't the way your subconscious prefers. Your subconscious thinks in terms of impressions, of concepts, of feelings. It prefers images to letters; it likes color and form over descriptions. A picture is worth a thousand words, it reasons; an image conveys so much. So, like an artist, its best method of communication is through vivid visual displays; through kaleidoscopes of hue and pattern projected on your mental screen; through magnificent, bizarre or terrifying dramas played on your psychic stage. That's what dreams are. They are your best means of imagery. That's why Freud called a dream "the royal road leading into the subconscious."

Dreams

It was Freud who systematically discovered that dreams reveal hidden impressions of your subconscious. Before his time dreams were thought to be instances of possession by demons, visitations from spirits or messages from the gods. Freud showed that they are basically your messages to yourself. In most cases these messages are presented with the mastery of a Broadway producer. But in a dream you are playwright, actor, and audience. And the casting is so perfect that, as you dream, the experiences are just as real to you then as your waking experience seems to you right now.

On rare occasions your dreams portray daily life with great accuracy. They don't differ much in content or excitement from daily living. Most people report them to be in black and white. But many dreams, though depicting daily life, seem absurd and confusing because they co-mingle day residues with repressed wish fulfillments. Often the meaning is disguised. It's telling you something your conscious doesn't want to face. Something that dares surface only in a dream. Your dream world is a world unto itself. It's a world of wishes, of fears, of cloak-and-dagger coverups, of eroticism, and of fond memories and loves. It is a world of symbols that your subconscious creates to express itself.

There is much wisdom in dreams. Psychiatrist Carl Jung believed a major purpose of dreams is to provide insight, at least insight for your subconscious. Your subconscious often worries about the same problems that your conscious does since it hears about them every day from your conscious. Since dreams tie in closely with your occupation, daily problems are often the subject matter, though this fact may be obscured. Unfinished activities are dreamed about more than completed ones. We all have deeply buried complexes which to some degree hinder our waking activity until they are resolved. Dreams resurrect these complexes. Your wishes, worries, warnings and traumas can all be mixed together in complicated scenes, sequences and whole dramas of seeming absurdity. Yet to you while you are the dreamer, they are real, possible and logical. When you dream, you are in a world of another dimension. But to you the dreamer, it's a real dimension.

Dreams about daily life, of unfinished activities and even those that resurrect buried fears are pretty typical. All of us experience most of them. You may have had them to a greater or lesser extent, and recalled them with different degrees of memory. Still, you have probably had one or more of the common dreams. Thus, they might be classified as "normal." But some people have more unusual dreams.

These are the type of dreams that can link your nocturnal adventures to the material world in a practical way. Many people have remembered where they misplaced objects by dreaming about them. Usually these dreams occur only after the dreamer has consciously fretted over a lost object, perhaps for several days. The same goes for dream creativity or problem solving. You have to have a question or be concerned about a problem. Then, when you least expect it, the answer may occur in a dream. Dreams have created music, machines, paintings, novels and sculpture. Robert Louis Stevenson, after years of trying to plot a story on the duality of man's personality, had revealed to him in a dream the tale of "Dr. Jekyll and Mr. Hyde." Coleridge dreamed up "Kubla Khan" during a nap and Goethe dreamed many of his poems. Marconi, Edison, Pasteur . . . many of the world's geniuses did some of their best creating while asleep.

Then there is an extremely rare type of dream that is not only strange, but downright awesome. The University of California's Dr. Charles Tart calls them "high" dreams. They could also be named "psychedelic" or "mind expanding" except for the negative drug connotation. They are so rare you probably don't know anyone who has had one, much less had one yourself. Tart defines a "high" dream as a sleeping experience in which you *know* you are in an altered state of consciousness, though you needn't know it is a dream. These experiences usually include fantastic revelations. They have cosmic or Divine overtones that go beyond reason. Still, while the dreams are in progress the sleepers receive the messages with complete clarity. These dreams are so outstanding that when the dreamers awaken they remember how awestruck they were. They recall how beautifully the dreams' messages were conveyed. They recollect the magnificence of creation that was revealed. Yet, as they awaken, no matter how desperately they try, they cannot for all their efforts hold on to the actual messages themselves as they evaporate like wisps of steam. It's as if the nature of the cosmos is so awesome that only intuition can understand it; that mankind's puny brain just doesn't have the mental circuitry or programing to process the material. Advanced mystics claim they sometimes receive these remarkable impressions during meditation, but it takes years of practice before they can remember much of what they experience. When they can, it's a fantastic adventure.

In fact, remembering and then being able to piece together the meaning of *any* dream or sequence of them is an adventure. The ancient rabbis used to say, "A dream that is not understood is like a letter not opened." The early psychology pioneers, Freud, Jung and Adler, all spoke out with similar messages. They all said that to understand your dreams means to understand yourself—so much so that modern researchers now believe that *no* dream is unimportant.

Contrary to many claims, there doesn't seem to be a universal code of dream symbols. Most dream analysts now realize this. They talk in terms of dream sequences rather than individual symbols. But even with analyzing sequences there doesn't seem to be much uniformity. Each analyst interprets in terms of his school of education, his theories and his own personality. That leads many psychologists to say that only *you* can properly interpret your dreams.

The mentality of the dreamer is the main factor in dream meaning. Simple people have simple dreams, and vice versa. Some symbols are more universal than others. Long instruments like swords and nails usually signify male. But does a broom handle? Only you can really understand what your dreams mean, and then usually in terms of your emotions as they occurred in the dreams. Remember, dreams are just stories. You react to them like other stories . . . in a specific way depending on your psychological history. It's your *reaction* to the story that tells you about your own subconscious. Other people will react differently to the same story. It is now believed this is why Freud found sexual meaning in all his patients' dreams. That it was probably Freud who had the sex hang-ups.

Many colleges of psychology offer courses in dream interpretation in which students recall and report their dreams to the class. But in some courses, instead of the class as a whole trying to interpret dreams for the dreamers, each student interprets them in light of his own personal psychology as if *he* had the dreams himself. This way each reported dream becomes a psychoanalytic tool for *all* the students. Truly unusual dreams can be resurrected years later for use as personal sounding boards for students of the future.

"Is dream recall practical?" you may ask. "Will it help me?" Well, if nothing else, it's a fascinating thing to do. To see your subconscious in action is like watching the antics of a bright and exuberant child. It darts here, loses interest and goes over there, then returns. It invents fairies, or demons, and fabulous exotic places. It is you at your most creative. But it's also you telling yourself something.

Dreams are a major way that your subconscious communicates with your conscious and gives it messages. But this communication works the other way around too. A case during World War II is an example. Then good liquor was hard to come by, especially for underage naval cadets. So on those few occasions when these young warriors threw a drinking bash, more than likely the important ingredient for their debauchery was inexpensive rot-gut gin. To disguise the taste, and also because they had just been weaned from milkshakes, one enterprising crew chose the sweetest punch mix they could find, namely many packages of Jello. With such a mix the booze couldn't be tasted. But that didn't matter. The purpose of these parties was not to savor a bouquet of spirits, it was to get roaring drunk.

During one such affair a cadet arrived late. He found his mates already well on the road to oblivion. With gusto he quickly caught up and even surpassed them. In fact, he got sloppy drunk. But the next morning was puzzling. Unlike the other cadets, he didn't have a herd of cattle stampeding in his head. At first he boastfully attributed this phenomenon to his stamina and physical condition. But soon the pride changed to chagrin. He learned that the party ran out of liquor long before he arrived. He had gotten drunk solely on harmless sweet punch, spiked with copious amounts of his own imagination.

We all tend to perceive things as we expect or would like them to be. Coffee grounds poured into boiling water taste great on a camping trip, but horrible at the breakfast table. We overlook guile from a candidate of our own political party, but pounce on anything his opponent does. And you are indeed rare if at some time you haven't increased your heart beat merely by thinking of a terrifying or trying situation. Suggestion is so powerful among certain Haitians that it produces death—by voodoo. Phenomena like these are called "psychogenic": of having mental origin—of being suggestive.

When your conscious mind is working, it receives, processes and analyzes all incoming data before passing it to your subconscious. Therefore, your subconscious is not in the habit (nor capable) of logically processing what it gets. What it does process is by trial and error, as in dream solutions. But usually it accepts with confidence whatever it receives. If you control the input to your subconscious, its output will normally be controlled. So you are like a programed computer, and your subconscious is the part of you that is suggestible.

Most people automatically condemn suggestibility as being undesirable. "It's just psychological" is an expression often considered synonymous with "mental weakness." This can be true. Hang-ups, bad habits and negative attitudes all result from suggestions that are accepted without your knowing it. Yet suggestibility can be a strength, too. But you must realize your suggestibility potential and use it positively. It is a potent form of imagination.

It was Dr. Norman Vincent Peale who coined the phrase "the power of positive thinking." You can literally persuade and program yourself to reject doubts, overcome negative beliefs and eliminate concepts of personal failure. But you can't just *think* positively. You have to behave positively . . . with your conscious and subconscious. Psychologists and physicians have observed this human potential for years. One way of doing this is through what Maxwell Maltz, M.D., calls synthetic experiences. All you need is a good imagination. Your subconscious will normally believe anything your conscious strongly impresses upon it. Perhaps you have observed athletes at a track meet who spend lots of time mentally warming up before competing. They are "psyching" themselves. They are mentally practicing their task before performing it. They are imagining every move, every phase of the upcoming event. They are having a synthetic experience. For many of them this improves their performance. The same goes for you. If you develop strong attitudes and ideas toward happiness, friendship, and health, these will automatically replace the negative concepts that may be programed into you. So, too, for success. Wasn't it Jesus who said, "If thou canst believe, all things are possible to him that believeth."?

But there is a more powerful way to create synthetic experiences. So powerful that its mysteries have awed people for thousands of years. It even awes today's experts who know how to use it. These, of course, are the hundreds of psychologists, physicians, dentists and other professionals across the land who practice hypnosis.

Hypnosis

Professional practitioners use hypnosis for all sorts of things. Not only can they use it to improve a person's self-image, but hypnotic marvels extend into medicine, learning, and mysticism. Biologist Julian Huxley, whose exploits in science match the literary kudos of his younger brother Aldous, was completely sold on hypnosis. He was so convinced of its benefits that he believed it "is in harmony with the future evolution of man." Now lots of other people feel the same way.

For all the enthusiasm about hypnosis, nobody really knows what it is. Many practitioners will tell you it's a situation where your awareness is keenly and narrowly focused, like a cat intensely watching mice. Yet it is also a state of complete relaxation; a condition when your conscious has temporarily stopped giving inputs to your subconscious even though the latter is still aware and alert. More than likely your subconscious is focused on a hypnotist's voice. Since your conscious is not providing inputs, your subconscious is at its most suggestible from other sources. It believes what the hypnotist says. Your conscious mind is standing in the wings watching your subconscious perform on stage to the instructions of another director, sometimes with complete amazement.

Over the years hypnosis got a bad reputation. Stage hypnotists made their subjects look like fools. Authors invented evil-eyed Svengalis who held innocent maidens in mental bondage. And until recently, medicine called hypnosis *humbug*. Only slowly are the myths about hypnosis being exposed for the fiction that they are.

.

Still, many people have concerns—very legitimate concerns. What if your hypnotist had a heart attack? Would you remain in a permanent mental void? Would you vainly wait for a wake-up order that would never come? Not at all. You would either fall into natural sleep from which you would soon waken, or you would get bored and break the trance. Another major concern is that you might be forced to do something under hypnosis that you don't want to do. Hypnotists vehemently deny this. True, your mental state isn't one of normal, everyday awareness. In hypnosis your awareness is centered *more* in your subconscious, but it *is* alert. Thus, you are aware of everything the hypnotist tells you and can reject whatever offends your basic morality. How about prolonged hypnosis? Can repeated hypnotic inductions weaken your will? Can you become subject to the will of another? Not really. Receiving numerous hypnotic inductions can be habit forming. But, so can riding a commuter bus. Hypnotists claim you can reject being hypnotized as easily as you can stop riding the bus to work. And though psychologists still debate whether under hypnosis you can be *fooled* into violating your ethics, there has never been a single documented case in which hypnosis, per se, directly caused permanent harm to an individual.

You may be wondering if you can be hypnotized. You have heard people adamantly say they can't be. Well, they are wrong. Everyone is hypnotizable to some degree. But only a few, about 10 percent, can go into somnambulism, that state in which truly spectacular feats are performed. The degree of suggestion people accept depends on their convictions and attitudes toward hypnosis. It is affected by how much their reason intercedes and on the extent their subconscious believes a suggestion. But these conditions aren't fixed since most people can increase their hypnotizability with training.

Perhaps the best known use for hypnosis, and historically the oldest, is for anesthesia. Many hypnotists, to demonstrate their skill at self-hypnosis, put out lighted cigarettes on the palm of their hand without pain or even raising a blister. However, your mind can do other feats besides cut off pain. The mere thought of a physical activity triggers tiny tensions in the muscles involved. These motor responses to your imagination are why athletes can practice mentally. They can literally train their muscles to react as if they were practicing physically. Some athletes actually participate in events in the state of hypnosis.

However, you may not like some of the physical things that result from mind power. Secreted fluids, like juices in your stomach that produce ulcers, mentally induced heart problems, or nerve impulses that cause ticks and jerks—all of these come from mind power—unwanted mind power. Because recent studies indicate this occurs often in medical patients, a growing number of physicians are joining a new medical fraternity called the Academy of Psychosomatic Medicine. These doctors firmly believe at least three-quarters of your illnesses are of mental origin. They think some physical deformities are too. Warts have been removed through hypnosis. You may not want to believe it, but next time you take to bed with a headache, when your nose swells with hay fever, when you break out with boils, more than likely your mind is playing tricks on you. Hypnosis has been used to correct many of these psychosomatic ailments.

One outstanding psychosomatic physician practices in Mill Valley, California. Peter Mutke is a surgeon, psychotherapist, and hypnotist. He handles hypnosis like other doctors use hypodermics. He hypnotically extracts psychic problems from patients' minds for analysis. Likewise, he injects suggestions as cures. His most spectacular hypnotic treatments have been with women with undersized breasts. First, through hypnoanalysis Dr. Mutke discovers the specific inhibitions that produced what he calls "mental disuse atrophy." These are complexes that cause a patient to subconsciously believe her breasts cannot or should not develop. In childhood she may have associated large breasts with promiscuity. Or her older sisters may have told her she would always have small breasts. Once the patient realizes her traumas and eliminates her inhibitions, Dr. Mutke hypnotically programs her mind with "bio-automation." He suggests that her breasts will grow. This creates subconscious hyperawareness of her organs, which in turn stimulates growth by subconscious direction of hormones, blood, and nutrients to the areas. It turns mind-power into woman power.

Though psychic problems that manifest as physical ailments can be treated hypnotically, more common are the strictly mental problems. Take Sergei Rachmaninoff, for instance. He wasn't always one of Russia's most renowned composers. His first concert was a dud. Rachmaninoff was so distraught over not being favorably accepted that he developed a psychotic gloom. In this state he couldn't compose at all. But his genius was salvaged by Dr. Nikoli Dahl, a hypnotist. For three months, in daily sessions, the physician treated his patient. He repeated over and over to the hypnotized composer, "You will write another concerto; you will work with great facility." Rachmaninoff slowly recovered from his depths of brooding and later went on to create many of the world's greatest musical masterpieces. He was so elated with his recovery that he dedicated his famous Concerto No. Two in C Minor to Dr. Dahl.

Whereas medical and psychiatric uses for hypnosis may have grown rapidly in recent years, its nontherapeutic applications have been more like an explosion in a powder magazine. Experimenters all across the land have found one application of hypnosis after another. Not only do athletes compete in events while hypnotized, but other people by the thousands are discovering what indredible gymnastics their subconscious minds can perform. Neurophysiologist Warren McCulloch of MIT demonstrated what a fantastic memory your subconscious has. He hypnotized several bricklayers and regressed each of them ten years. They were then instructed to describe a specific brick in a specific row which they had laid one decade before. Since bricks all have flaws that are easily detected, each description was verified later as being accurate by simply checking the actual brickwork. The brick experiment was just a stunt. Still, total recall does have practical implications . . . like remembering where valuable objects have been misplaced, or dredging up important long-forgotten facts. Hypnotic memory has even resolved court disputes. And Aldous Huxley was able to resurrect years-old research while in a deep trance. He could read verbatim the hallucinated pages of books he had not seen for over twenty years.

Reliving the past has always been an exciting hypnotic experience. Who wouldn't thrill at being regressed to childhood, or even to what appear to have been previous lives? These things are possible to some degree for anyone who willingly accepts hypnosis and is cooperative. The experience of age regression varies from just fair memory with little or no visual imagery to actually reliving past events as if they were real. And no matter how accurately you can recall what happened so long ago under hypnosis, it is still astounding to those who experience it.

Then there is time-distortion hypnosis. With this you can review major portions of your life in just minutes. Also experiments in creativity have been successful with time distortion. In one experiment hypnotized girls were told to design a dress and to take one hour to do the job. But what the hypnotized subjects thought to be six-minute intervals were counted off aloud every second. After ten seconds the subjects awakened thinking they had been hypnotized for an hour. Yet all could accurately draw the dress design they had created. The same has been done with song writing. And time-warp hypnosis has compressed one year of art classes into a few hours—at least that's what one mind laboratory in New York claims.

But you're reading this book to find out about personal growth, about spiritual development, about self-realization. So you are probably wondering if hypnosis can help you in these areas. Very likely. It is a perfect tool for examining your deeper being, for learning to know yourself, and for giving you the stamina to improve. In the hypnotic search for your true identity, spiritual and mystical experiences sometimes occur. Bernard Aaronson, Ph.D., has used hypnotically created time and visual depth distortion to generate feelings of intense euphoria. Many people have hypnotically relived past psychedelic experiences and then learned to induce through self-hypnosis a similar mental condition in which they had new experiences. For those who enjoy the glories of meditation, self-hypnosis is a fast way to enter the meditative state of mind. It can also create the will to persevere in such practices. Hypnosis is a powerful tool for spiritual enlightenment.

The major thrust in hypnosis now is toward self-hypnosis. Actually, most of us do this all the time. Usually it is negative self-hypnosis resulting in psychosomatic illness or other unpleasantries. Occasionally it's just humorous, like if you are a naval cadet. But it can be applied positively, and it can do anything heterohypnosis (being hypnotized by someone else) can do. You can hypnotize yourself any time you want, and once you are past the expenses of learning how, it's absolutely free. Sexual inhibitions, weight control, smoking, moodiness and anxiety are all candidates for self-hypnosis. So are introversion and other negative outlooks on life. Through self-hypnosis you can implant goals in your subconscious as catalysts to trigger your natural success drives. And it is a powerful means of producing synthetic experiences of yourself performing perfectly. You can develop the capacity to visualize, to create, to draw upon all the strength of your subconscious. Many forms of yoga are really just self-hypnosis. That's why adept yogis have such amazing control over their heartbeat, their breathing, their body temperature and can even control how much blood circulates within a certain limb.

In heterohypnosis your subconscious accepts directed suggestions and instructions from another person while your conscious stands by. In self-hypnosis you play a game with yourself. Your conscious and subconscious make a contract that after certain rituals and signals your subconscious will accept as true some untruths your conscious may suggest. This takes time to learn. The reaction of your subconscious in this case is really a conditioned response similar to Pavlov's dogs getting hungry every time they heard a bell.

There are several ways to learn self-hypnosis. Libraries and bookstores overflow with books purporting to tell you how to go into a deep trance in just minutes. Some people can learn to hypnotize themselves from these books. The more clearly defined and illustrated the exercises are, the better. One of the best books on the subject is *Self-hypnosis—a Conditioned Response Technique* by Laurance Sparks.* It gives several techniques for inducing a trance through images. It also provides methods for dealing with a variety of mental problems after you have mastered going into a trance. But don't be disappointed if you can't attain deep hypnotic states. People who don't respond well to a hypnotist can't be expected to do any better by themselves. In fact, learning self-hypnosis by yourself is the hardest way to learn it.

That's why some hypnotists put their voices on records or tapes. This more closely simulates having a hypnotist right in your room. These inductions are recorded for a general audience. More than likely they don't quite suit your specific personality and situation. Also, they are limited to fifteen or thirty minutes a side. This may not be enough time for induction, demonstration and wake-up for you. Still, with repetition, recordings can be effective.

---

* Hardcover: Grune & Stratton, Inc., 381 Park Avenue South, New York, N.Y. Softcover: Wilshire Book Company, 8721 Sunset Blvd., Los Angeles, CA. 90069.

Several of these records and tapes are on the market. An occasional bookstore carrying metaphysical and psychic material may have them. Magazines specializing in hypnosis and psychic phenomena often print advertisements telling where you can get them. The Wilshire Book Company markets a hypnosis recording by its founder, Melvin Powers. If you have a tape recorder, you can be your own hypnotist. Laurance Sparks provides several scripts in his book which you can read onto tape. If these don't work, you can always make up recordings of your own. But don't be foolish enough to do this unless you *really* know what you are doing.

The very best way to learn self-hypnosis is to go to a professional hypnotist. Everyone has heard of posthypnotic suggestions. These are instructions hypnotists implant in your mind while you are hypnotized. They create a strong urge in you to react in a certain manner after you awaken. This reaction is usually coupled to some type of signal or ritual. The hypnotist might say, "When you hear the count of three you will have an irresistible urge to get a drink of water." Sure enough, when you come out of the trance and hear the count of three, you feel like a sun-bleached skeleton in the middle of Death Valley. We are back to Pavlov again. Posthypnotic suggestions are really powerful one-time forms of conditioning. The most common use of posthypnotic suggestion is to condition subjects to go immediately into trance at a special signal. This saves countless hours of hypnotic induction. But a hypnotist can give you a posthypnotic suggestion that *you*, not the hypnotist, will give the trance signal. This is the most potent way of getting your subconscious to react to your desires and instructions.

Learning self-hypnosis from a hypnotist has other dividends too. Professionals can teach you the basics of hypnosis: how to use it for your specific needs and what the pitfalls are. Also, any special problems or requirements you have can be explored personally with the instructor. Their resolutions can be specially adapted to you.

The price for learning self-hypnosis can be high. Naturally, the most expensive way is to have private instruction. This costs from $25 to $75 an hour. But this is also the most effective way of learning. Professionals working alone with you can use techniques designed just for you. They can observe your reactions and alter the procedure accordingly, and they can terminate the instruction as soon as you have learned specifically what you want to learn. But it's possible that your cost may run as high as $1,000 before you and your hypnotist decide you are performing as well as you ever will.

Most people learn self-hypnosis in a course consisting of several lessons. Though not as effective as private instruction, a lot of the material covered is the same. Yet you and all the members of your class share the cost of your instructor. Still the price can be high. $600 is what one extensive course costs. $200 is more typical and $30 to $50 is what fledgling psychology students charge before their professors catch them at it.

A typical professional course ($150–$250) might have from eight to twenty students who meet once a week for eight evening sessions of two or three hours each. The students get extensive reference material and a book in self-hypnosis. Along with theory they receive new experiences each week including relaxation, hand levitation, anesthesia, recall, age regression, time distortion, speed reading, visualization and hallucination. They are taught how to hypnotize themselves, how to deepen the hypnosis, how to recognize positive and negative thinking and the causes of emotion or psychosomatic illness. Another type of course, in fact one taught by the previously mentioned Dr. Mutke, is a weekend marathon of approximately twenty hours. The students learn basic techniques of self-hypnosis along with theory. Repetition of this seminar often results in marked improvement in your self-hypnotizability. The price, including bed and board, is under $200. At the low end of the cost spectrum are courses that may not provide much theory, but they do teach relaxation, posthypnotic suggestion, self-suggestion and hypnotic deepening. If they are run by college students, most of the clientele will be from a nearby campus. These courses may not be as professional or structured as others, but they can teach you self-hypnosis. Also they are a lot of fun because the participants are mostly energetic young people who are there more out of curiosity than because of emotional problems.

Where do you find these people who can teach you to do such wondrous things with your mind? Physicians and dentists do not advertise. However, by phoning your local medical or dental society you can be put in touch with doctors who practice hypnosis. Most who do are too busy with sick patients to take you on, but may be helpful in recommending another physician or someone else they consider competent. Of course, many psychiatrists are adept at hypnosis. They are usually quite willing to accept you as a pupil for private instruction. So are many psychologists. The same for professional hypnotists. These and some psychologists are listed in your yellow pages under "hypnotism." Many states have hypnosis associations. Though these aren't official state organizations, most qualified and ethical hypnotists belong to them. Check with your library to find the names and addresses of these groups. They, in turn, can tell you who is a member in your local area.

Classes in self-hypnosis are sometimes listed in phone book yellow pages. More often they are advertised in your local newspaper. Self-hypnosis intrigues venturesome young people. Therefore the student paper of your nearest college probably carries advertisements by professional hypnotists. Certainly, courses taught by psychology students are included in its pages, though students seldom include their names. Often secretaries in psychology departments are aware of self-hypnosis classes, so you might phone them. They are usually quite helpful. If you want color, go to your nearest campus and scan the bulletin boards. Self-hypnosis courses are often announced on posters tacked up alongside the numerous other announcements on yoga, Zen, meditation, aikido and everything else imaginable. Even if you aren't interested in self-hypnosis, it's an adventure just to read a college bulletin board. You might find some other mental discipline that's even more exciting than hypnosis.

Silva Mind Control

Many people will tell you Silva Mind Control is even more exciting than hypnosis. Its creator, Jose Silva, claims that the core of Mind Control is learning to *guide* your awareness from its natural conscious abode into other levels of consciousness. Most of what you call thinking is done with your conscious mind. In this state your brain emits electrical impulses predominantly in a frequency range called "Beta." By getting your brain to produce lower frequencies you can operate in an entirely different spectrum of mentation. Silva Mind Control claims that with special training anyone can learn to consciously function at lower brain frequencies. These include the "alpha" frequency of meditation and even the "theta" of subconscious creativity. Electrical devices using the biofeedback principle can teach you this too, but Mind Control enthusiasts say machines are not necessary. However, the organization does market a low-priced biofeedback device which its graduates can use for special training and experimental purposes.

Silva Mind Control didn't just happen. It evolved. Starting in Laredo, Texas, Mr. Silva studied different techniques of hypnosis. He also experimented with what hypnosis can accomplish. After twenty-two years he arrived at a science which he named "Psychorientology," a technique of mental conditioning through gentle self-suggestion. It can produce a subjective-intuitive mental state in which astounding feats are possible. By 1966 the method was perfected and was made available to the public.

The basic Silva Mind Control instruction consists of four sequential courses which can be taken individually or as a unit. The entire series takes less than a week and is presented during the day or in evening classes, culminating in two ten-hour sessions over a weekend. Total time: forty-eight hours of intensive instruction. Most class sizes range from five to twenty people. That way they are friendly and cozy.

If you expect the heavy doses of training, and they are heavy, to be exhausting, you are wrong. They are pleasant and soothing. From the very start you are taught to relax. Then you are verbally guided to different mental "levels." The deeper the levels you achieve, the more effectively you perform and, theoretically, the lower your brain wave frequency. The basic technique of instruction is by "voice programing." You are talked down deep within your psyche by the instructor to the beat of a metronome. At the same time you mentally count down along with the instructor. This develops a habit pattern, a conditioned response. You are conscious all the time and learn to count yourself back out. By repeating the process, first slowly and deliberately, then more rapidly for up to fifty times during the course, you become proficient at the technique. Throughout the course the instructor guides you in many different mental experiences, all the while giving positive suggestions to enhance your capability.

The Silva course does lots of things. Are you beset with tensions? Silva may be able to help you. How about migraines? Again, the course has techniques for this. Insomnia? You are taught sleep and wake control, even dream recall and problem solving. There is a technique for improving memory too. Mind Control can do many things self-hypnosis can do. In fact, it resembles self-hypnosis on a low-key basis.

The central theme of Mind Control is visualization. You learn to see with your mind's eye. This may sound ludicrous if you have never been able to visualize in your life. Lots of people truly believe they can't. Yet with Mind Control you soon get a demonstration that you can visualize, poorly as it may be. The instructor might say, "Now close your eyes, and the one thing that you mustn't do is see a pink elephant." He pauses, then asks, "Which way was the elephant facing?" Everyone can answer. Each did in some mental way picture an elephant. From this starting point the class is taken to deeper psychic levels. You are verbally guided through visualizing first colors, then familiar objects like flowers, and eventually whole scenes. With repetition everyone improves. Some people see literally. Most visualize in a hazy fashion. A few enhance their visualization with imagined sounds and aromas. But all learn to visualize to some degree.

From here your instructor gets into your imagined goals. You literally create images of them mentally. Because you are functioning at subjective levels of consciousness, these synthetic experiences are tremendously powerful. If you are overweight, you visualize yourself as being pencil-lead thin. In your mind you willfully refuse that piece of cake. Similar corrective visions work for smokers and insomniacs. Some people claim to become so adept at envisioning what they want by Mind Control methods that they can influence future events. They believe they can mentally alter the course of their lives and can attract to themselves happiness, prestige, and even prosperity.

Jose Silva says Mind Control is so effective that anyone can learn to use it to improve his extrasensory perception. However, he prefers the term "subjective communication." He even guarantees that after completing his course you will to some degree have developed ESP capability. This is considered so important that the last two days are devoted to mental projection into objects and living things. This way you supposedly experience their basic natures through intuition. You are instructed how to visualize the internal structure of different materials. You vividly imagine the "atomic" taste, the sound, the aroma. This is subjective learning. No two people imagine exactly the same properties. However, once having established your *own* imagined "reference points," you will mentally recall these same characteristics whenever you intuitively sense that particular material again. Some people are amazingly accurate in sensing unknown materials in an envelope or otherwise hidden from view. A few students, after learning this technique, claim to intuitively detect defects in electronic or mechanical equipment and to pinpoint where the trouble is.

The main thrust of Mind Control's intuitive sensing is on animal life—primarily human. The principle is the same. You intuitively sense a particular biological situation, then let your imagination create an image, or reference point, for it. Images created by laymen may differ sharply from those of biologists or physicians. But no matter how bizarre, whenever you intuitively sense a particular situation, your subconscious supposedly will project that image to your consciousness. The ultimate goal is to apply the technique to people who are ill. It is claimed you learn to detect ailments psychically from afar; somewhat like Edgar Cayce did.

But ailments detected are still ailments until they are corrected. Mind Control teaches that corrections can be accomplished by using synthetic experiences. You just vividly imagine the sick person as being well. You mentally heal diseased organs. You psychically set broken bones. The entire final day is devoted to envisioning potential patients and practicing psychic healings on them. One purpose of Silva Mind Control is to establish a cadre of psychic healers around the world.

Most students are not instant Edgar Cayces in their detection. Many are completely wrong. When successful "hits" do occur, often the student got some unwitting (even witting) clues. Nevertheless, the ability of the classes as a whole seems to far exceed normal probability in specifying details completely unknown to the students. The correction rates are not well documented, but Jose Silva believes that if enough trainees practice on any particular person, his recovery certainly won't be slowed, and it may be hastened.

Students are admonished *not* to inform people they are being worked on psychically. If you don't have the ability to heal, you shouldn't give people false hope. You shouldn't in any way dissuade them from seeking professional therapy. Also, if people know they are being worked on, they will naturally want to know what was found. Many beginning healers are grossly inaccurate. By telling people they have illnesses they may not have, the healer would just reinforce the negative. Above all, Mind Control instructors say, don't try to psychically analyze yourself. Coupling faulty imagery with your own possible psychosomatic fancy could result in spiraling negative problems.

What does all this cost? It varies locally, but the full 48 class hours run from $150 to $200—there are discounts for students and families. One nice thing about Silva Mind Control is that once you have taken the series you are free to repeat it at any time, anywhere, as often as you wish at no extra charge. Many graduates repeatedly take advantage of this offer. Not only can you repeat a class when it is given in your area, but Silva Mind Control has over twenty-five centers in major metropolitan areas. You can attend weekly practice sessions here too—all for free.

No matter where you live, a Silva Mind Control course is given somewhere near your home. Over 500 accredited instructors throughout the country bring the teachings to thousands of students. Courses are offered in every one of the 50 states as well as Alberta, Ontario, and Quebec in Canada. The same for a few countries abroad. At intervals courses are repeated in most communities. They are usually well advertised in local newspapers beforehand. If you haven't seen an ad, you can inquire by writing Silva Mind Control in Laredo.

There are also advanced courses. On a yearly basis Mr. Silva himself teaches a 35-hour graduate course in many localities for $200. Also there are specialized courses for executives, mining engineers, schoolteachers, salesmen, etc. Each concentrates on subliminal levels of consciousness as applied to personal improvement and subjective intuition in that special field of endeavor. Mining engineers are taught to use intuition in prospecting. Teachers learn to achieve rapport psychically with their pupils. Prices for these specialized courses vary.

Some of Mind Control's graduates aren't content with just taking a course, or repeating it over and over. They want innovations. So lots of them have lively get-togethers in one another's living rooms. It is with these groups that potential instructors get part of their experience. All such groups practice health cases. But they add other exercises with individual participants tape recording special experiments for the group to try. Thus, the graduates not only practice their healing exercises but have a glorious time being psychically creative in the arts and music, regressing in age (even to what appear to them as past lives), visualizing journeys into the future and taking psychic out-of-body trips. For many graduates, Silva Mind Control not only helps them in daily life, but becomes an exotic fun trip whenever they meet with their fellows.

If you ask most people if getting rid of anxieties will relieve their burden in life; if you ask if developing positive attitudes is a milestone on the road to success; even if you ask if just creating fun trips is a major improvement over their former selves, you will get a resounding Yes. Most people would be quite content to achieve any one of these objectives. And they would be justified in selecting these levels of advancement as resting places on the long road to self-improvement—to self-knowledge. But there is much more to self-knowledge.

Mainly it's to go beyond manipulating your mind. You must *learn* about your hidden self. This secret part of you consists of attitudes, prejudices and even strange personalities buried deep within your psyche. You absorbed lots of these as an immature child. You have never let go. It's because of this that even though people age, they don't really become *true* adults. They are more like grown-up children. Their outwardly mature selves are but masks of the child-adults beneath.

Fortunately, there are ways to become an adult-adult. Today numerous schools exist that can rid you of childish ways, that can teach you how to live, that can show you the refreshing joys of truly growing up.

Chapter 2

GROWTH TRIPS

By the summer of 1946, World War II was over. The bands had stopped playing and most of the GI's were home. At last domestic problems, especially racial conflict, held center stage. So thirty concerned people gathered at State Teachers College in New Britain, Connecticut to learn how to cope with racial discrimination. Little did they realize that an innocuous by-product of their efforts would evolve into the most potent tool that humanistic psychology had seen.

The participants were mostly educators and social workers, with a smattering of other interested citizens thrown in. There was nothing unusual about this except for one thing. Along with the participants were observers, psychologists who wanted to see how groups worked. They wanted to know how ideas were developed, and how the participants got along with each other. They wanted to learn what made a group function.

Every day the psychologist observers sat and listened and tape recorded. Every night in private they analyzed the tapes, often until even the crickets had gone to bed. They discussed and carefully noted individual qualities and interactions of the participants like leadership, jealousies, misunderstandings, arguments, loyalties and teamwork.

But the participants got curious about what was being learned.

One night a few asked to attend an evening analysis session. With some foreboding the observers granted their wish. The effect was electrifying. As the participants heard the tapes, as they listened to comments by the analysts, as they recalled the day's travails, its skirmishes, its victories, its hurts, its misunderstandings and angry words, they discovered personality traits in themselves they weren't aware of before. They began to understand their hidden selves. Within days all participants were attending the evening sessions more enthusiastically than the daytime ones. They had lively discussions about their earlier behavior. They argued about what they had really meant in an earlier statement. They confessed how they *felt* toward another's remarks, and what their emotional state was at different times of the day. History books don't record if interracial breakthroughs occurred that summer, but the participants got a tremendous personal dividend from the frank evening evaluations. The observing psychologists got even more.

They had accidentally seen feedback in action—feedback from the rich environment of group interaction that permitted understanding oneself and other people. They had discovered a new way of learning, a new way of social growth.

The very next summer three of the participating psychologists organized another training program. This one would emphasize feedback. It would also emphasize intimacy and dependence. Thus, it should be held in an environment of beauty far removed from disturbing social influences. The quaint little town of Bethel, Maine at the base of the White Mountains was chosen as the locale. For lack of a better designation this three-week session was called a "training group," or T-group. Because the training involved observation and analysis, the term "laboratory" was also used. To this day T-groups use the laboratory method, or what is more commonly referred to now as Sensitivity Training.

NTL Institute

The experiment was a success. So successful that from that early Bethel episode the original researchers went on to found the National Training Laboratories Institute for Applied Behavioral Sciences (NTL). Yearly summer training was continued at Bethel while NTL branched into research at MIT and the University of

Michigan. For the next twenty-five years NTL expanded and changed. At this writing it can serve you through three separate divisions or centers. The Professional Development Division trains group leaders and other professionals in the behavioral sciences. The Contracts and Consultation Division emphasizes social problems of managers, executives, educators and organizational groups. It is also involved with organization development and system changes. But what probably is of most interest to you is the ever-brightening star of NTL, its Programs and Laboratories Division. Here the emphasis is on enriched relationships between individuals. It stretches your potential. It deepens your understanding of individual viewpoints. Yet it focuses on you. And all this within the context of a small group.

NTL is a unique organization. Only the administrative staff headquartered in a Virginia suburb of Washington, D.C. is full time. The training personnel are spread all over the country. Most are permanent employees of colleges, universities, industry, clinics, and consulting firms. This far-flung adjunct staff includes over 200 highly qualified professional psychologists and therapists who participate only at certain times of the year. They are collectively known as the NTL Network.

A substantial number of NTL programs still focus on Bethel, Maine, the only place it owns any real estate. There is a training center right in town, with additional rented facilities at Gould Academy, a nearby private school available during the summer. But there are other places where you can get training. The major Western location in summer is at Kresge College nestled among the redwoods on the University of California campus at Santa Cruz. T-groups of many types also take place in conference centers, hotels, motels and resorts throughout the country.

No matter where they are conducted, or who conducts them, T-groups everywhere are very similar and their basic goals are the same. NTL's Programs and Laboratories director, Barry Certner, says, "The basic goal of a T-group is that participants have the opportunity to learn about themselves and other people experientially; that they learn how groups of people function and how they as individuals function in interpersonal and group contexts."

Central to all T-groups is feedback. Feedback is a basic tool for learning. That's how your skills are developed. That's how you pick up bad habits too. But if you are receptive, feedback can be extremely positive. In the T-group you get feedback in two ways. First there are feelings. These are valuable during highly charged interactions. Your subconscious uses them as indicators of positive or negative situations. And these feelings can inhibit or enhance your receptivity and learning. By *consciously* recognizing your feelings and the circumstances that evoked them, you can control your responses. The T-group is designed to expose you to numerous feelings so that you learn to recognize them. The T-group also gives you feedback by having other participants recount what they thought you said or felt. Then they explain what their own words and actions really meant. Lots of T-group time is spent in plain talk, straight-from-the-shoulder communication. Rules of convention and politeness don't apply, just realistic response. Honesty and openness are the goals. This way you learn to communicate at a basic level. You understand what was meant, and what wasn't. You see how you unintentionally stir up a variety of responses in others. You see how your actions generate affection, rejection, anger or respect. And you learn how these feelings are created in you.

Most NTL participants start with the Basic Human Interaction Laboratory. This program often accommodates seventy or more trainees at a time, along with six staff members. The laboratories are usually split into smaller T-groups, each acting independently most of the time. There is no guarantee what the result of any T-group will be since they aren't very structured. Nor are they designed to solve specific problems like marital difficulties or sexual hang-ups. They are experiences with people. So they can go any direction the participants take them. In fact, the T-groups have no "leaders" per se. The staff, called Trainers or Facilitators, help participants maximize what can be learned from group interaction. They give just enough guidance to make certain the group meets its basic goals and doesn't get hung up on a specific problem or too much intellectualizing.

Right after a group is formed there is usually confusion. But the facilitator doesn't interfere. Eventually the participants discover they have to move the group forward themselves. Then follows a period of sparring and feeling each other out . . . of petty power struggles, of resolving who becomes leader, of selecting the pecking order, and what issues will be considered. At this stage the accent is negative. Then, as defenses are let down and the participants discover they all have similar concerns, feelings become important.

Gut feelings are often shared. The group atmosphere usually becomes honest and open. A sense of unity, mutual trust and respect unfolds. In some groups the sharing is so deep that it takes on a mystical quality. Then comes mutual expression of deep personal feelings. This is when the feedback is most important, and when it is most powerful. As participants openly talk out their pains and feelings, deep affections develop. By the time the program ends, such a rapport has developed that most members want to meet again sometime. They make elaborate plans to do so. But, as with most well-laid plans, the reunions seldom occur.

Though the smaller T-group is central to Human Interaction Laboratories, there are large group activities too. Seminars, lectures, intergroup exercises, and community activity round out the program. Included in the training, both small and large group, is role playing and nonverbal activity. Occasionally techniques developed for other purposes in other parts of the country are used. These include physical activities like pillow-pounding or wrestling to release bottled up energy. And, of course, there is verbal confrontation. But assault tactics are discouraged. NTL is not interested in breaking down people's defenses, something that distinguishes it from many other training philosophies. NTL considers its most outstanding characteristic to be that of providing participants with a unique environment where they can learn with others—a context that allows personal choice and integrity in the process. NTL workshops are relatively gentle.

This may explain why certain people like NTL. In addition to its divisions focusing on professional systems and social problems, NTL processes over 2,100 people every year in the Programs Laboratory Sessions. Many people go to Bethel for the training. No wonder! It's a delightful community. Charming New England homes and large old shade trees line the streets. The days are warm and the evenings cool. Wooded uplands stretch in all directions. NTL's facilities in town match the charm of Bethel. The stately brick buildings of Gould Academy provide comfortable dormitories and spacious meeting rooms. The lawns and gardens are perfect for wandering and meditating. A ten-minute walk away is the NTL Conference Center, a gracious Victorian mansion that is handily accessible to a golf course. Nearby is the large dining room where most participants take their meals.

The laboratories at Bethel last eleven days. Though they run longer than twelve hours every weekday, ample time is provided for being alone or for recreation. During these free periods, if you get bored with yourself, there is tennis, golf, handball, squash, and a gymnasium. On weekends the blue lakes nearby are ideal for fishing and chilly swims. Pine forests are at hand to hike in and offer occasional views of the distant White Mountains.

Eleven days of training at Bethel will cost you around $350. If NTL provides room and meals, you pay more. Participants are encouraged to use NTL rooms and meals because communal living fosters greater intimacy. However, different arrangements can be made. If your whole family goes to Bethel, homes of vacationing locals are available for rent. And the youngsters aren't forgotten. Special laboratories have been designed just for children and for teens.

Kresge College in California is another place where the eleven-day Basic Human Interaction Laboratory is conducted. Shorter basic labs are held throughout the country. Six and eight-day labs (priced proportionately) are conducted at locations like Miami; Denver; Dellroy, OH; Stony Point, NY; Portland, OR; Montreat, NC; and others that change from year to year. Also there are weekend workshops in Washington, D.C. and near New York City which cost only $100 plus room and meals. More towns are scheduled for the same thing. And if you are a skier, you can spend six days at Bethel's winter lab for $250. Room, meals and tows are extra.

After you complete the six or eleven-day basic lab, more advanced workshops are available. These provide deeper introspection employing methods like fantasy, body movement, art, drama and other non-verbal techniques. They are available at Bethel as well as in Massachusetts, Illinois, New York, California and in the Deep South. There are also management-focused programs catering to institutional and community growth that deal strictly with material world problems. Though some of these are conducted at Bethel, the majority are held in numerous other cities. Their prices and locations vary depending on demand. By writing the NTL Institute in Arlington, VA, you can find out about all workshops, locations and prices. Well, almost all prices. Cost of the *Corporation Presidents Conference* at the Cotton Bay Club in the Bahamas is discreetly omitted from the catalog.

At NTL, the T-group is still the central training tool. The

method is to immerse you in dynamic group activity. The result is your improved understanding of how you relate to others, and how they affect you. The T-group is social psychology. This is very popular in many parts of the country, especially the East. But group participation needn't be limited to making you a nice person to have around. Groups can be applied to all sorts of understanding. This is especially true for understanding yourself; for discovering your inner troubles; for discovering your personality. Groups are great for growing up.

"Personality" is an important word in the growth movement. It is believed to have come from the Latin *persona*, which meant a mask that actors wore when playing a role before an audience. All people play roles—usually for other people's sake. They play different roles under different circumstances, and they wear different masks with each role.

All their lives people relate to others and to themselves through personality masks. Your masks at first may be conscious efforts to hide your deficiencies from other people. Later these become unconscious habits. Extraversion and introversion are often unconscious masks to hide the same complex—inferiority. Aggressiveness does the same. Akin to masks are fantasy, sour grapes, isolation, rationalization. All are powerful forces that mold your personality. They are defense mechanisms, face savers that hide the real you from the world and from yourself.

Employed properly, these defense mechanisms help you discover your personality. Group setting therapy is the catalyst that can make this happen. Its not that all the other participants recognize and inform you of your masks and your role playing. This does occur, true, but the main benefit of group therapy is the stress it produces. Stress brings out defense mechanisms. It shows up the flaws in your masks. Specially designed group activities can offer numerous situations that bring out different defense mechanisms. Skilled group leaders can recognize these. But only you can unravel their mysteries because only you have the memories of what produced them. So you are the one who must eventually discover what is deep within you. By using group stress as a tool, a good leader can actually feed your hang-ups. He can cause the stress to build. Eventually your defenses become so powerful that even you see them. Then you understand. Then you realize what the stresses are all about. Then you can begin to resolve your hidden problems. The method is known as group therapy. It's also called "Encounter."

Sensitivity training and encounter are often confused. Some people claim they are the same thing. An early pioneer in the growth movement, Carl Rogers, is one of these. However, most other people in the field make a distinction. But that doesn't mean they agree on the distinction. You ask several "experts" how sensitivity training and encounter differ and each has a different idea. In fact, sometimes they seem to contradict one another. But most have one concept in common. They say, "What's done at NTL is sensitivity training. What's called the 'West Coast Growth Trip' is encounter." That's the clue to the difference. Sensitivity training is educational. Encounter is oriented to behavioral changes. Sensitivity training is for social purposes. Encounter is growth oriented. In sensitivity training you become sensitive to others. In encounter you encounter and relate to yourself.

Types of Growth Therapy

Encounter groups, being so inner awareness oriented, rely strongly on qualified therapists for leadership. The groups must have a structure that best induces inner awareness situations. They have to be guided to provide planned feedback to participants. Unlike T-groups, the leaders have more control. Thus the original loose T-group evolved into the structured encounter group with strong leadership. Special techniques were added, and over time, different leaders developed different techniques.

So encounter training has changed a lot over the years. Modern encounter groups relate to the whole you. They employ what psychologist Dr. William Schutz calls the "body-mind" concept. When your emotions are aroused, you are urged to feel what tensions are generated. You should locate them in your body. It is a *feeling* process, not an intellectual approach. In Will Schutz's view, action is always better than words. Whatever you feel, you should convert to action. These are the most lasting experiences. Wrestling, pillow-pounding, screaming, touching, hugging and chanting—all are part of what he calls the "Open Encounter" . . .

that is, open to using all methods of therapy—and also open to innovations.

"Open Encounter" is just another way of saying "many forms of growing." Sometimes these techniques are combined; sometimes not. Most of the methods used are powerful therapies in their own right. Core therapy is a derivation of Gestalt therapy. This, in turn, is remotely related to the approach of insight called gestalt psychology. However, some techniques are more basic than others since they designate principles in the growth movement spectrum just as red, yellow, and blue specify basic divisions of the color spectrum. Gestalt therapy is one of these.

The father of Gestalt therapy was an ex-Freudian psychotherapist, Frederick (Fritz) Perls. His method has spread across the country. *Gestalt* is a German word that loosely translates as being a synthesis of experiences, emotions, body movements and sensations. These constitute a whole experience different and usually greater than its separate parts, just as a well-executed football play is more than just eleven men running around on a field. Gestaltists frown on analytical approaches to therapy because they believe your actions, your thoughts and your feelings are more than just a record of independent events in your life—that you as a person must be considered as an operating whole. Gestalt therapy does not stress intellectual understanding. It emphasizes emotional awareness . . . becoming aware of yourself. Why you experience something is unimportant. *How* you experience it is. And so is the insight this brings about.

Perls claimed that "nothing exists except in the here-and-now." Even memory and expectation are here-and-now experiences. Since your only awareness exists in the present, your problems must be resolved in the present. He strongly disapproved of Freud's free-association procedure, claiming memories evoked by psychoanalysis are false memories, lies you hang onto to justify your failures or unwillingness to grow up. To mature, you must take responsibility for your own life. Psychoanalysis does just the opposite. It provides you with a *past* that is responsible for your present problems. Gestalt therapy makes you face these problems *now*, problems that were never completely experienced and thus never completely resolved. It won't let you flee from them until they are experienced and resolved.

Gestalt therapy often takes place in a group setting. Still, it is usually a one-to-one relation between participant and therapist. Others in the group observe, sometimes experiencing their own problems in the process, while one person is being probed on the "hot seat." Probing occurs in many ways. There might be direct questioning, such as "Why are you frowning?" You are asked to describe what frowning feels like, and what internal feeling would make it go away. You might be told to imagine different people inside your body, each supporting a different side of an internal conflict. This play-acting shows up the nature of your conflict. Fantasy is another approach. You might imagine a wise man within you and ask him questions. This is relying on the same subconscious wisdom that you may have experienced in dreams. Perls also strongly believed in re-experiencing dreams. If his subjects had dreams that weren't complete, he had them fill in the gaps and fantasize *feelings* in dreams. Experiencing feeling is basic to Gestalt therapy.

Gestalt therapy shares many of its techniques with another form of treatment called Psychodrama. Psychodrama uses the psychological principle of transference. Most of us have experienced it subconsciously. Invariably the result was negative. Your hostility toward the boss during the morning may be taken out on your family at day's end. Dependence on a protective mother may be transferred to your therapist many years later. Jealousies, love and fears can all be transferred. Psychodrama does this therapeutically.

Psychodrama workshops are group activities. Participants alternate from supportive roles to being the star performer, or "protagonist." Psychodrama hinges around the protagonist. You play-act previous painful encounters with other people. You transfer resurrected feelings of hostility, guilt, fear, and other emotions to other psychodrama participants. They, in turn, act out the roles of people associated with your emotional problems. There is lots of role changing as people in the audience spontaneously join the drama. The director and his assistants take various roles too, even yours. They may stand behind you and act as your double, injecting comments from what they glean to be your hidden personality. These moments are usually charged with emotion, with crying, screaming, anger, sometimes actual hatred. By acting several parts, including those of former adversaries, you recall not only how you felt, but may discover that old opponents had a justifiable viewpoint. They may not have been as demonic as you remember them. As these powerful dramas unfold, so too does your self-enlightenment as you relive experiences with a new maturity and replace old memory traces with new ones.

Psychodrama is designed to bring repressed emotions and thoughts to the surface. But *true* past experiences aren't the only subject matter. In replaying an event, you as protagonist don't have to follow the script. You might prefer to change the actual story to end the way you would like it now. Then there is dream psychodrama, or just plain absurd-statement psychodrama; any form of drama that gets your subconscious to express itself. This builds a living picture of your secret world. Psychodrama is not just verbalization. More often now it is incorporated into open encounter workshops rather than being used as a therapy unto itself. So it includes gestures, movements and even dance. And though during any specific drama the protagonist benefits most, all participants are caught up in the emotions and feelings too. To each of them, a little bit of their own self unfolds.

Most psychological therapies search for emotional problems in the hidden recesses of your mind. Yet Fritz Perls claimed a lot of you is open for all to see. He believed your personality shows up in your voice, your facial expressions, your movement, your posture and in psychosomatic illness. He got the idea from Wilhelm Reich. Dr. Reich had discovered that psychological repression of emotions like fear and hate is accompanied by physical change. It's as if your psychic energy, which Freud called libido and Hindus label as prana, is transformed into physical energy. In fact, Carl Jung suggested that psychic energy may be related to physical energy. This transformation causes some of your muscles to constrict. If this happens often enough and over extended periods of time it becomes spastic. You get a permanent muscular contraction and, just like your heartbeat, this becomes totally unconscious. That's why children raised in puritanical households may develop a permanent sour look. In adulthood it's known as <u>Presbyterian frown</u>. The same with pugnacious jaw, the result of a little child trying not to cry. Your body is so affected by misdirected psychic energy that psychiatrist Alexander Lowen claims *all* neurotic problems manifest themselves in the structure and functioning of your tissues. Thus walking, posture, facial expression and handwriting, all are clues to your personality.

Since body and psyche are inextricably linked, awareness of

one provides knowledge of the other. Bioenergetics is one way to pay attention to body signals. The therapist might first note your posture, observing how you raise your arms when told to reach for something, or seeing how you react when asked to fall down. Therapists can determine whether you are overly protective of yourself or want to show your bravery. They can tell if you are trusting or suspicious. You are asked to tell how you felt during all these experiences. In bioenergetics, breathing, stressful exercises and difficult postures are emphasized. This physical activity hyperventilates and exhausts you. Your emotions flow more freely this way. Pounding, kicking, and screaming are also ways of letting go. When these are intense, your ego gives way to your body. Your body then responds freely, and long-forgotten memories, especially feelings, may spring into consciousness.

Another way of using your body to explore your psyche was created by a biochemist, Ida Rolf. The process is officially known as Structural Integration, but is more popularly called Rolfing. Dr. Rolf's philosophy is that most human bodies are tense and distorted in some way because of the trials of life. Your body has to contort itself to stay upright against gravity. If you have a sunken chest, you invariably thrust out your head to compensate. So, too, with other distortions.

Around all muscles is a flexible connective tissue called fascia. When your muscles become permanently tense, the fascia, no longer in flexure, hardens. Then your tensed muscles and fascia are permanently locked unless relaxed by stimulation, pressure, and fresh blood. Vigorous massage, in fact, kneading, is needed to do this. Over time such a procedure can literally realign your distorted body. Sometimes the process is extremely painful. But it can also be enlightening.

Most psychologically contracted muscles can be relaxed. When this happens, you often recall the feelings that originally tensed those muscles; emotions that were frozen into your distorted body many years before. Sometimes you just feel physical and psychological relief. Other times there are sudden intense releases of fears and emotions. A qualified therapist can help you work through these problems right on the spot. Then you achieve permanent mental well-being with complete muscular relaxation and realignment at the same time.

One patient while having her leg Rolfed, suddenly screamed

wildly. She had recalled a terror years before as an infant in her crib. As the massage continued she saw her nursery in flames. She was alone and frantic. She was pushing vainly with her tiny legs against the slats. Eventually she was rescued, but her terror at the time had blotted from her memory all but the fire. So, from that childhood experience in her crib on, anytime she was alone, her legs tensed, a condition only to be relieved on a massage table 40 years later.

A typical Rolfing program consists of ten one-hour sessions, each designed to work on specific muscles and movements. If you complete the whole series, you will undoubtedly improve your posture, and more than likely resolve several major personality problems. It will cost around $300 and is available from many therapists and growth centers. However, if you want to be a Rolfing instructor, you have to learn from a certified instructor or Dr. Rolf herself. You can get this latter training at the Ida P. Rolf Foundation in Boulder, Colorado.

Of the many methods for growth used in the encounter movement, most focus on your unsavory side. They work through tons of psychic junk. They dispose of mounds of personal garbage. But only a masochist wants to wallow all the time in a psychic sewer. Most people like to smell roses too. There are forms of experience that let you do just that. The most famous of these, and one of the most popular, is Sensory Awareness.

Sad to say, most of us have lost awareness of the beauties and delights all around us. Repetitions in daily life and the constraints of society all dull our observation. You are probably oblivious to most of your environment—and oblivious that others are oblivious. The next time you take a commuter train, or a subway, or a bus, look at the numerous blank eyes around you, just staring and not seeing. Notice how you yourself are hearing, but not listening. Most of the time you seldom *notice* aromas, textures and visual joys. Nor do you recognize sensations aroused by other people. Sensory awareness is a way to rediscover the rich world around you, just like you discovered new things as a child.

Children do most of their learning through their senses: touching, tasting, observing, listening, and trying new things with their bodies. They *feel* their environments. As they grow older, society discourages this. It foists intellectualization on them. So most people develop concepts of things and events as they *should* or *shouldn't* be, not as they really are. Sensory awareness techniques allow you to discover again how things really are, (how your environment really feels. It lets you feel your environment.) It lets you build on your sensations. Yet, you are discouraged from evaluating or expecting; you lose the concept of pleasant or unpleasant.

The training doesn't enhance your sensing abilities; it just makes you more aware that you have them. You may be told to experience gravity—to feel what it is like to lie on the floor or sit in a chair. You may be asked to observe how it feels to stand. What is your posture? What psychic problems have affected your posture? By touching other people you can feel their skin, finger their bodily softness or firmness, sense their vital forces and overcome the American phobia of bodily contact. A little tapping, or even slapping, conveys gentleness or aggression. Sensory awareness also introduces you to a treasure trove of sensations that you always took for granted and didn't appreciate. Seeing without focusing on specific objects produces impressions that long escaped your notice. Colors, light and shadow, shapes and movement—all develop new and different meanings. With your eyes closed, your senses can be tremendously enhanced as you passively listen, taste, feel and smell your environment. Sensory awareness makes life new and exciting.

In fact, the whole gamut of growth experiences is new and exciting. As the movement grew, different group leaders experimented; they changed techniques and they added new ones. Often leaders banded together and pooled their various methods and styles to provide even greater richness for participants. This was expecially popular in California, and the collaborations that formed became known as growth centers. Without question, the largest and most famous of all growth centers is Esalen Institute.

Esalen Institute

Esalen is also the oldest growth center. All other growth centers are patterned on the concept that developed from seminars held at Esalen's Big Sur, California facility. Esalen at Big Sur is really a small community, a delightful collection of rustic wooden buildings surrounded by gardens and redwoods just steps away from both hot sulphur springs and cold rushing streams. All this is perched precariously on the brink of rugged, rocky cliffs in earshot of the pounding Pacific surf two hundred feet below.

Esalen Institute was the brainchild of two Stanford graduates in psychology. Neither was satisfied with the modern methods of mental therapy. Nor were they happy with the concept that only sick people should benefit from therapeutic methods. So they began a search for other means of self-improvement, including practices of Oriental mystery and yogic schools. Then came the big chance. One of them, Michael Murphy, inherited from his grandfather a small rundown resort on the Big Sur Coast. From that beginning along with some brainstorming with partner Richard Price came the idea of the growth center. The concept was to provide an ideal growth environment by combining a remote setting and proven or experimental psychological methods along with techniques of Oriental origin.

The first seminar was held in 1962. It wasn't an instant winner since it took some time for the novel idea to catch on. So President Murphy held workshops and waited tables. Vice-president Price served as chief grounds keeper as well as being a group leader. But in time the word spread. By 1973 Esalen was a success, and over 25,000 people had gotten some form of training from the Institute. Now 10,000 participate every year.

Until recently all training was at Big Sur where participants took up temporary residence. But that is expensive. So Esalen added another center in San Francisco which does not require living in. It now serves as the Institute's headquarters. The facilities on Union Street aren't as serene as those at Big Sur, but the charm of these newly remodeled and brightly painted Victorian homes is ideal for a non-live-in center. This is a real cost boon for people lucky enough to live nearby.

Esalen is truly unique. It brings psychologists, masseurs and even mystics together as faculty. The trainees are mostly middle class people who for one reason or another want more from life. Many people like encounter training just for the lift it gives them. Other people have psychological problems and go to Esalen for pure therapy. A few enjoy encounter because it is different and seems to be anti-establishment. These latter, sometimes called "encounter bums," often repeat workshops over and over without getting much real benefit. A few people just like the environment of Big Sur. They live on the grounds but seldom participate in any workshops. Some devotees who can't normally afford Esalen programs work at Big Sur in return for room, board, and an occasional workshop.

Esalen doesn't have a specific philosophy. It's too eclectic for that. Nearly anything goes except drugs. As Mike Murphy said, "All life is a process of unfoldment." At Esalen you can unfold in as many ways as are possible, and then some. Murphy sees Esalen as being similar to a university, offering a non-dogmatic diversification of courses, methods and instructors. Of the permanent staff, many are specialists in specific growth techniques and have developed strong followings. Will Schutz is an Esalen resident who combines writing with full-time group leadership in open encounter. Fritz Perls refined gestalt therapy while he was a resident group leader. And structural integration had its unfolding at Esalen because Ida Rolf was a long-time staff member. In addition to its staff, Esalen hosts a constant parade of big-name lecturers and group leaders who visit from all over the country. They too give workshops and courses. It is this adjunct staff of famous names that attracts many people to Esalen. Luminaries such as Dr. Stanley Krippner, Dr. Rammurti Mishra, Dr. John Lilly, Charles Berner and even David Meggyesy, the ex-pro football player, all have their followings . . . and their unique programs. So Esalen might be likened to a marketplace where different merchants present their wares.

Though no longer dominant, still the most popular Esalen workshops are the encounter groups. In them participants interact with one another as *feeling* beings. Honesty is the watchword. Tell-it-like-it-is becomes the rule. You feel; you emote. Raw emotions range from fury to intimate affection. From these you learn about yourself. You realize your self-deceptions. You recognize your inherent abilities. You usually discover that you are more worthwhile than you thought. Above all, you learn that you are not a victim of outside forces. You learn that ultimately you are responsible for how your life turns out.

It didn't take group leaders long to discover that intensive workshops over several consecutive days are far more valuable than years of periodic short-term therapy. Thus, most encounter workshops at Esalen are either weekend or five-day sessions. Still there is quite a range. A full day session in the city will cost you $20 and up. A weekend at Big Sur with room and board runs in the neighborhood of $100 while five days ranges up to $300. The culmination is a four-week Big Sur residence program priced around $900.

Esalen has numerous programs that range from exotic and unusual experiences to practical exercises useful in every day life. There are dream workshops, warm sulphur baths, massage sessions, enriched relationship groups and even meditation. There are workshops for singles, couples, families, strangers, professionals, specific organizations and just general interest. So you will discover the menu for mentation not only offers such staples as encounter, psychodrama and gestalt therapy, but there are fancy dishes with strange names.

A quick look at one Esalen catalog (it changes every quarter) reveals a tremendous variety of far-out titles along with equal variety in cost. In San Francisco there's a one-day session in "Body Music" for $20 or a weekend of "Fair Fight Training for Couples" at $50. "Mountain Aesthetics Along the Big Sur Coast" is a mountain and shore weekend experience costing $100. Other Big Sur weekends include a "Workshop for Gay People" ($100), "Gestalt Tarot" ($90) or "You Don't Have to Suffer to Feel Good" ($110). If you can spend a full week, you might be interested in a "Tender Invitation" ($220), "Freeing the Voice" ($280) or in a unique approach to illumination called "Endarkenment" ($300).

Esalen is also into sports. Because its athletically inclined director, Mike Murphy, sees sports as a Western form of yoga to coordinate mind and body, he adapted regular Esalen techniques to the playing field. Athletes trained in these methods actually change their time sense so they can respond more rapidly to fast-moving situations. Esalen's new Sports Institute now trains amateur and professional athletes. It's available to you too. Included in its workshops are Hatha Yoga, Aikido, T'ai Chi Ch'uan, Rolling Movement, and Dance.

Esalen also has its spiritual side. This is becoming more important every year. Many group leaders are into yoga, Zen or some other form of deep self-realization and often experiment with these on their groups. Also specific workshops in Universal Centering, the Human Biofield, Biofeedback Training, Hypnosis, Dream Analysis and Meditation are available at both Big Sur and San Francisco. Then there is a form of training that combines many of the previously discussed techniques along with lots of others, and can be adapted to your individual needs. This is Psychosynthesis. It is fast becoming one of Esalen's mainstays, and workshops in it are conducted by specially trained leaders. Other than to say that it is a powerful process of development, further discussion of this very important growth program is deferred until Chapter 8 where it more appropriately belongs.

If just experiencing all the foregoing isn't enough, Esalen has figured how you can get academic credit for it in the process. Several colleges and universities give you credit for a semester or longer spent at Esalen under the tutelage of an Esalen advisor. For information, write the Director—Esalen College Program.

The phenomenon that started at Big Sur eventually swept the nation. The first growth center patterned after Esalen was Kairos, established in San Diego in 1967. Three years later more than one hundred centers were active throughout the country. By 1974 the number was well over 300, and ten million people had participated in growth programs of some sort. One million new participants join the ranks every year. It shouldn't be surprising that, just like spiritual centers, over a third of the growth movement is in California.

Some growth centers are marketplaces à la Esalen. Others have small permanent staffs that conduct a limited number of workshops. Still others concentrate on specialties like gestalt, sensory awareness or even specific types of yoga. In size and quality the range is extensive. No other growth center compares in size to Esalen with its permanent staff of eighty people along with numerous "circuit riders." Compared with other growth organizations, the Center for Human Communication in San Francisco's distant suburb of Los Gatos, with its staff of eleven professional therapists and counselors, is considered large. The other extreme is typified by one small commune living according to Jesus' law. They practice a little encounter on each other, but their main goal is a trip to Bermuda—as soon as they parlay their $13 bank account into enough money to buy a boat.

Encounter Pitfalls

The growth movement is new, very new. It is dynamic. It is exciting. It is restless and changing. It is a living, evolving drama.

And, as with every process that evolves, it has its oddities, its freaks, and its tragedies. The drawbacks to the growth movement are many. Most are the result of immature participants and incompetent or inexperienced group leaders. Encounter encourages—or excuses, depending on your viewpoint—straightforward dialogue. It throws a wet blanket on subtlety and tact. Therefore, honest and direct qualities you may develop in workshops often backfire. They are seldom appreciated by people living with real-world problems and unacquainted with masks, hangups, and role playing. Even within workshops there can be problems. It's difficult to screen out neurotics, the very people most subject to emotional breakdown and often attracted to workshops. The charged atmosphere of encounter workshops is not therapy for them. Nor are all "normal" people constituted the same way. Some are shattered by strong attack. Others retaliate with blind rage. Overly sensitive people may be permanently harmed if rejected by the group. Yet inexperienced group leaders who can't differentiate personality types often encourage just these things against the wrong people. Impulsive participants usually get just the opposite guidance from what they need. They are encouraged to display their emotions when really they should learn to curb them. *New York Times* writer Leo Litwak believes encounter-oriented students had a major influence on the chaos that reigned at San Francisco State College during its notorious riots.

When real troubles arise in encounter sessions, it is usually the fault of the leader. Many of these people are self-styled therapists without professional degrees or licenses. Some become group leaders after participating in just a few workshops. They often experiment on their classes with techniques they have heard about but never experienced themselves. These leaders seldom know how to handle unexpected side effects. Aggressive charismatic leaders cause the most casualties since they have tremendous influence on a group. Their interests become the group's interests. Their targets become the group's targets. Some of these leaders use their central positions for their own self-aggrandizement. Consciously or not, they elicit unwarranted emotion from participants to satisfy their own egos. Some unhinged leaders get kicks out of forcing strong men to cry, or worse, to extract confessions of homosexuality. This is seldom done for the sake of therapy. The effect of aggressive leadership is so pronounced that one encounter group follow-up study showed that leaderless groups have more lasting benefit than those conducted by leaders who are insensitive to the needs of participants.

Stanford University researchers claim that about 10 percent of encounter participants studied become casualties. Some become neurotic. It's not clear if they had neurotic tendencies in the first place. University of Chicago psychologists found up to 80 percent of encounter applicants have been involved in psychotherapy. Moreover, if physical activity isn't controlled, participants can get hurt. Bruises and scratches abound. Some people actually suffer broken bones. One author-psychologist is so put off encounter that he claims 44 percent of participants in some encounter groups have been mentally or physically harmed. Of course, he's not an encounter fan. Dr. William Schutz of Esalen doesn't have figures that high. He has written, "My impression is that the results of encounter groups are overwhelmingly positive (83 percent positive, 15 percent no change, 2 percent negative)." But remember, he is a professional psychologist with twenty years of research and teaching. His contemporaries at Esalen are also well qualified. Many centers can't brag about such excellence.

Good growth centers, like good physicians, are usually discovered by word of mouth. If you have friends involved in the growth movement, by all means tell them what you are looking for. If that doesn't work, look up psychologists in your local yellow pages. Centers with licensed professional staffs often list themselves under this category. Perhaps the best and most up to date list of growth centers is kept by the Association of Humanistic Psychology. A simple letter to the San Francisco headquarters will get you their current list of numerous growth centers. The list changes yearly and AHP doesn't guarantee the quality of these centers since any group of persons can call themselves a growth center.

Unfortunately there is not yet a reliable way to measure or judge quality. The type of growth centers that cause psychiatrists and psychologists to climb the walls are those run by amateurs. These often have student leaders or are experiments in communal living. If you are brave enough to try them, check the underground papers or your local college bulletin board.

Growth centers aren't the only way to grow. There are other ways of interpersonal participation. These usually cost less too. If you like excitement, emotion and sometimes pain, try the Synanon Game. It was originally devised as a communication avenue to junkies, people who live with physical and mental pain and have been forced into a life of lies. Many people think of it as attack therapy—"Assault therapy" might be a better term. The game is a leaderless encounter between 5 to 15 people. Anything goes short of physical violence. This game is available to you at just a few professional growth centers. Amateur centers are more likely to feature it.

Synanon

But if you live near Santa Monica, Oakland, San Francisco, Detroit or New York, why not play with the pros? The real Synanon was created to rehabilitate alcoholics and drug addicts. It has clubs in these cities. But the game to members of Synanon is not considered therapy; it is thought of as just a game . . . a game of communication. Synanon's non-resident game-clubs allow anyone to participate. These are like windows to the Synanon life style. One penny a month entitles you to drop by whenever you like and join the games. Larger donations are accepted. There's no problem in making contact; all Synanon facilities are listed in their respective phone books.

Humanism

A very different organization is that of the Humanists. Most of them are agnostics. They take the position that there is no personal God—that there is no human personality independent of body and brain—that death is final.

Instead of seeking God, Humanists search for meaning and values in naturalistic philosophy. They are concerned with ethics and virtues. Their creed is that service to man must replace service to God. They are actively involved in social and legal affairs. Women's liberation, planned parenthood, antipoverty, environmentalism, civil liberties, amnesty for draft evaders—all are strongly supported by the Humanists.

But the members don't concentrate just on social action. They emphasize self-discovery and assisting others in self-discovery. Most affiliated Humanist centers throughout the country offer some form of self-evaluation and growth training. The minimum cost is $15 ($7.50 for low-income individuals) per year for subscribing members and up to $100 if you are generous enough to be a sponsor. For your fee you become a member of the national organization and receive both bimonthly publications, *The Free Mind* and *The Humanist*. To join write the American Humanist Association in San Francisco or the Humanist Association of Canada.

Membership in one of the many local centers is extra. Prices vary. So do activities. San Jose's chapter is an example. It charges $7 more a year plus extra fees to participate in the different encounter programs. The encounter sessions are leaderless, confidential, open ended and usually more gentle than other types of encounter. San Jose supplements its encounter sessions with marathons, humanist festivals, seminars, family counselling and micro labs. All programs encourage honesty, trust, deep feelings and the here-and-now. Their goal is to enrich your life, to build your trust, to expand all human potential.

The growth movement is still very young. It is still evolving, still learning what it is. It certainly has weaknesses. But of those who have participated, by far the majority are profuse with praise. Most people who have completed a workshop report feeling more open and honest. They seem to understand themselves better. They see others in a different and better light. And most are better able to communicate with their families and fellow workers. Those who sought therapy are usually relieved of some phobias, others of complexes, still more of common emotional problems. Some people get such a lift from encounter that they make it a life-style. Many eventually move into deeper forms of therapy. Some go on to find happiness in religion.

Esalen's Dr. Schutz recognizes this. He makes no claim that encounter is the ultimate method for attaining your maximum potential. He sees it merely as part of a spectrum of growth methods, its goals as being part of a bigger goal. He has written, "As I gain experience with encounter, it becomes clearer that the encounter goal of realizing one's potential is virtually identical with the religious goal of finding the God within."

Indeed, scientists and therapists have discovered there is something within much deeper than most encounter workshops can penetrate. It is both awesome and frightening. If you penetrate your psyche to this deeper self, your outlook toward life will change fantastically. You will realize who and what you really are. You will see the grandeur of yourself.

There are several ways you can do this.

Chapter 3

FINDING THE REAL YOU

Freud believed most of your inner problems, your complexes, guilts and fears, developed from early experiences starting with birth. He saw several separate stages in this childhood development, and identified different problems related with each. Childhood sexual conflicts, failure to satisfy infantile wants and imbalance of fundamental drives were the things Freud looked for in his patients. Even today many psychologists and psychiatrists hold views similar to Freud's. They believe that in your early years your mind was too unsophisticated to understand the real nature of problems that came up. So problems that weren't resolved have remained in your subconscious, and they will remain there and fester until you understand them in the context of adult maturity. At least that's what the psychoanalysts say.

But some mental scientists say there are other subconscious elements that aren't a part of your individual history alone. These seem to be common to everyone. Psychiatrist Carl Jung first discovered them in dreams. He called them archetypes and thought they were inherited primordial images. He claimed your psyche is not only related to the present but that it reaches back to prehistoric times. Jung speaks of your archetypes, not as being inherited ideas, but as psychic pathways, indwelling forces that guide you. They have a numinous spiritual quality and in fact they often appear as spirits in dreams. They have been referred to in holy scriptures and may be the source of many revelations. Jung says of the archetype, "It mobilizes philosophical and religious convictions in the very people who deem themselves miles above such fits of weakness. Often it drives with unexampled passion and remorseless logic toward its goal and draws the subject under its spell, from which despite the most desperate resistance he is unable and finally no longer even willing, to break free, because the experience brings with it a depth and fullness of meaning that was unthinkable before."

Well, what are these archetypes? What do they look like? Are they just symbols? Are they abstract concepts of philosophy, of emotion, of pleasure and pain? They appear as images, in whatever form your subconscious wants to display them. They may appear in terms of your own personal history and be clothed in your own perceptions. Yet they are basic to all mankind, and they seem to be urges to *experience* different traits and principles. The principle of evil might present itself, depending on your background, as Nero, the devil, or Jack the Ripper. Your struggle in life may be symbolized by a mountain climb, a wild stagecoach ride or a ship tossing on a stormy sea. Archetypes like these are often present in dreams. The deeper ones, such as the authoritarian old man or the principle of the universal creative mother, usually need more coaxing to emerge. They manifest as Zeus or Moses, Mother Nature or an earth goddess. Innocence, purity, heroism, guilt—human traits of all sorts, concrete or abstract, are buried deep within your psyche as archetypes.

At least one group of people has become acquainted with these inner phenomena. Amateur experimenters with LSD report dragging up from their psyche not only repressed resentment toward their parents or anxieties stemming from early encounters with kindergarten classmates, but they often have strange philosophical insights. Some people suddenly see their entire lives in a different light. A few recognize a universal oneness in all of creativity. Yet most people who experiment with psychedelic chemicals can't anticipate what will occur. Will their experience be exotic, blissful or revealing? Or will it be sheer horror? To them, an acid trip is an adventure somewhere. But few people know where somewhere is.

Some scientists do. At least they know where a controlled series of LSD encounters may lead. They know that LSD doesn't *cause* you to have certain experiences. Rather it is a powerful amplifier of your own mental processes. As such it can open your deepest psychic spaces to awareness, and over time can do this in some sort of pattern. So a few psychiatrists have used psychedelic drugs therapeutically since they act as a powerful psychic purgative on disturbed patients.

One of these psychiatrists is Stanislav Grof. His early work started in Czechoslovakia and continued at the Maryland Psychiatric Research Center. First he developed a method of treatment called Psycholytic Therapy with LSD. It involves a psychiatric preparatory period followed by from 15 to 80 sessions where the patient receives median doses of LSD once every week or two. He discovered that as the therapy sessions unfold, patients experience bit by bit what is buried in their psyches. It is like peeling an onion layer by layer with each layer disclosing something deeper within. But Dr. Grof found that with psycholytic therapy the onion of your mind unpeels in a specific manner. That there are stages in how you can discover yourself.

The first stage of the therapy exposes your childhood problems. It resurrects childhood traumas, Oedipus complexes, weaning training, juvenile diseases and surgical experiences. It vividly recalls to memory abuses you endured when young. Generally this stage differs for each patient because each person lived a different childhood.

But that's just the beginning. Dr. Grof wrote, "As far as the psycholytic treatment with LSD is concerned, only its first stage can be considered therapy in the conventional sense. The following two stages transcend the framework of therapy and resemble strikingly the procedures that have been used over millennia in various countries of the world in temple mysteries and initiation rites as methods of spiritual awakening and enlightenment."

Beyond this first stage Dr. Grof says your experiences get into the transpersonal realm. These he emphasizes don't show any continuity with what you call your ego. They don't seem to be related to your experiences in the material world. In this stage LSD therapy dissolves time and space. It distorts, and eventually shatters, your ego. Dr. Grof says, "It shows the human mind as a gigantic iceberg with elements of individual and collective unconscious as well as ancient phylogenetic (evolutionary) memories buried in the depths. From the point of view of the experiences in repeated LSD sessions even the 'depth psychological approach' of the classical Freudian analysis barely scratches the surface."

That's an understatement. The second stage is rife with much more fundamental experiences. You may relive prenatal and birth agonies. You experience death and rebirth, again and again. You are caught up in medieval battles or you may be seared in the blinding holocaust at Hiroshima. Your anxieties build to a peak, then they settle down for a while. You may have soothing experiences of beautiful forests, of starry skies, of aromatic flowers and great works of art. Myriad psychic phenomena come to the surface in an alternating, vibrant kaleidoscope of heaven and hell. There are combinations of agonies and raptures so powerful it is hard to tell them apart. They merge into what Dr. Grof calls volcanic ecstasy. And there is an agonizing search for the meaning in life.

Beyond this words can't describe your experiences. The archetypal portrayals are so abstract they seem like the "high" dreams described in Chapter 1. You witness cosmic wars between good and evil. You battle powerful demons as you reunite your soul with the Divine consciousness. The phenomena are embryonic; they are ancestral; they spell out your whole evolution . . . even to the point that you can identify with lower mammals, with reptiles, or even with protozoa.

Also you seem to be reliving past lives. "Reliving these experiences," Dr. Grof says, "is often accompanied by purging 'karmic hurricanes,' winds blowing as if through centuries and tearing karmic bonds. This ends in an experience of irrational bliss, purity and relief from a 'timeless curse'—a triumph over a fundamental achievement that has been attempted for centuries without success."

In this latter stage you have intuitive knowledge, apparent insights into the basic nature of man and the universe itself. You realize the relativity of values. You identify with opposites. You see the yin and yang of life—and you understand what they mean. Finally you go beyond the framework of your individual self. You become one with all. You see the universe as a single unity. You experience the ecstasy of wholeness. As Dr. Grof describes it, "The positive experiences involve a type of ecstasy that is very distinct from the 'volcanic ecstasy' described above. It could be labelled 'unitive,' 'melted,' or 'All is One' ecstasy. The subjects experiencing it feel that they have transcended the dichotomy between the ego and the external world and they experience blissful unity with other people, Nature, Universe and God."

If you are like most people, your guilts, fears, drives and archetypes are a real part of you. They mold your thoughts. They guide your actions. Only when you have recognized them with a mature mind, or have so thoroughly experienced them that their psychic energy is dissipated can you be said to be rid of them. When that happens, a little recognized and hidden center which Jung called the "Self" becomes apparent. This is your basic and pure self . . . your *real self.* Your ego, though still a conscious part of you, now becomes subordinate to the now powerful "Self." You as a person then become spiritually *reborn* with a new outlook on life.

There are other ways to achieve this new outlook on life. Dr. Grof refined the psycholytic treatments into a therapy requiring far fewer sessions, one which bypasses the childhood traumas. This still involves difficult prenatal and transpersonal experiences, but he discovered that larger doses of LSD result in your having more universal and fundamental experiences. That patients exposed to music and settings conducive to religious experiences evidence dramatic changes in personality. This occurs usually in from one to three sessions. Yet both forms of therapy get to and expunge your deepest psychic problems. So from what he observed from both types of therapy Dr. Grof concluded, "Man in his innermost nature appears as a being that is fundamentally in harmony with his environment and is governed by intrinsic high and universal values."

And so what are the results of successful LSD therapy? What are humans once their innermost nature becomes dominant? For one thing, psychotic symptoms are reduced. Anxiety, guilt, tension and depression may virtually disappear. Increased relaxation, serenity and inner peace are the rule. People feel purified; they are more in tune with nature and have a better self-image; they feel more zest for life; they exhibit improved health and enjoy a freer and more potent sexuality. It's like having a film removed from all their senses. Also these people are more tolerant, more understanding, more loving than before. Art, nature, the simple things in life become meaningful. The same occurs with religion, philosophy and mysticism. Above all, these people accept themselves as they really are. They no longer have unrealistic goals and ambitions, and they think in terms of the here and now. Many have a greater urge to be creative; they want to be more productive. . . . They get into the crafts, invention and helping others. They want to cope with *real* problems, not neurotic ones.

But if you have the idea of getting a few acid trips from your psychiatrist in the name of psycholytic or psychedelic therapy, don't waste your time. Only two institutions in the United States and one in Canada are authorized to administer psychedelic drugs. Then you have to be emotionally disturbed to qualify. Federal law frowns on "normal" people trying to become enlightened chemically. No! You haven't a chance. So right now, as far as seeking enlightenment is concerned, LSD can't be of much help.

That's probably just as well. It gives you a chance to explore other ways to enlightenment. In fact, mystics and spiritual leaders claim there are much better and more permanent ways. Still LSD therapy and the research that accompanies it have opened up the human psyche as no other psychological tool can do. It has given psychologists and psychiatrists in the transpersonal movement a new understanding of the awesome magnitude and depth of your psychic manifestations. And their findings can be used as a sounding board for comparing other methods of psychic growth. That shouldn't be difficult. Dr. Willis Harmon of Stanford Research Institute says there are no psychedelic drug experiences that can't be duplicated in some other way.

Church of Scientology

Scientology is one way of showing you what is deep down inside yourself. And it's a popular way. The Church of Scientology is one of the fastest growing religious organizations in America. Its members consider their philosophy to be a new 20th century religion—an approach to spirituality *and* psychology that is totally different from anything theology or science has ever known. To Scientologists, it is the most potent way to self-knowledge, and the only way to salvation.

The high priest of Scientology is Lafayette Ronald Hubbard . . . Ron or L. R. H. to his admiring followers. His abode is the 4,000 ton, 300 feet long Apollo that plies the warm Mediterranean waters, a yacht that once buoyed up the private parties of Winston

Churchill. In his youth Hubbard traveled through Northern China and India where he met several lamas and priests. Later he became an engineer, explorer and science writer. During World War II he was skipper of naval escort vessels.

Ron Hubbard's spiritual awakening really started when he made several startling inner discoveries in a Naval Hospital while enduring the terribly lonely and introspective world of a man temporarily blinded by a depth charge. Upon recovery, he combined these discoveries with his knowledge of Buddhism and his technical know-how, then seasoned the mixture with that creativity which only a science writer can have. The result was the science of Dianetics, a philosophy of mind-control-over-body. By 1952, Ron Hubbard had made another discovery. He concluded that the source of all minds is spiritual. This philosophy and the method of how to personally recognize this he called Scientology.

Hubbard asserts that men are really gods, or at least godly manifestations. It is they who created the world, and this they did as a game. But they fell so in love with the game that they developed amnesia and the game became reality. All of us will continue on this worldly merry-go-round until we stop dreaming and realize the world is an illusion. Shades of Oriental mysticism? Hubbard is quite specific about what you are really like. He says you don't *have* a soul; you *are* a soul. He calls this soul "Thetan." It is a "spiritual agent of infinite creative potential that acts in, but is not part of, the physical universe." Spiritual man, he says, is pure thought—and is immortal. That's why Scientology puts so much emphasis on reincarnation and recalling past lives to explain why you are what you are in this life. This philosophy isn't official doctrine, however, since you are supposed to find your own truth. Many Scientologists even keep their former church affiliations.

Scientology is both a religion (in the Buddhist sense) and a working psychology. In fact, it's quite a challenge to orthodox psychology. It speaks of the same psychological elements, but gives them different names and assigns slightly different properties to them. You have an "Analytical Mind"—your thinker, and a "Reactive Mind"—your emoter. During moments of stress, severely painful sensations and perceptions are stored in your reactive mind as unprocessed, unanalyzed and unobserved image pictures called "engrams." When you later experience similar stress situations, the engrams force you into what your Reactive Mind considers survival responses. These automatic behavior patterns are inappropriate for the new situation so they create new engrams and secondary anxieties. Over time, whole engram chains can build up to the point that any situation slightly resembling the original stress will trigger emotional upwellings. A mother whose child died in a house fire may re-experience horror the next time she sees a home burn, adding another traumatic experience to the original one. Over time any fire may trigger a painful emotion. But this can be overcome. To negate any engramic effects, even archetypal effects, you must become aware of the engrams behind them. And you have to re-experience the engram, completely.

This is done by "Auditing." It's also called pastoral counseling. An auditor is a listener who listens with a specific purpose. He gets you to talk about yourself. This has been likened to the Roman Catholic confessional, but it's not the same. Your auditor guides you into peeling off layers of your psychic onion, helping you bring your engrams to consciousness where they can be re-experienced and then discarded. The goal of pastoral counseling is permanent erasure of the effects of painful experiences in your lifetime. Your auditor does this by asking the right questions. There is a long prescribed list of processes. Everywhere in the world Scientology auditors use the same processes. From this inventory they open up your mind so *you* can find the answers. Just like Gestalt therapy, just like Socratic dialogue, just like Zen, Scientology has no answers— just questions. Only you have the answers about yourself. You have hundreds of answers, but you need someone to ask the right questions. Your auditor is specially trained to do just that.

He also uses a special tool. Scientologists call it a twentieth-century religious artifact and claim it's a modernized version of Buddhism's prayer wheel. Some people say it's a lie detector. Actually, it's an electronic device called an E-meter or Confessional Aid. It measures electrical resistance in the palms of your hands and like other galvanic skin response (GSR) machines, it registers your emotional state. It doesn't really detect lies, but when you have an experience that affects you emotionally, the meter will register it. The same occurs if you just think about the experience. Your auditor uses this technique to discover which questions touch on sensitive emotional areas. This shows fruitful stress areas that should be explored. It also indicates when you have worked through a particularly emotionally charged memory and are "released" from a specific psychic problem. Thus, auditing techniques coupled with Scientologists' acquired ability to imagine and reinact past events create mental episodes almost as real and exciting as LSD dramas.

This was amply demonstrated during one auditing session with a twenty-seven-year-old man named Larry. Larry was to re-experience as many events as necessary in what he believed to be his myriad incarnations to "release" him from engrams associated with guilt.

As the auditor quietly reminded him of the auditing rules, Larry firmly grasped the electrodes of the Confessional Aid. He was asked if he had broken the rules by taking alcohol, drugs, or anything like that within the last twenty-four hours.

"No," he answered.

The meter indicated no emotion in his response. Then the auditor said, "Can you recall any occasions in which you generated guilt in another person?"

Larry closed his eyes, nodded a little, and finally said, "Yes." The meter agreed.

"When was this?"

"About four hundred years ago."

"Would you go to the beginning of the episode?"

"Yes."

"Would you describe what you see?"

Larry hesitated. Though his eyes were closed, it was apparent that he was straining to see through four centuries of history. The needle on the meter registered strong emotion. Then Larry said, "I see a woman kneeling in front of me. There are cobblestones around. She has black hair. She looks Spanish. She is crying. I am making her feel guilty in some way. I think I am a priest. Yes! Yes! I am a priest. And she's crying and I am saying, 'You're guilty aren't you? You're guilty aren't you?' She's crying and confesses, 'Yes—yes, I am. I am.' Then I see some soldiers around. And there are lots of other people like this woman. Some are kneeling; some are standing. The soldiers are holding them prisoner. They are kind of out on a big square . . . a courtyard. Well . . . I guess that's about it."

Then the auditor asked Larry to relive the episode carefully; to recall in as much detail as possible what had occurred. Larry squinted his closed eyes, wrinkled his brow and faded back into time. For a few moments he was still; then he thrashed his arms and squirmed in the chair, all the time keeping his eyes tightly closed and firmly gripping the electrodes. Again the meter showed powerful emotion. Finally, with a crisp "OK," Larry indicated the episode had been relived.

The auditor asked him what happened.

"I was a priest, and I remember I started yelling at her, 'Confess! Confess! You are guilty, aren't you? Aren't you?' She cried back, 'No. No.' I pulled her head back and made her look me in the face and I said, 'You're guilty aren't you? You're guilty.' And then she finally screamed, 'Yes. Yes—I am guilty.' Then she cried. And I felt good about this. I really felt *good*."

Again the auditor asked Larry to repeat the episode to pick up any missed details. Again Larry squirmed. Then he said, "OK, I'm there."

"What did you experience?"

"Just about the same. There really wasn't much difference at all. I remember the soldiers were bringing more people to me . . . for me to make them confess. And it really felt good. It really felt good."

That episode concluded, the auditor asked Larry to remember another experience further back. This one turned out to have occurred twenty thousand years ago. Larry was a young bowman in a forest. He was chasing a man who had intruded into his tribe's territory. He caught him. He vividly recalled beating the man's head against a log, all the time accusing him of being "guilty." And it felt good the whole time.

Then back still further. Much further, over a hundred thousand years ago. Now Larry's descriptions were far-out. He was in a lost civilization. He was an official. He was humiliating people. He was making them feel guilty . . . and he was enjoying it to the hilt.

Then another event, this time a hundred and fifty million years into earth's murky past. He was in a dark tunnel. He was there clandestinely. He met a girl. He was angry. He accused her of being unfaithful. He berated her. All the while she was begging, "Forgive me. Forgive me." But he continued to make her feel guilty. He even refused to sleep with her that night. He felt very righteous. And he felt very *good* every minute of the encounter.

That's when Larry let out an uncomfortable laugh. He looked

up, and with a sense of enlightenment, said, "You know, before this auditing thing happened, I've done a lot of bad things. I've committed harmful things to other people. Now I just realized that I had to somehow justify doing those things . . . like minimizing them . . . like making them seem smaller to me than they were. So I guess I subconsciously decided to do it by making people feel guilty. That's why it felt good.

"What a weird thing to do, now that I look at it. God, it feels good to know that. It's good too, to know that now, maybe, I can be more in control of myself."

That's what Larry got from his session. He felt a sense of relief with his discovery. And the auditor said, "Your needle is floating. You are released."

Larry is a good visualizer. He practically lived those exciting episodes as he would have in a dream. He saw, he heard, he felt those years back in time. Whether he relived real incarnations or vividly imagined them is unimportant. He benefited from them. His subconscious was purged of engrams because of the exercises. That's the purpose of Scientology.

The first instruction on the long road to discovering yourself in Scientology is in communication. This $35 course lasts two weeks and takes about fifteen hours. In it you learn how to understand and convey ideas. You learn that communication is the responsibility of the communicater. Then you are ready to talk about yourself—and learn about yourself.

You can learn about yourself by following one of two routes. The "Training" route is a book-learning process, and is a stepping stone to becoming a minister in the church. You learn about the church's many philosophies, its theories, and its processing methods. You learn how to audit, and you get audited too, since all students practice on one another. The Training route is educational and professional preparation, and requires full-time participation during each stage of your progress.

The other route, "Processing," is more therapeutic, aimed at growth and self-awareness. Most people take it part-time. It too is educational to some degree, in that you attend lectures and work closely with other students. Yet the heart of Processing is having private sessions with some of Scientology's 100,000 professional auditors who take you over a prescribed series of sessions that cost from $25 to $50 an hour. This route is not cheap, but you have more control of the timing and benefit substantially from the one-to-one relationship with the auditor.

Whichever route you elect, you must start with Dianetics, the foundation of Scientology. Dianetics deals with your emotional condition and how your mind affects your body. Its goal is your emotional and physical well-being. This is where you first learn to consciously re-experience those painful past events that trigger irrational actions of your Reactive Mind. These experiences of the source of upsets or problems are always accompanied by revelations and heightened awareness. Some Dianetics students actually experience a change in their bodies. It's a mental way of Rolfing. There is no specific time limit on auditing; you progress at your own rate. But figure on fifteen to sixty hours over two to six months if you are following the Processing route and a flat $500 if you are a student in Dianetic Training.

Whereas Dianetics deals with how your mind affects the physical you, Scientology is concerned with your spiritual self. This includes your manifestation in the physical universe and how you relate to other spiritual beings. Its goal is spiritual freedom. It is the study of knowing how to know, of greater perception, of finding spiritual values. Its processing route involves auditors just as in Dianetics. This unpeeling of your psychic layers rehabilitates your memory, breaks down psychological barriers and revives your creative power. You relive and take responsibility for past misdeeds and thus resurrect and eradicate old traumas and even archetypes. There are eight steps, called grades of release, to the first major milestone in Scientology. Ron Hubbard calls this milestone "Clear." To be Clear means that no programing remains in your psyche that is not under your own control. It means that your mind is no longer cluttered; it is free of uncontrolled stimulus-responses. Rather than *re*acting, you are *acting*. The Training route in Scientology also has eight phases to reach Clear, but the last four are the same as in Processing. As with Dianetics, Scientology Training places more emphasis on learning than does Processing, and it is cheaper because students audit one another.

"So," you ask, "what is the difference in costs between Training and Processing?" That's a good question. The first four stages of Scientology Processing will cost you $125 or more a stage. Student Training is exactly $125 a stage. Beyond that, both routes to Clear may take from $1\frac{1}{2}$ to $2\frac{1}{2}$ years of auditing and can cost from $1,500 to $5,000. This may seem high, but your fees may be paid out over a long period of time. Over 6,000 people felt it was worthwhile and have become Clear.

Cost is one reason the church encourages the Training route. Auditing is inexpensive because students work with one another and you can also reduce cost more by working for the church selling literature and doing general administrative work. Better yet, become a full-time staff member and get your training free.

Once Clear, the real you—the thetan—is now uncluttered. You are able to operate as a purely spiritual being. That's Operating Thetan, or OT. Still, you have to learn about your newly discovered self and how to operate it. It's like being born again. The real you, the thetan, is neither body nor mind. The real you is pure spirit. There are eight more levels of Scientology advancement before you really know how this spiritual self works. At the top of this ladder, it is claimed, you will have complete mastery of yourself, of destiny, of space, time, matter, and energy. You will recognize your divinity.

OT training is given only in Los Angeles or at the international headquarters in England. The price? It averages $2,500 extended over one to two years. But members say money doesn't bother most OT's. By this stage they are no longer playing the money game, or they have become so successful that price is no object.

With the exception of advanced levels, instruction is available all over the United States and in some cities abroad. There are 25 major churches of Scientology along with over 200 missions in the United States and Canada. Then there is the fleet. Seven ships serve as floating monasteries for the churches' elite, the Sea Orgs (as in Organization). These are the 3,000 extremely dedicated full-time members (by invitation only) who get Dianetics, Scientology or OT Training while at the same time developing teamwork and hardiness by meeting the challenge of the sea. Needless to say, they are Ron's fair-haired favorites.

What do Scientology's members get for all their effort? All their time? All their money? Quite a bit. For one thing, as a Scientologist you learn that you really do count in this world. You also learn that you created your own situation. When you become Clear, you reach that plateau which Abraham Maslow called "Self-actualization" and Carl Jung described as the state of recognizing your real self. Clears can love or hate without remorse. They can take pride in their sex, yet enjoy the traits of the opposite sex. They can be intellectual and rational, yet become deeply emotional—all with no inner conflict. Clears learn to reveal and control the personality *they* want. It's a new state of heightened responsibility to yourself. Clears' bodies change, too, just as in bioenergetics. Posture, health and even vision are reported to improve with Clearing. So does IQ, Scientologists claim.

What about Operating Thetans? Well, their wants are just different from most people's. They aren't interested in the pleasure goals of normal worldly folk. They have graduated to other mental realms. Scientologists claim advanced OTs can communicate telepathically, perform psychokinesis and mentally materialize things. They have no more engrams; they have no more archetypes; they have no more fetters; they are finally free. They have completed the human trip. To Scientologists, discovering how to operate as a Thetan is salvation. They no longer think of themselves as Homo Sapiens. They are Homo Novus.

You have probably heard rumors that not all the world is enchanted with the Church of Scientology—that, in fact, some people are downright hostile to it. And, of course, you would have heard correctly. This may stem in part from Scientology's crusade against some medical practices like brain surgery and chemical or electrical shock therapy. The medical profession has countered that Scientology made unfounded claims that its Dianetics methods could heal and branded the organization a serious threat to health. The Food and Drug Administration even seized a load of E-meters. Furthermore, a few churches got up-tight over Scientology's unorthodoxy. This antagonism spilled over from the United States to other nations. For a while Scientology received a lot of international static. But in a court case Judge Gerhard Gesell ruled that E-meters should be returned to the church if used for purely religious purposes—though he did caution Scientologists against making any claims of healing. The church now admonishes all participants to seek medical advice for physical illnesses. Much of the ruckus has died down and Scientology concepts are not only being accepted as adjuncts to orthodox religion, but a few psychiatrists are recognizing and employing some of the practices too. So now Scientology can get on with its self-imposed task of Clearing all of mankind . . . of getting each and all individuals to drop their irrational habits and conditioned responses . . . to teach them to take control of their lives . . . to become responsible.

There's another way to learn to do these things. And its discoverer is an excellent example of a person who mastered his life. Werner Erhard readily admits he used to smoke five packs of cigarettes a day. And he used to get high on thirty cups of coffee during the daytime and come down in the evenings on several martinis. Today he doesn't smoke at all. He is moderate in the other two for social purposes, and he lost ten pounds in the process. Yet he never did *stop* doing these things—he just eliminated the desire to do them. That happened only after he had spent several years getting into all sorts of growth trips. He tried Zen, meditation, Gestalt, bioenergetics, body awareness, primal therapy, and sensory awareness. Then in a moment of clarity he saw how they all fit together. He synthesized them and applied the results to his habits. From this evolved what he calls Erhard Seminars Training. It's now available to the public.

EST

est

Werner Erhard's method is usually abbreviated *est.* That's also the Latin way of saying "It is." As Werner said, "In life you wind up with one of two things—the results or the reasons why you don't have the results. Results don't have to be explained. They just are. *est* is."

est was an immediate winner. In the first three years since the program got under way in 1971 Erhard produced over 30,000 graduates. *est* now turns out 1,500 more each month, in several American cities. The concept behind *est* is simple. You are responsible for how your life is. All your physical and emotional problems are manifestations of your mind at some level of consciousness. You as an entity are already perfect, but you don't experience your perfection because of mental barriers. In *est* training you begin to recognize these barriers and start to dissolve them. You start becoming responsible for your life.

According to *est* theory, when you encounter a worldly problem, you flatten like a rubber ball thrown against a wall. When the problem is past, you often fail to completely unflatten. This means some emotional energy remains locked within your mind. In Erhard's training you learn the process of releasing that energy. *est* allows you to recognize that your mind creates a headache; that tension or nervousness don't. This theory is based on the principle of stored emotional memories. If you don't consciously experience an emotion, it is stored as a subconscious memory where it can fester and cause trouble. And it can be warehoused in numerous spaces at different levels of your psyche.

Erhard's concept is that only by fully experiencing all these stored emotional memories can you eliminate them. He reasons that since no two things can exist in the same space at the same time, if you mentally create an image of the old experience, and experience it fully this time, it will dissolve the buried memory. The analogy is similar to the mutual annihilation of matter and antimatter. Another way of putting it is that by synthetically creating an old experience in your imagination strongly enough, you become consciously satiated with the experience. For instance, do you have a craving to overeat? *est* processes recreate your experience of hunger. This may then erase the symptoms that *cause* you to eat since you are conscious of and are concentrating on the physical sensations and thoughts associated with hunger. These are not experiences of eating, but of the desire to eat.

The same goes for other habits. Werner, as his followers call him, says, "We don't ever tell people they should *stop* smoking. What we find in the training is that, after the training, a person may so totally experience the *desire* to smoke that he erases the desire to smoke." Thus, *est* does not recondition, it deconditions; it dehypnotizes; it deprograms your computerlike mind. This is just the opposite of hypnosis, which plants suggestions. *est* removes suggestions by duplication—by satiation. To erase insomnia, for example, you recreate the sensations, the thoughts and the past experiences associated with sleeplessness. You synthetically experience sleeplessness. The same for headaches, for anxiety, for fear, and even for severe complexes. The feeling of restricted breath that you may experience when confronted by a stern boss can be completely recreated and re-experienced. When fully re-experienced, the difficulty should go away.

Lots of your training with *est* gets into those locked-in body tensions that Ida Rolf talks about. Erhard's method gives you an orderly pattern of techniques to relax and to expand your consciousness. This lets you observe obscure muscles under tension. You feel these tensions and eventually experience the feelings that have tensed the muscles. By discovering the emotional patterns built into your body, you can free your body from them . . . and thus free your consciousness for other things, like coping with everyday life.

You also learn to deal with frustrations. Between an incoming stimulus and your normal automatic response there is a space where you may choose to act or react. You learn that *you* should control when you go to the bathroom, not your bladder. Also you can develop a new outlook toward difficulties. You discover that things are the way they are; that frustration is just a waste of time. You may want to play tennis, but it's raining. With *est* training you may still want to play tennis, but you learn not to be disappointed when you can't. There's that Zen showing through: "non-expecting" becomes a part of your life-style. Things are.

The purpose of *est* is not just to rid you of hang-ups or make you smarter. It may assist you in accomplishing these, but more important, it is designed to alter the quality of your life. The stated purpose of the training is to open additional dimensions of living to your awareness. *est* emphasizes that you have created your environment and that *you* must accept responsibility for it. Then your life-style can become more spontaneous as you find yourself eliminating old patterns and habits. You can discover your true nature. *est* lets you come face to face with your false self and shows you the real one. As Werner says, "You will laugh for three days at your old self when you realize your true self."

Actually *est* training doesn't resurrect your real self for you. *est* isn't like LSD therapy where you go through several stages of psychic discovery before you graduate. Nor is it like Scientology where you have specific well-defined grades that you must pass. *est* training isn't processing per se. It shows you how to process yourself. Most graduates continue their private processing long after finishing the basic training seminar. Still, that brief sixty hours of instruction can make a major change in your personality and your outlook on life. Even the first day can. At least that was the view of a cocktail waitress, Polly, when she said, "One time that really struck me during the training; it was Saturday evening of the first training. We did a process that was just really strong. When I walked out of that hotel, it was like the world was really made for me. I had to walk from the Commodore Hotel, which is in kind of a respectable part of New York, all through the downtown night-scene into 'Hell's Kitchen.' That night I just walked down the street and people just cleared out of the way. I mean it wasn't like I was just walking. I felt like superwoman. And I still get senseless at that."

The standard training usually consists of two full weekends of intensive instruction along with one mid-week evening seminar. The price is $250. Most likely the setting is a large hotel ballroom filled with over two hundred housewives, physicians, hard hats, longhairs, and lots of regular hairs. Up front a dynamic instructor communicates by combining the crusty language of a top sergeant with the koans (questions) of a Zen master. Also he demonstrates the processes, often using lots of chalk and blackboard, or he takes the class through a process, urging the trainees to observe their experiences without evaluation. This way they learn to look at the reality of their experiences.

And like Silva Mind Control, there are processes involving relaxation, memory, psychically experiencing materials and substances. Then there are those Zen-like koans to shatter belief patterns and intellectual conditioned responses. Lots of time is spent sharing experiences with others in the group, though you don't have to if you don't want. You experience your complete range of emotion—apathy, excitement, elation and rage. You are guided into recalling particular instances of your life. You recreate them exactly. You observe them. You don't analyze them, just experience them—experience them until you are full of them—so full that they just go away.

Graduates may repeat the training at a reduced price. And they can get more than just the standard training. *est* has a variety of evening seminars in which graduates continue to master themselves and their environments, but in different ways. Seminars like "Self Expression," "About Sex," "Body Series" and "Be Here & Now" are held once a week and cost only $2.50 per session. It's in these seminars that you really put the training into practice. Like the standard training, they are available in many California cities. *est* has also spread to Honolulu, New York, Boston, Washington, D.C., Denver, and Aspen, Colorado. More cities are in the future.

In addition to the standard training and seminars, there is special professional training. Physicians, nurses, psychologists, educators and entertainers can all find something specially adapted to them. There are also courses for the whole family. An eight-day intensive Teen Training Course was introduced in 1974. Couples, parents, children and teens—all can find a course of training to help them better cope with life.

What, you might ask, is the end product of *est* training? For one answer, here's what a graduate, Christine, had to say. "Now I have quite a reputation for laughing all the time. Not only around the *est* office, but where I work too. People just hear my laugh and they come up and say, 'How come you're smiling all the time?' It's really far out." Dave, a salesman emphasized other improvements when he said, "I find that negatives seem to be positives. When negatives come along, I'm able to handle them more readily. I experience my life as plateaus. I feel that I go up on a plateau and I'll have a peak experience that will really get me high. Then I'll go along for a little while, then there'll be another peak experience. My life still seesaws, but it is basically experiences of positive growth up, like a step ladder. Before I used to have long periods of depression and go maybe for a week and not be able to sleep. That's not true anymore. My energy level is very, very high at all times."

These self-assessments were similar to findings by an independent psychological testing firm, Behaviordyne in Palo Alto. What it found is impressive. Males in general had boosted their self-images, were less anxious and less dependent. Also they assumed more responsibility, felt less guilt and fears, coped better with life, and were much happier. Women improved similarly, but got a couple of dividends since they developed more ambition and made greater demands on themselves than they did prior to training. Some people develop posture changes just as in Rolfing. The most obvious physical changes are in mobility—like the boy who started training with a sunken chest and didn't swing his arms as he walked. After just two weekends of the standard training he had thrust out his chest and moved his arms normally. Even improvement in eyesight has been observed.

Dramatic changes in personality and attitudes about life can occur as a person confronts his own psychic barriers and moves through them. Over time, the real self emerges. It is the same real self that other in-depth therapies produce—Maslow's "self-actualization" and Scientology's "Clear". It is a here-and-now consciousness, and a sense of responsibility. It is understanding, tolerance and love. It's an outpouring of joy and exuberance. It's a personality that everybody likes to be around. Yet those who have stripped away their false selves and advance to this psychic level all seem so similar; it's as if they are all stereotypes of goodness . . . as if there is something hidden behind their outward personality so pure that it is basic to all mankind . . . as if their real self is the same in all people . . . as if they are no longer stuck on a separate personality.

Werner Erhard explains this strange phenomenon this way, "As people become more unblocked, their individuality is in the *experience* of themselves rather than in the appearance of themselves. So they may *look* stereotyped, but their experiences are very individual, whereas the blocked person is exactly the opposite. His outward appearance is bizarrely different. His inward experience is very much the same in terms of its monotony, deadness and for some people, suffering. So it's just a reverse. As you become more unblocked you become *apparently* similar to your fellows and *inwardly* richer in your experience."

To put it another way, the outwardly stereotyped appearance of the self-actualized person is akin to the dullness that children find in adults because they aren't screaming, running and playing in the mud. But the adults are having intellectual experiences of which the children are totally incapable. And self-actualized people have spiritual adventures beyond most people's comprehension. Their inner lives are fantastically exciting.

Not many people, no matter what type of training they take, totally achieve this state of self-actualization. Still, they will probably have developed their real selves into truly mature selves. If you are one of them, you will no longer crave prestige, nor personal gain, nor ego fulfillment, nor material pleasure. You will discover that true living is not accumulation of material things and incessant activity. It is calmness, peace, love, and untold joy. Your awareness will merge with your real self and you will become confident and never afraid. You will no longer be anxious about life. You will lose your concern for the future. Gone will be the fear of death. Now you will see there is yet a higher entity, a Being deep within your psyche that is wiser and grander than you had ever imagined, a self far greater than even your real self, a vitality that suggests immortality . . . and divinity.

Chapter 4

THE DIVINE EXPERIENCE

It has been argued by materialists that religion is purely the invention of mankind; that belief in a comforter, a protector, a way out of the worldly mess is necessary for most people so they can maintain sanity and hope; that religion's purpose is to satisfy basic psychological needs. But critics of religion have never explained *why* those needs. Is it perhaps because what the religions teach is basically true? Is it possible that deep down in every human subconscious there is an understanding of the reality of the cosmos? Could not this knowledge or reality be filtered up through the levels of consciousness as beliefs rather than exact understanding? And could not this subconscious knowledge be common to all mankind?

Ralph Waldo Emerson thought so. He said, "There is one mind common to all individual men." Thomas Edison felt the same. So did Dr. J. B. Rhine of parapsychology fame. Psychiatrist Carl Jung even claimed to have found this common mind.

Jung once had a dream. It was one of those creative dreams, the type that disgorged years of absorbed knowledge in one succinct picture. But, like most dreams, it was disguised. In it Jung saw a house with many basements, each older and more primitive than the one above. The last was in complete disarray and seemed infinite. This experience gave him a clue to the nature of consciousness. Yet several more years were to pass before Jung finally understood the clue and formed his final concept of mind. What he ultimately envisioned was three levels of your psyche. Uppermost is a shallow mantel of consciousness. Under this is a much thicker layer of *personal* unconscious which includes Freud's concepts of preconscious and unconscious. All of these Jung considered as individual in nature, unique to each person. Below all this he postulated an infinite *collective* unconscious, something greater than individual life forces. The collective unconscious is not considered a group mind. It is generic to all people and its genesis predates individual experience. It is urges, feelings, instincts, memories and the whole assemblage of archetypes. It is also undreamed-of beauties. It is ecstasy beyond imagination. It is undiminished love. And it is consciousness that is universal. Some people call this superconsciousness. Others prefer the term cosmic consciousness. A few look upon it as being something even higher. The founder of Science of Mind, Dr. Ernest Holmes, said, "There is that within every individual which partakes of the nature of the Universal Wholeness and insofar as it operates—is God."

Most mystics agree. God is within you. And they claim to know. Many of them have penetrated the filtering process of their various levels of consciousness. They have seen firsthand what lies beyond individual mind. As Saint Augustine wrote, "I, Lord, went wandering like a strayed sheep seeking thee with anxious reasoning without, whilst thou wast within me . . . and I found thee not, because in vain I sought for him who was within myself."

One person in this century who discovered that is an Indonesian named Muhammad Subuh. He was a twenty-four-year-old bookkeeper when he received a spontaneous revelation. It came as a glorious ball of brilliant light. In utter shock, he thought he was having a heart attack. Instead an inner voice told him of a way to inwardly experience God. It also told him he would die at age 32. From that moment Subuh had exciting and beautiful inner experiences of God every day. Then, three years later, the inner divine visitations stopped as suddenly as they started. Subuh returned to a normal life, though measurably changed. In June of 1933, as predicted, at age thirty-two he died. He died mystically, that is; but he was spiritually reborn. This time he got a special divine message. It spelled out his new mission in life: he was to share his gift with the rest of the world. Thus began the practice of Subud.

Subud

The word is a contraction of *Susila Budhi Dharma*, and roughly translates as "following God's will through divine revelation by totally surrendering to the Will of God in order to live rightly by the Grace of God." Subud is a way of life in the material world while at the same time being an experience of what Subud interprets to be God.

At first Muhammad Subud's following was small and limited to the Orient. It wasn't until 1947 that the movement really got under way in the West. By 1958, Subud was established in San Francisco, Sacramento, Carmel and Los Angeles. Then it spread across the United States. Now there is a Subud center in almost every major American city, and in many other cities throughout the world. And everywhere in the world members call their founder *Bapak*—"Honored father from Indonesia." Some say, "Bapak is like the sun; members are like his rays."

What is so unique about Subud that its founder should be considered an honored father and be likened to the sun? What has he given his followers that is so wonderful? Illumination, that's all . . . divine illumination, they say. Subud is not a religion, but it is a means of awakening your spirituality. In Subud the human soul is considered separate from God. Yet a Great Life Force flows through everything and everyone. According to Bapak, mankind originally had open channels to the Source of this Great Life Force. But alas, as so many other creeds will tell you, mankind developed impurities that eventually clogged those channels. To know God again you must clear out these impurities. Subud is considered God's way of doing it for you. Sure, you may eventually get salvation (return to God) by your own efforts, like serving mankind or submitting to religious disciplines. But in these other ways you *strive* to experience God. In Subud you do *nothing*. That's right—absolutely nothing. In Subud, the members say, all you do is abdicate your will to God; just surrender; just open up to God's Grace; just silently and without desire await the divine gift.

The vehicle for doing this "nothing" is the latihan. That roughly translates as "spiritual exercise." It's a form of worship—not worship because God needs it, but because you do. It is considered the quickest road back to the Source. It is the road of the ordinary man, not of the intellectual person. In the latihan you don't think, you just experience. What you experience is entirely the will of God. This is God's way of introducing you to yourself, of getting rid of your impurities. The latihan, though performed in groups, is really your personal form of worship. And on occasions your personal experience is awesome. As one member put it, "Sometimes you'll get a knowing within you about something you just can't put into words. You can't even tell yourself what it is. But you can *feel* the experience. You know it's happening. It's something very private. It's something that's just yours. It's being given to you only."

But it's not being given lightly. Bapak discovered early in Subud's history that this sort of experience is a serious business. That's why you can't become an instant member. There is a three-month probationary period so you can decide if Subud is really for you. You need to understand what occurs during the latihan. Otherwise you might not be able to cope with the strange and sometimes awesome experiences you may have.

During your first three months Subud provides you with experienced members called helpers to advise and instruct you. They will try to answer *all* your questions. Subud has absolutely no secrets. The helpers will share with you their experiences during the latihan. They will tell you what to expect. Some Subud centers have scheduled lectures. Others arrange talks with you privately. Above all, you are encouraged to sit outside the latihan hall on several occasions and listen. What you hear may shake you a bit. Occasionally there is just silence. More often you will hear singing . . . or laughing . . . or crying . . . or shouting . . . or speaking in tongues. At times there is the noise of movement, of falling, of stomping feet. What you hear is preparation for your coming adventure—not an intellectual adventure, but a feeling adventure.

It is spiritually much like the Christian baptism, an expression of faith in the Grace of God. There is no special ceremony, no ritual. You just join the others in the latihan. But this first time is special. It is called a Contact or Opening. And you are opened by one of the helpers, opened up to the Grace of God. That's a major feature of Subud philosophy. Supposedly Subud can be transmitted from one human to another and without any loss of its power.

When you enter the latihan hall, your probationary period will have prepared you for what is to come. You will see that only members of your own sex are present. There's a good reason for that. Opposite sexes are distracting. And when things get emotional or extremely active, this practice insures no improprieties. First off, you will sit quietly so your body and mind can become stilled. That way the spirit can express itself. Then all members stand, arms at their sides. From this point on the latihan is a period when you just drop out of the material world. Things start to happen. People begin to *feel,* and they respond to their feelings. There may be spontaneous moans and groans. Members may express joy at the top of their voices. Others might grunt or cry out. Sometimes it gets vigorous. Some members quiver, quake, vibrate, jump up and down or roll on the floor. Then abruptly, at a specified time, the activity ends. The members politely say good-bye and leave the hall. The latihan is over.

You are probably wondering what these strange happenings feel like. Robert Knill, an old hand at the latihan, explains it this way. "Some of the experiences, especially in the beginning, you really don't know what they are. Like I might experience my arm waving in a certain manner. Yet I don't know why it's waving that way. But it just does. Subud is actually beyond man's mind; it really is. When you are doing your latihan, you are very very bright. Your mind is really sharp. So you might ask, 'What the heck am I doing this for?' Or you are doing something and you might think, 'Wow, that was pretty good.' You just observe yourself. Sometimes it's like you're not in your body. I've felt like I was standing back watching myself."

Subud is not considered a therapy in the sense that Gestalt or Encounter are. Still, it does reach into deep chambers of your psyche. Over time most people will discover their basic animal instincts and archetypes. These usually manifest as writhing, grunting, and rolling on the floor. Often complexes are discovered that trigger despondency and fear. Occasionally, problems are repeated in latihan after latihan until they are resolved . . . until they are cleansed from your soul. But mostly the latihans are a joyous experience. When they are over you feel relaxed and clean.

Some participants describe feeling a glow all over their bodies. They feel vibrant and wide-awake, like they had just come from a cold shower. But most important, as one enthusiastic member said, "I feel that when I'm in the latihan, I'm plugging into the forces of the universe."

Newcomers are encouraged to practice the latihan only in Subud groups. This way you allay any confusions that surface by asking questions. But participation in too many group latihans is considered stressful. To start, you are advised that two latihans a week is adequate. With time you will discover that the latihan doesn't belong to Subud. It becomes your *own* method of worship. It is God telling you about yourself. When you can sense this, then you may practice the latihan in the privacy of your home. Eventually the latihan state carries over into daily life. You begin to live in a permanent latihan. You become, in Maslow's terms, "self-actualized." You see the world anew. You see your body in a new state of health, while at the same time your family and social relationships improve dramatically. Most important of all, says Bapak, you develop a new outlook toward the spiritual world.

That brings us to the next question. What does this road to enlightenment entail? How much time? How much money? As far as time is concerned, you are on your own. There is no attendance requirement. The latihans are held twice a week for half an hour each. It's up to you. Since most Subud centers don't have their own meeting place, they rent a hall. This averages about $10 a month per member, but the price is at your option since a free-will collection box outside the latihan hall is the only source of funds.

Where do you find Subud? If there is a center in your town, it's listed in the phone book. If not, write Subud headquarters in San Raphael, California, for the nearest one to you. If you become a member you will be a welcome brother or sister to any of the hundreds of latihans in twenty countries around the world. They usually start everywhere about 8:30 p.m. local time. And, of course, the latihan has no language barrier.

The only requirement for membership in Subud is to ask. In fact, the Subud Contact can't be given unless you ask. The members don't sell Subud. They only talk if you ask them to. They *will not* proselytize. They don't even like to be written about because that might be construed as proselytizing. However, Subud should not be mixed with any other spiritual discipline. The passivity of

Subud alternated with other types of training, especially those employing willpower, only results in confusion and anxiety. The conditioning needed to let go completely would constantly be countered by the conditioning of other methods. You have to make a choice. The choice doesn't have to be permanent, of course. You are always free to drop Subud, but you are advised to give it a reasonable amount of time. Bapak says, "Don't believe me—try it."

Hasidism

There was another spiritual leader who asked his followers to try his methods. But the reason was vastly different. During the 18th Century hordes of Cossacks swept into Poland to pillage, rape and murder. Polish Jews suffered the most. Many of them had been steeped in a Jewish holy book, the Kabbala, which teaches how God built the physical and spiritual worlds. But the great book didn't tell them how to get relief from their suffering, or from their persecutions and from the numerous false Messiahs that were springing up in their moment of trial. The Kabbala wasn't much help to their low morale. They needed something that wedded the spiritual realm with the hardships of worldly life.

Rabbi Israel ben Elizar had an answer. The Baal Shem Tov, Good Master of the Holy Name, as he was called, revived and revised a 3rd century mystical philosophy called Hasidism (Chassidism) and its followers were known as Hasids (Chassidim), or Holy Ones. Baal Shem's Hasidism was directed primarily at the living conditions of Eastern European Jews. Even today the distinctive characteristic of Hasidism is its dual role of ministering to both the spiritual and material needs of Jews.

Hasidism is based in Ahavas Yisroel (love of fellow Jews). This means to love them completely and unconditionally. Thus Hasidism changed the Jewish religious fervor from the future orientation of waiting for the Messiah to a here-and-now outlook. The concept is to help others. Hasids consider helpful relations with other people to be a way they can approach God in this world.

And they say, you can enjoy everything in this world within the guidelines of the Torah. Sadness has no place in service to God. "Serve God with joy" became a goal to strive for. To Hasids the worship of God is joy. That's why singing, dancing and loving are considered forms of prayer. At any level that you are capable of worshiping, do it with joy. And Hasidism emphasized that you can fulfill your duty to God by worshiping at *any* level that you can. Rabbi Lisbon of Berkeley emphasized this when he said, "Chassidim are taught that not only the scholar who is well versed in the literature and writings can learn and elevate himself spiritually, but the simple Jew who doesn't have that capacity of intellectual study can too." Then Rabbi Lisbon told how, "You can learn from nature; from watching a single leaf flutter to the ground. There is another way. From a simple tale, a simple little story, one can learn great things. And by thinking about it, he can also gain insight of his spiritual level from a tale which is easily understood by simple folk. That was the advantage in what Baal Shem taught—that for every thing that happens in this world, a little story, not necessarily with the deep insights of the Bible, will help an individual to reach his completion and fulfillment."

The following tale of the Polish shepherd shows how sincerity at any spiritual level is worship of God. One day this poor man said in his prayer, "God, I am not a literary man. Though I know the alphabet, I can't read or write. But you, God, you know everything. So I will say the alphabet out loud, and since you know how to write, please put together the nicest words to make up the most beautiful prayer."

Such Hasidic tales aren't just cute stories. They are for you to contemplate. The philosophy is that the better you understand, the more fully you experience and appreciate the world. The tales give you something to study so you can understand, not only the world, but your own inner psyche too. It's not hard to see what deep contemplation on a variety of tales similar to the following would do for your own self-understanding.

Yudel was a man well renowned for his fear of God. He was also known for the severe penances he imposed on himself. So once when he came for a visit, the Rabbi Mikhal immediately admonished him, "Yudel, you are wearing a hair shirt against your flesh. If you were not given to sudden anger, you would not need it." Yudel nodded. Then the rabbi continued, "And since you *are* given to such anger, it will not help you."

There are several Hasidic sects in the world. But the largest one is called Chabad, an acronym for the Hebrew words meaning Wisdom, Understanding and Knowledge. A century after Hasidism was renewed, Rabbi Schneur Zalman added to Baal Shem's teaching. Whereas Baal Shem declared that everyone *can* worship God, Rabbi Schneur Zalman taught them how to do it. The Chabad Movement centered around Lubavitch in Russia for nearly a hundred years before it spread to the world. Now the Lubavitch Chabad Movement claims to be one of the most powerful influences on world Jewry.

Rabbi Schneur Zalman emphasized a deeply mystical view of God and Creation. But like his predecessor, he taught in terms that can be understood by the average person. And, like his predecessor, he emphasized the here-and-now. Rabbi Lisbon points out, "At the very same time when one is dealing with high mystical interpretations and deep contemplations, he is very much a part of this world. That's what some people are afraid of. They wonder, that in dealing with the mystical, how can they deal with the physical on the living end? Chabad teaches that both are not contradictory. On the contrary, they both complement one another."

The most effective way of achieving the fusion of spirituality with wordly life is by performing the Mitzvoth. These are Judaism's rules of conduct and observances such as regular prayers, following dietary laws and observing holy days. As Chabad followers will tell you, "Hasidic 'joy' is both ecstatic spiritual communion and lifting oneself up to God with the knowledge that observation of Mitzvoth brings God down into the world and affects our day-to-day lives."

Hasidism is an ongoing practice. Though there are levels of spiritual development, there are no milestones, no stopping places, no awards or degrees. When one potential Hasid approached his Rabbi and proudly proclaimed he had learned the whole Torah, the Rabbi answered, "Well, maybe you have learned the whole Torah, but what did the Torah *teach* you?" You can always learn more from the Torah; there is no end to Hasidism. And as one avid Hasid said, "Learning the Torah and understanding the word of God is really the biggest trip you can get as far as spirituality is concerned; even more so than prayer."

An Hasidic service is a mighty kinetic force in action. Men and women both participate fully, though they are separated in the synagogues. The types of people you find at the services are as varied as their personalities. But they are all there for the same purpose. They sway, nod and chant in Hebrew, completely lost in their personal prayer and oblivious to all around them. To many this is a fantastically rapturous worship. Often participants have the realization of the presence of God. At less formal gatherings the participants might be seen singing, telling Hasidic tales and offering toasts of wine to supplement their happy mood. Many are adept at ecstatic Hasidic dances where individuals whirl round and round as their joy pours out of them . . . and as they are filled with the spirit of God.

But they also study. Lots of time is spent poring over the Hasidic Discourses. These are based on excerpts from the Kabbala that give interpretations and insights into the Torah. There is a lot of plain psychology in them too. They cover such subjects as how to serve God by overcoming laziness, improving character, improving self-respect and increasing respect for other persons and their desires. Each Discourse ends with the question of how its message can be applied to your personal life. Chabad teaches that in dealing with interpersonal relations you must start with yourself. You must understand how you *feel*, or what you *mean* when you speak. The objective is to eventually get you in touch with, and in complete command of, your real self.

Well, you may ask, who is eligible to become an Hasid? What are the prerequisites? Mainly, you have to be a Jew. In fact, you have to be an Orthodox Jew. But there's a twist. Whereas Orthodox Judaism accents the *letter* of Jewish law, Hasidism, though not deviating one iota from the letter of the law, is concerned primarily with the spirit of the law. Hasids believe that feeling, enthusiasm, and joy should go with the regular law. They not only observe the law, but they enjoy the law.

Where will you find Hasids? Mostly in Israel and New York City. The Satmer, the Belz, and the Brestlau sects are in these places. But the Chabad Movement is everywhere. One rabbi commented that there were two things he could count on finding all over the world—Pepsi Cola signs and Chabad. But instead of looking, you can just write to the three-story brick Tudor building in Brooklyn that serves as the Movement's worldwide headquarters. You will get an answer telling of the nearest Yeshivo (Chapter) near you. There is a Chabad emissary in every major city of the United States and Canada.

Now there are hundreds of thousands of Hasids throughout the world, most of them in the Chabad Movement. And their influence has spread from the Hasidic community into the mainstream of

Jewish life. Their Rebbe is a leading Jewish spiritual leader in the world today. In fact, the present Rebbe has made it his personal goal to make traditional Judaism accessible to all North American Jews by supplementing their religion with the joy and warmth of Hasidism.

He accomplishes this through his followers who range all over the continent conducting Hebrew schools, adult education, day schools and overnight camps. The Rebbe formed a Jewish "Peace Corps" of hundreds of students who spend their summers visiting cities and small towns reaching Jews everywhere and bring joyous Hasidism into their lives. And on occasions the Rebbe speaks from New York by simultaneous phone connections to loud-speakers set up in Chabad centers all over the world. The last time he did it, his inspiring dissertation went for six hours without let-up.

One of the most effective means of spreading Hasidism is through the Chabad college campus program. Over a dozen Chabad Houses minister to the needs of 2,000 students throughout the United States and Canada. The programs provide worship every morning along with evening classes, lectures and films on Hasidic interpretations of various aspects of Judaism. Some universities give academic credit for Chabad courses. Then there are the weekly Shabbats which include Chabad services. Also the Chabad Houses provide counselling and the invariable rap sessions that are a must on every campus. A few even prepare kosher lunches at reasonable prices for students from Orthodox homes. But you don't have to be Orthodox to be welcome. Chabad Houses are open to all students who want to identify with their Jewishness.

There is another spiritual movement that focuses on identity. In this case it's identity with Jesus Christ. That's what the Jesus Movement is all about. Its members are known as Jesus People. To them identity with Jesus, acceptance of Christ and his ways, is a road to salvation. To most, it is the only road. To the young people of the Evangelical Jesus Movement, not only is identity and acceptance of Jesus Christ the only way, but devoting their life-style to his calling is a must too. Jesus People adhere to the doctrine, "Verily, verily, I say unto thee, except a man be born again, he cannot see the kingdom of God."

Psychologists might construe the concept of rebirth as an

allegory to unblock your subconscious so higher awareness can come through. Subud might consider it another way of surrendering to God. And Oriental doctrines might link it to karma. Whoever is right, the concept has been around for a long time. The old Egyptian cult of Osiris taught of death and resurrection. The Dionysian mysteries of ancient Greece had death and rebirth rituals. So did the Orphic and Eleusian mystical schools. But the most significant death and resurrection drama of all was acted out by Jesus of Nazareth first on a Roman cross, then from the tomb of an Arimathean named Joseph. To America's growing numbers of Jesus People this mighty drama, coupled with strict interpretation of the Bible, constitutes the core of the movement . . . and the pattern for their lives.

The Jesus Movement

Al Lewis, Director of Global Youth Evangelism, sums up the Jesus Movement this way: "We literally believe that Jesus Christ was not only God incarnate in the flesh—lived, died, suffered, was crucified, buried, raised from the dead and ascended unto the Father—but, and this is the mystical aspect of it, we believe that Christ is literally born in our hearts just as Christ was conceived in the womb of the Virgin Mary." Then, to emphasize this, Al continues, "We believe just as literally, but spiritually speaking, that Christ is born in the heart of a believer when he has this personal encounter. . . . So this is what happens—a new birth. This is when a transformation takes place. Literally, the very spirit of Christ comes in and takes up its habitation. 'All things pass away, and all things become new' . . . not because of some psychological experience, but because of a divine encounter with Christ. You actually are conscious of His presence right there more so than you are conscious of a person standing next to you. It's right there, not only with you, but *in* you."

That's not hard to believe if you have ever attended a Global Youth Evangelism service. No two worshipers have the same experiences. Most express what they are feeling in a physical way, but some may show their devotion through absolute silence. More often they are vocal. It's not unusual during a sermon to hear shouts of "Hallelujah", or "Praise the Lord" or even "Right on."

Sometimes the cries of "Praise the Lord" become contagious and the entire congregation is swept up in joyous shouting. Then come other utterances, the speaking in tongues. The shouting builds. People quake. Some hear music from heaven and dance in the aisles. Others are thrown to the floor, completely prostrate under the power of God. Some do indeed appear to be infused with divine spirits. Numerous Christian mystics of the past reported being filled with an inner fire emanating from God. Saint Theresa described being immersed in the ocean of God, and Saint Francis of Assisi so identified with Christ that stigmata appeared on his body. In fact, a rare few people today do produce this phenomenon.

Do all these experiences result from mere uncontrolled emotionalism? Are the feelings nothing but vivid imaginings or hallucinations? Are the vibrations, the quivering and the prostration, just products of hysteria? Most behavioral psychologists would probably say, "yes". Transpersonal psychologists might feel that in giving yourself to Christ, your ego just vanishes; that your traumas, complexes, archetypes, masks and desires—all the things that make up your personality, your ego—just melt into the collective unconscious. But to Jesus People there is a biblical answer. The second chapter of the Book of Acts describes such activities by followers of Jesus when, during the Pentecost, He returns to them in the spirit. Those present, but not filled with this spirit, wondered if such carryings on weren't the result of too much wine. But in the Bible Peter says, "No". And Jesus People know this to be true. So when they experience this revelation of Christ, to them this is reality . . . the ultimate reality . . . the actual Christ.

Few Jesus People have profound mystical experiences. Only the most Pentecostally oriented speak in tongues or are prostrated by the power of God. Most of Christ's new and zealous followers aren't even looking for these experiences. What they seek is a new life, a new outlook; something in which they can find beauty and nobility; something which will give them faith that things will be better.

One devout member of the Christian World Liberation Front put it this way: "What's really moving about the Jesus Movement is there is something being born; there is something that is here in embryo. The kingdom of God, the doctrine of Jesus Christ, is not simply the forgiveness of sin. It is that, but also much more. It is that there is a kingdom. We have a foretaste of it in our Fellowship, in the body of Christ that is present in the World today. But there is coming a kingdom in which Jesus Christ is king, and in which He is going to rule over the entire earth. You know, it's a little bit like the Marxist idea. In fact, Marx probably got it from his Judeo-Christian heritage . . . of the new society being formed in the shell of the old. The old society is corrupt; extremely corrupt; extremely hollow. This whole shell is not going to endure. There is a new society being formed, the society made up of the children of God. We are going to join in that kingdom. We are going to rule and reign with Christ in this world. That's what we look forward to."

Does that sound exciting? To many people it does. So maybe your next thought is, how do you join this new kingdom? How do you find your promised spiritual land? How do you participate? And how do people prove worthy of being included?

Jesus People do it through prayer. They worship. They praise the Lord. They witness to all who will listen. And most important, they read the Word. To most devotees of the Movement their Bible tells all, all that is necessary for their lives. Strict interpretation is the rule—to Jesus People the Bible is literal truth. But there is more to living Christianity than just intellectualizing. Christ must be experienced. Christ is considered a living divine personality, not just a consciousness you can tap into. Christ is a here-and-now supernatural Being that guides your every move, that demands your burning love, that can lead you to eternal salvation. One devout follower expressed it in this eloquent way: "We come down with humble hearts before what we believe to be God, the omnipotent, omniscient, immutable creator of the universe who spoke the worlds into existence and set the stars on their course. We believe at that moment when we come into His presence that He not only accepts us and forgives us for what we are, but He also at the same instant gives us *power* to become what we know we ought to be. Repentance is essential. It's a first step, but it's not all there is. Repentance takes care of the past, but the joy comes when we commit our future."

And what is that future? It depends on where you end up in the Movement. The Jesus Movement is an amalgam consisting of Evangelists, Conservatives, Liberals, Neo-Pentacostalists, and Fundamentalists. To the participants the Movement appears to be infused with something supernatural which they can only sense. "The Movement is not humanly organized," they say, "God's spirit is behind the Movement. Christ is with us now. 'Where two or three are gathered together in my name, there I am in the midst of them.' "

The Movement started spontaneously in 1969 with three or four seed groups springing up on the West Coast. Then it exploded across the land, offering the United States and Canada every conceivable type of gathering place for young people. There are Christian prayer groups, coffeehouses, communes, farms and Bible schools. Since baptism is symbolic of rebirth, young converts by the thousands are immersed in lakes, oceans, rivers, ponds, swimming pools and even public fountains. Other activities include Bible classes, Christ rallies, demonstrations against pornography and witnessing (proclaiming the glories of Christ) on street corners. One Berkeley group, the Street Theater, takes its message to the University of California campus with props and costumes to give impromptu performances before crowds of 200 to 400 bemused and sometimes impressed students. The Jesus Movement is fun. It is gatherings, like the old-time camp meetings out in the open where you can see God's creations in nature. It is readings and singing and making testimony to the Lord Jesus Christ. And it is putting psalms to modern rock music. The Jesus Movement is a *living* religion.

One end of the spectrum of people living this new Christianity is called Young Life. Its lively meetings occur in over 1,300 homes across the land every week, and are packed with 60 to 80 high school students singing hymns to the strumming of guitars. Or the students might be listening to lectures on the principles and practical aspects of Christianity. The meetings are free to all students from local participating high schools. The same holds for Youth for Christ, which meets weekly in homes or meeting halls in 300 major cities. It has clubs in over 2,000 high schools. Both Young Life and Youth for Christ are listed in the phone books of cities where they have clubs.

Beyond the high school level are an infinite variety of Christian experiences for young people. They vary from simple meeting houses, to clusters of families living near one another, to large remote communes. Some are strict and authoritarian. Others are practically leaderless. A few demand that you share all your personal wealth with your fellows. Estimates of the numbers of these different groups vary almost as much as do the life-styles of the groups themselves. Probably at any one time up to 1,000 are in operation somewhere in the U.S. and Canada. But they come and go rapidly. About half go out of existence while an equal number spring up every two or three years. The names of these Christian houses are as varied and unique as the life-styles they support. A few have straightforward names like Crusaders for Christ, Calvary Fellowship or Jesus Center. Others are more imaginative, like the Love Inn or Adam's Apple. Some combine whimsy with scripture— Lord's Fish House, Needle's Eye Coffeehouse and The Holy Ghost Repair Service. Some just say what they are. Wheaton, Illinois has its Jesus People and Lansing, Michigan boasts a group just called Christians. But all are serious about their belief. They think in terms of sharing and love. Theirs is a faith in God through Christ.

So now the words "Praise the Lord" are heard all over the land. They are getting louder and louder as more and more young people shout them. The Jesus Movement is growing. It's getting big. That's why lots of young people are confused about it. They don't know where to turn. They are asking, "How can I find out what's going on? How in God's name can I discover the right Jesus group for me?" Most Jesus People will answer, "*Ask* in God's name." They mean of course for you to pray. To ask for God's guidance. Many Jesus People claim they found their way into the Movement just that way—that Divine guidance put them where they are. However, most will concede there are other ways too. You might drop into a religious bookstore and ask where Jesus People hang out. Local churches can be helpful too, especially those that aren't too hung up on long hair. In college towns the student newspapers often carry news about Bible meetings and other goings on. Also, on most campuses you will find a Campus Crusade for Christ or an Intervarsity Christian Fellowship. Either one can put you in touch with many groups in the Movement.

Or you can look to the Jesus press. There are over a hundred newspapers and magazines catering to the evangelical movement. They all carry news and other information about various organizations.

When you look into it, you will discover that the Jesus Movement is, indeed, diverse. Its organizations come in almost any style, in any make-up and are located nearly any place you want. So take your pick. Members of the Open Door, Inc. live in Alaska; some Vermonters frequent His Church; and in California you will find Jews for Jesus. And that brings Christianity back full circle, doesn't it? That's how the whole thing got started in the first place: Jews for Jesus, circa 33 A.D.

No one will dispute that's how Christianity got started. But there is another beginning that is questioned. And it is an important beginning too. Scientists, philosophers and lots of plain ordinary folk have asked many questions about it. Those questions boil down to "What is reality? What is the World? How did it all begin?"

Most adherents to Western faiths are materialistically oriented. To them, matter is real. The world is hard, concrete, something of substance. Yet their own scriptures tell them that at least its genesis was not so substantive. As that Jesus Person so poetically said, "God *spoke* the worlds into existence. . . ." Physicist Sir James Jeans put it another way when he observed, "The universe looks more like a great thought than a great machine." Teilhard de Chardin, too, pointed out that though most people think of the material world as being *real*, a large number believes that it is all mental . . . that creation is a divine dream. Mystics fall into this latter class.

Some mystical theories hold that an object, a person or an activity you observe, feel, taste, hear or smell during waking consciousness is no more substantive than one you dream about in sleep. They seem equally real to your consciousness of the moment. The only difference, mystics say, is that your waking illusion is more persistent than the nightly one. All of what you call nature, what you define as the universe, is looked upon by mystics as a mental thing, a construct of Divine Mind. And they emphasize that *you* are a part of that Divine Mind—so much so that Democritus felt that *he* himself was that mind, the only mind, and that *he* had dreamed all of creation. He saw creation as symbolic of Divine Mind just as your dreams symbolize your nocturnal mentation. Pre-Christian Gnostics had a similar idea. They believed that just as you dress up in clothes, Consciousness dresses up in matter . . . but it is nevertheless all mental matter.

That brings us to the most unorthodox Christian church of them all. Its history began on a wintry day in 1866 in Lynn,

Massachusetts. Mary Baker Eddy, then a partial invalid of forty-five, slipped on the ice. This was no ordinary fall. She was hurt badly and was taken into a house nearby. The internal injuries she suffered made it impossible to move her, and after three days her doctor declared he could do nothing to help. Having come from a devout scripture-reading family, Mrs. Eddy asked for a Bible. She turned to the Book of Matthew which describes how Christ healed a palsied man. Suddenly, while reading, Mrs. Eddy was flooded with the presence of God. She got an insight into Christ's method of healing. At that instant her injuries, along with an old spinal problem, vanished. She was healed.

In thinking about the incident later, Mrs. Eddy recalled that healing had been prevalent from the beginning of Christianity through the third century. However, she reasoned that miracles are impossible, that God's laws are immutable. When Jesus healed, therefore, he must have known how to apply the laws. So Mrs. Eddy spent the next three years intensely researching both the Old and the New Testament to discover the fundamental spiritual laws and truths that Jesus knew. She concluded that you are a divine mental concept. Your body and all that you experience exist in thought. It is thought that needs healing, not matter. And the remedy lies in learning to think God's thoughts. Christianity is truly a science, Mrs. Eddy said. And also it is teachable and provable by any sincere student. Six more years went by as she demonstrated, proved, taught and healed. She even taught others to heal. Then she put all this knowledge, all the evidence, all the methods into writing, in her most famous work, *Science and Health with Key to the Scriptures.*

Church of Christ, Scientist

By 1876 Mrs. Eddy had a dedicated and enthusiastic following. So she founded a church in Boston based on this rediscovered Christian Science and became its leader. The Church of Christ, Scientist is not much different today than it was nearly a century ago. True, the original little Romanesque structure on Norway Street has expanded into a multimillion-dollar complex of church buildings, Sunday school, publishing house, reflecting pool, fountain and a twenty-eight story steel and glass administration building. The small congregation has grown to over 3,000 churches, societies and college organizations in the United States and Canada, plus many more abroad. And the membership numbers in the hundreds of thousands. But the doctrines and practices are the same. In fact, "Scientists" claim the doctrines are the same as Christian doctrines of 33 A.D.

What is the Christian Science version of the teachings of Jesus? What is this something that the early Christians were supposed to have known and practiced? What is the secret that today's Christian Scientists now possess? First off, they make a distinction between Christ and Jesus. "Christ" was a title bestowed on a man named Jesus—he was originally called Jesus, the Christ. The Christ is absolute Divine *truth*. Jesus was a man, a special man, true, but nevertheless a man. Therefore, to Christian Scientists Christ is the Divine message: Jesus just the messenger. Jesus is looked upon as the way-shower to salvation. But Christ is the way. The message that Jesus taught is venerated—not merely because he said it, but because it is believed to be true. To Christian Scientists the Christ is a Divine idea. It is a concept of the nature of being, a model of the universe. To them God is *all* . . . there is nothing more. God is the only true *Mind* . . . there is nothing more. God is infinite intelligence . . . there is nothing more. Matter is a false sense of mind called "mental" mind. The material world is unreal. It is but the product of Divine thought.

Christian Science holds that God is perfect, that nothing in God can be in error. Mary Baker Eddy wrote in *Science and Health*, "Under divine Providence there can be no accidents, since there is no room for imperfection in perfection." Therefore illness and hardship *must* be illusions. They must be *mankind's* errors. This is likened to the principle of mathematics. Mathematics is perfect. If your phone bill has been added up wrong, it isn't the principle of mathematics that's at fault, it's the computer or accountant at the phone company. Proper application of the principle will give a correct total. God is looked upon like a mathematical principle . . . as perfect. And God, like a mathematical principle, is not even aware of error. God is *im*personal. People are aware of their imperfection, but God isn't.

That brings us to another basic difference between Christian Science and orthodox Christianity. Christian Scientists have no Satan; no Prince of Darkness playing tug-of-war with the Prince of

Peace for your soul; no eternal damnation in Lucifer's fiery ovens. To them evil is not real. It is a mental state, an attitude—an attitude contrary to the truth about God's nature. Therefore, evil can be rejected from your consciousness. Truth can mentally eliminate all evil that befalls you. Your problems are *all* created by false belief, by mortal mind. Heaven and hell are mental states. They are here and now. Mrs. Eddy stressed that since God is all there is, you have nothing to fear. You can gain your salvation here and now. But you have to work for it.

Christian Science applies the laws of spirit the way a physicist employs the laws of matter. Christian Scientists consider the Bible their textbook on how to bring their lives into accord with spiritual laws. They learn from it just as the physicist learned his trade from physics texts. That's why the practices are called a science—they are scientific applications of the Divine law of thought.

The other text in Christian Science, *Science and Health,* is a guidebook to the Bible. Together, these two texts teach you how to see the perfection of Divine Mind, and how to accept that your ills and reverses are the result of false beliefs. This isn't suggestion, hypnosis or psychosomatic medicine, they maintain. It doesn't rely on your mind as the curative agent to reprogram your thinking. It is not will power or Power of Positive Thinking. It is just opening your mind to God's perfection. As Mrs. Eddy wrote, "Beloved Christian Scientists, keep your minds so filled with Truth and Love, that sin, disease, and death cannot enter them. It is plain that nothing can be added to a mind already full."

This principle was well illustrated to Robert Newell of San Francisco after he was stricken with an incurable illness. He describes it this way:

"I had the experience of winding up in a hospital totally paralyzed from the neck down. I had no feeling in my body below the neck. It was brought on, the doctor said, by a burst artery in the brain. He showed me x-rays of my brain pointing out that the area containing the motor center of the body had been severely damaged. He said it could not be repaired surgically, would not heal itself, and therefore, I would never be able to use my arms or legs again.

"Although I had been studying Christan Science for a few years, that was the first time I ever turned to God for healing. As my thoughts went out to God in deep, humble prayer, I became increasingly aware of the perfect, divine laws of creation and that I received my existence from God alone, that nothing in matter could interfere with my full expression of God's qualities. The statement of Jesus, 'It is the spirit that quickeneth; the flesh profiteth nothing,' took on real meaning. I ceased to think about healing a physical condition and became filled with a deep sense of gratitude through the conviction that my real selfhood, my mental or spiritual consciousness, was still perfect, whole, active, and free of any limitation. My thoughts became flooded with an awareness of the presence and love of God. I saw that I could express all the qualities of God, perfectly, without using physicality, because those qualities were mental, and therefore I was not handicapped or paralyzed.

"It was during a state of inspired, elevated prayer of gratitude that I became aware that a physical healing was taking place. It felt as though someone were pouring warm water over my body. Then my hands and feet began to tingle. I realized I again had feeling in my body and when I tried to move my arms and legs they functioned perfectly. I sat up in bed and did a few calisthenics to make sure that everything was working fine. The healing occurred in less than thirty minutes after the doctor had given the medical verdict. There was no period of recovery. It was just like that."

Just like that! Well, not always. Most healings aren't that dramatic, nor as rapid. Sometimes cases take years of faith and prayer. Actually, it's not your body that becomes regenerated according to Christian Scientists, it's your mind. It's your character that regenerates. When that happens, your body follows suit.

You can't have two masters in Christian Science. Faith in two different ways of healing is thought to cancel out both of them. That's why Christian Science and medicine are incompatible. Christian Science is not critical of medicine. Doctors are thought of as doing the best that they know how. "Scientists" never ridicule or deride the medical profession. In fact, medical abstinence is not even obligatory. You can choose the method of healing that you think best. But Christian Science veterans consider their unique method of prayer to be the most reliable form of medicine.

In fact, physical healing is just the top of Christian Science's iceberg—and intentionally so. It is stressed because that is the most impressive and demonstrable way of showing healing through prayer. As Mrs. Eddy wrote, "Healing physical sickness is the smallest part of Christian Science. It is only the bugle call to thought and action, in the higher range of infinite goodness." Healing in Christian Science terminology includes not only health problems, but also deals with social, economic, moral and intellectual ones. It's involved with mortgages, car payments, marriages, jobs. One testimony that appeared in the *Christian Science Sentinel* dealt with practical down-to-earth problems this way: "Four years ago, while at college, the desire for Mother Church membership rid me in an instant of the desire for social drinking, and later that same year of the smoking habit. . . . One difficult situation centering around sharing an apartment with four other girls was completely resolved after one night of prayer and study, and in a way no person could have outlined or even predicted." Another person got social healing this way: "A marriage counselor had not helped our unhappy situation; but from the day my wife began reading the Bible and *Science and Health* by Mrs. Eddy our marriage grew in mutual respect and love. I attribute our very happy marriage to our honest desire for spiritual growth."

Unfortunately many Christian Scientists, especially the newcomers, haven't developed the understanding and faith that healing requires. But, according to Christian Science, individuals can help one another through the Divine Mind. That's how some people can heal others. Not that they themselves do the healing—the Christ power does that. But a healer opens the patient's mind to receive the Christ. The patient can become aware of a truth that the healer is thinking. These healers, called practitioners, are specially trained by the Church and are licensed to practice.

Practitioners are very much like physicians. They devote full time to healing. They set their own fees. You can have a personal visit or contact them by phone. Unlike physicians, practitioners don't heal by consultation or advice. What they do is pray. There is no laying on of the hands or even focusing on the problems. They focus on spiritual perfection. They try to awaken the patient's awareness of perfection. Above all, they try to overcome the patient's fear.

Along with practitioners, the Church trains nurses. Except for not administering medicine, these nurses receive three years' experience in sick-room care just like any other nurse. Their purpose? To relieve a patient of discomfort and to provide moral support to overcome fear. Christian Science practitioners and nurses seem to have proven their worth, not only to Christian

Scientists, but to the rest of the world. Now, most insurance companies recognize, and will pay for, Christian Science practitioners and nurses in lieu of medical treatment.

Of course, an important aim of the Church is to help *you* grow spiritually so that you can treat *yourself.* Christian Science has an elaborate organization to do this. There is the original Mother Church in Boston, from which the workings of the entire worldwide network are directed. This is what makes the Christian Science machine hum. But this machine reaches you mostly at local outlets. There are branch churches in numerous communities throughout the United States and Canada, sometimes up to 25 in a single large city. It's in these facilities that Christian Scientists worship and to a great extent learn their lessons.

Mrs. Eddy divided the biblical teachings into twenty-six categories. They focus on God, man, and the nature of reality. She believed that if you understand these basic subjects, you can cope with all problems that might trouble you. The study of them is simple. Every day of each week members study passages from the Bible and from *Science and Health.* These passages are specially selected by scholars from the Mother Church. The following Sunday, everywhere in the world, the same passages are read aloud to local church congregations. No sermons, no rituals, no symbols—just the reading and prayer. Before each service the members are reminded, "The Bible and the Christian Science textbook are our only preachers." The purpose of Christian Science is personal understanding of spiritual truths, not someone else's interpretation of them.

The concept that healing through religion should be a *normal* part of worship distinguishes Christian Science from most other faiths. This is epitomized at another Christian Science service, the Wednesday night Testimony Meeting. This service is really a way of glorifying God. Though testimonies are descriptions of how problems were resolved through Christian Science methods, they are given as expressions of gratitude for God's healing. Testimony meetings are "giving" occasions—times to express joy for spiritual development and healing that members experienced during the week. They are opportunities to praise God and give encouragement to others. Also many written testimonies, after being thoroughly verified, are published in the Church's magazines. Over

45,000 testimonies have been published, while many times more remain unrecorded.

The Church also has still other ways of providing instruction to its flock. Sunday Schools are for young people aged three through twenty. On many college campuses you can find a Christian Science College Organization for students and faculty. The purpose is to bring the Testimony Meeting atmosphere to students who might be reluctant to attend normal testimonies where the membership is considerably older. And there is instruction for veteran "Scientists" too. Those who are serious and really want get even deeper into Christian Science can take Primary Class Instruction. It's a two-week intensive program under authorized teachers. The price is $100 for the one-shot course, but participants are encouraged to meet as a group with the instructor once a year thereafter for a refresher. This is also an expression of faith because the instructor is not really considered the teacher, but merely an avenue for God's word.

To Christian Scientists, how you become a Church member is extremely important. You have to join of your own choice. Children can't be automatically baptized into the Church. Membership isn't taken that lightly. Since liquor, tobacco and other drugs are considered false gods, you will have to give them up. You will be urged to work on committees, perhaps become elected as a "reader" at Sunday services, and, of course, you will be expected to contribute to the financial support of the Church.

But you don't have to join the Church to practice Christian Science. You can use the reading rooms whenever you want, and you aren't expected to accept all the abstentions right off the bat. Whatever your creed, your seriousness, or your degree of devotion, Christian Scientists say, "You are welcome."

Chapter 5

THE METAPHYSICAL SCHOOLS

Can you keep a secret? Even if it means enduring torture? Or death? That's the way it used to be if you were worthy enough to learn the most revered and sacred mysteries known to mankind. Fortunately, today nobody expects such sacrifices in order to protect mystical secrets. But centuries ago things were different. The old metaphysical schools, especially those in Western cultures, were all secret societies—so secret that they were called mystery schools. Their masters carefully limited the memberships to an elect few whom they knew had sufficient morality and intellect to guard and preserve the innermost secrets of the universe. All other people were excluded from this guarded knowledge. Only the priests of Egypt's Temple of Karnak were permitted in the inner sanctum. The ancient Hebrew priesthood alone could approach the Ark of the Covenant. Even early Christianity had its secrets which Saint Augustine claimed were too awesome for normal comprehension. Only the initiated could share them. Because of this the Church remained partially secret through the 7th century when its last vestiges of esoteric knowledge were eventually lost. Only in 692 A.D. were all believers admitted to full membership in the Church. Even today, priests of the Greek Orthodox Church worship apart from the congregation behind a curtain.

Why all the mystery? Why all the exclusiveness? Because it

had to be. Ancient populations were generally too illiterate, ignorant, and superstitious to be trusted with the secrets of the universe. They just couldn't comprehend the awesome nature of Being and the grandeur of Existence. These things cannot be explained in words. They have to be experienced. Ignorance and superstition inhibit the experience of reality. Also, experiencing takes time . . . lots of time. And the poverty of the masses demanded all their time just so they could survive. Antiquity could not afford many people spending their lives in pursuit of enlightenment.

Still, the masses needed something concrete they could grasp, something tangible to guide them. They had to have something to believe in, no matter how magical or supernatural. So the mystics, the keepers of the secrets, gave them something solid. They gave them an inkling of reality; they gave them hints of the true nature of the universe . . . but they conveyed this in diverse terms that different cultures could absorb and accept. Mysticism was taught to different societies through analogies, or myths, or parables. That's how the various religions were born. That's why the same truths, once committed to scripture, seem so disguised and different among various cultures. That's why all mystical schools have essentially the same philosophies, while most religions don't.

Most theologies were meant to guide and inspire the masses to greater heights of morality and spirituality without actually disclosing the esoteric teachings. The great teacher, Jesus, spoke in parables and cautioned that revealing the great truths was like casting pearls before swine who might even turn upon and attack those with the knowledge. In fact, that happened time and time again throughout history. Devoutly spiritual mystics often unwittingly surrendered their positions in the religious hierachies to more worldly priests whose life goals included wealth, power and position. Truth and spiritual knowledge didn't fit that pattern. So understanding of the original teaching gave way to dogma and authority. The eternal truths were lost by most churches. When that happened, the apparent strangeness of those who still pursued mysticism seemed like a threat. In religious circles threats were called sacrileges. And those who committed sacrileges were destroyed.

Thus, religions turned on the mystery schools at every opportunity. Churches deplored philosophies that didn't need priests to intervene between man and God. So until now, Western mysticism and its practices have been carefully guarded so the great truths might escape the ravages of dogmatic zealots of all faiths . . . of the followers of Ra or Baal or Jehovah . . . of devotees of Mohammad, Christ and even Karl Marx.

Fortunately, today's society is more tolerant, more enlightened, and certainly more accustomed to the assault of new ideas. Today's citizen has heard of psychoanalysis, of repressed fears, drives, complexes and traumas, all phenomena very much interwoven with mysticism, and modern science is more willing to embrace different concepts about the human psyche and its relationship to the universe. So followers of ancient mystical traditions now feel freer to reveal their esoteric wisdom. Now the doors of numerous metaphysical schools are open to you. In fact, you can learn some of the great mysteries by mail.

You may have seen advertisements in psychic or occult magazines showing a man standing alone amid windswept mountains, his arms raised to a light radiating from the sky. He appears to be searching for eternal wisdom. The caption invites you to write for a brochure telling how you can do the same. What you receive in the mail sounds even more exciting. It asks you questions like "Can you do these things? . . . Solve a problem by dismissing it? . . . See without eyes by inner perception . . . Live a thousand lives in one lifetime . . . Journey into another world yet remain in this one? . . . Transform your personality—actually become another person? . . . Search for the unknown and know when you find it?" If you follow up on this brochure by joining the organization that printed it, you will become a Rosicrucian.

Actually, there are three Rosicrucian organizations in the United States. All claim to be the legitimate descendant of the original Rosicrucians of yore. The smallest, and least known to the public, is the Rosicrucian Fraternity. It focuses on what it calls Ethical Soul Culture and Creative Law which, along with many of its philosophies and practices, derive from the ancient Masonic crafts. Most of its teaching is devoted to showing you how to live a constructive life. These teachings are available by mail for a modest fee.

Number two in the Rosicrucian pecking order is the Rosicrucian Fellowship. It, too, offers correspondence courses—several of them. They cover Rosicrucian philosophy, astrology and the Bible. All are free, but dedicated students are expected to support the Fellowship through purchases of books and astrology charts, and through free-will offerings. What you learn relates to evolution, rebirth, occult forces, and the esoteric nature of the universe. There is strong emphasis on astrology and vegetarian nutrition. You can also receive class instruction at the Fellowship's Oceanside, California headquarters.

A.M.O.R.C.

But the Big Daddy of the Rosicrucians is A.M.O.R.C. That stands for Ancient Mystical Order Rosae Crucis. It has well over one hundred thousand members and numerous centers all around the world. Its public relations budget alone exceeds the total financial outlay of the other Rosicrucians by many fold. And its mailroom handles more than six million pieces of literature and correspondence material a year.

A.M.O.R.C. claims to be the world's oldest and largest fraternity devoted to personal development through mind-power. Though not a religion, its philosophy supports all religions. A.M.O.R.C. teaches of God; of one God; of one God within you. Its ethics are similar to Christianity's, and it claims to be a direct channel to spiritual councils of enlightened souls called the Great Masters and the Great White Brotherhood. And this channel requires no change in your business, social, or religious life. All you have to do is put in a few hours of study each week.

A.M.O.R.C. (also called Rosicrucian Order) is a school of metaphysics. It deals in mental science, numerology and alchemy. It combines the esoteric with the material sciences. Its purpose is to awaken dormant faculties in individuals. In fact, it is very strong on psychic phenomena. But it does not get into such things as astrology, spirit communication or fortune telling. Actually, A.M.O.R.C. claims to be an updated extension of ancient doctrines compiled by Hermes Trismegistus.

Whether Hermes Trismegistus (Thrice Greatest Hermes) ever existed has never been established. Was he man or god? No one knows. Was he Greek or Egyptian? Again the same answer. But what he supposedly produced is known. Doctrines attributed to him introduced Mediterranean peoples to alchemy, astrology and many other occult sciences. The culture most receptive to these teachings was that of the ancient Egyptians. The Rosicrucians, and thus A.M.O.R.C., trace their origin directly to mystery schools that thrived on the Nile in the reign of Thutmose III about 1500 B.C. The first members of the Order are believed to have met in secret chambers of the Great Pyramid. However, Rosicrucians look upon Pharaoh Akhnaton (1355 B.C.) as their traditional first Grand Master because of his strong belief in a single god. When Akhnaton was overthrown and polytheism was once again established, the Rosicrucians began a see-saw history of secrecy and openness dictated by ever-changing political and theological climates. The teachings of this brotherhood spread to Greece and Rome. When Emperor Justinian, in the Sixth Century A.D. abolished mystery schools as heresies, the Rosicrucians went totally underground and remained so for most of the next 1,100 years. Still, their influence spread throughout Europe, eventually to be a potent force on such greats as Leonardo da Vinci, Francis Bacon, Isaac Newton, Claude Debussy, René Descartes and Jacob Böhme. In 1694 Johann Kelpius, master of a European Rosicrucian lodge, founded a new lodge in what is now the Fairmont Park area of Philadelphia. Purportedly Roger Williams, Thomas Paine, Thomas Jefferson and Benjamin Franklin were initiated through this lodge.

But time doesn't stand still, not even for esoteric orders. By Rosicrucian law, the Order can be active for only 108 years, then it must remain dormant for another 108 years. The Order began its present active cycle in 1909 and today is the only legitimate American Rosicrucian movement accredited by the International Council of A.M.O.R.C. Its headquarters were first in San Francisco, then in Miami, and were finally established its present location at Rosicrucian Park in San Jose.

Don't think that just because society no longer persecutes mystery schools there still aren't mystical secrets. To join A.M.O.R.C. you have to take a pledge of secrecy, just like your predecessors did. You are still required to guard esoteric wisdom from the profane world. There is good reason for this. Esoteric, though meaning secret, doesn't imply that knowledge should be arbitrarily withheld from society. It means that it is incomprehensible to those not on the road to spiritual enlightenment. Just as the choicest and tastiest food, if gulped too fast or in bites too large, causes you to choke, so concepts too strange or awesome will turn potential students away from the greatest of truths. Even initiates are fed knowledge at a rate that allows easy assimilation and understanding. This also keeps up their interest—it's always exciting to learn a new secret. Besides, there is that little bit of snobbery in all of us that likes to say, "I know something that you don't know."

Some ancients claimed that only the dead really know. That's why lots of Rosicrucian teaching is based on the mysteries that derive from the Egyptian Book of the Dead. Its secrets were read aloud to dying people to program their spiritual selves (or souls) for what was ahead. Thus, it was thought that even without physical brains to reason, souls could operate and control their experiences in the future life. Most of this Egyptian wisdom is applicable in earthly life too. So is alchemy. But Rosicrucian alchemy goes beyond primitive chemistry. Spiritual alchemy is not of the material world, but is the science of transforming evil thought into nobility . . . of transmuting your base metal of worldly consciousness into the pure gold of cosmic consciousness. A.M.O.R.C. explains cosmic consciousness and the nature of the universe in other ways too. One of the most authoritative sources is the Holy Kabbalah. This sacred Jewish work, though compiled by two rabbis at the beginning of the Christian era, is just an extension of far more ancient wisdom. Its message is given mainly through symbolism. What it teaches is that God is all—nothing exists that is not part of God; and that all nature is due to the *self*-development of God. It describes in detail how God created the physical and spiritual worlds. The ten sephiroth of the Sepher Yetzirah (Book of Creation) explain this numerically. So A.M.O.R.C. teaches esoteric numerology too. And all of this is yours for $5.00 each month.

The principal conduit for the Rosicrucian teachings is through your mailman. So long as your dues are paid up you receive a weekly correspondence lesson along with a monthly magazine. You start out with three Neophyte courses, or degrees, that sum up what's ahead for you. Then starts three intensive years of study about the esoteric nature of the universe. This includes the next nine degrees which are basically intellectual. They emphasize explanations rather than teaching you how to experience. But they do have some experiments you can perform to develop your latent abilities with ESP. The meat and exciting part of the lessons is what A.M.O.R.C. teaches about the unseen nature of the cosmos and how the material world interacts with other levels of existence. You discover the esoteric nature of matter, soul and spirit. You are taught the secrets of symbols. You study various levels of consciousness, the laws of the universe and evolution, the meaning of polarities and opposites, what the life force is and how to control it. A whole degree is devoted to philosophies of the ancient world. Another one covers diet, breath, health and healing. This healing isn't like that of Christian Science. Rather, it relies on controlling the life force that courses through the sympathetic nervous system in your spine. You learn about your psychic body and your aura, and how they are affected by mystical sounds. Astral projection is touched on too. You explore past incarnations, immortality and the purpose of your soul. Then, you finally learn about your relation to God, and how to psychically control natural events. You discover the true meaning of spiritual alchemy.

Beyond the ninth degree are three more levels of teaching. The tenth, eleventh, and twelfth degrees delve much deeper into your psyche. In fact, you must have proven yourself in the prior studies before you can receive this higher learning. It is claimed that much of this higher knowledge comes to you by psychic illumination; that you actually attend meetings in various parts of the world and receive instruction from the greatest of masters . . . all by astral projection. You supposedly gain membership in the Illuminati. The length of this latter training is indefinite.

Many mystical societies frown on ritual. They disdain ceremony and call it mumbo-jumbo. They say it distracts from spiritual goals. But other people claim just the opposite. They believe ritual focuses your mind on the subject, thus impressing it on your subconscious. Ritual overcomes your need to intellectualize everything; you learn to *feel* the meaning of the ceremonies. Also rituals are a form of conditioning that, after sufficient exposure, trigger special attitudes and even altered states of consciousness. Many creative geniuses triggered their inspirations with some form of ritual exercises. Rachmaninoff liked to walk in the country. Robert Louis Stevenson always slept with his head pointed north (Hindus have other explanations for this) and author and dramatist Johann Schiller couldn't write a word unless there was a rotten apple on his desk. As psychologists would say, ritual is a serial emotional exposure to heighten the receptivity of your subconscious.

So A.M.O.R.C. has all kinds of rituals. At the beginning of each degree you receive instructions on how to initiate yourself at home. You learn how to lay out your sanctum, where to place the altar, the chairs and candles. You learn affirmations, motions, oaths and other ritualistic procedures. It is claimed that through this you learn to attune your inner consciousness with the higher principles of the universe.

A.M.O.R.C. has even more impressive initiations. The Order maintains over eighteen lodges throughout the United States and Canada where initiations are performed. Weekly meetings with their attendant rituals are held in the Lodges as well as in over forty-six additional chapters across the continent. The lodges and chapters maintain temples designed in elaborate Egyptian architectural styles. They are laid out with mystical symbolism involving various designs and the four points of the compass. They have altars, sanctums, sacred triangles and incense to represent the Vestal Fire. They even have Vestal Virgins who are the young daughters of members. Along with the elaborate ceremonies that include symbolic regalia, affirmations and pageantry, there are passwords, secret grips, salutations, and signs. This may seem unappealing to lots of "erudite" people, but almost half of A.M.O.R.C.'s membership is college-educated of which, surprisingly, nearly two-thirds of the members are men. So to Rosicrucians, it is the members who live near a lodge or chapter who are lucky, because they can add depths of emotion to their studies. Members of this great fraternity are welcome to ceremonies in any Lodge or other A.M.O.R.C. meeting place to which their degree of advancement entitles them . . . anywhere in the country . . . anywhere in the world.

If you are a Rosicrucian with many years in the Order, you will undoubtedly have visited the finest of the lodges, the Grand Lodge of Rosicrucian Park in San Jose. Its imposing structures patterned on the architecture of ancient Karnak symbolize A.M.O.R.C.'s heritage and are used for the annual convention. Hundreds of Rosicrucians from around the world convene here every year for one or more weeks of learning, ceremony, and festivity. Most who attend the convention also attend summer school at Rose-Croix University where they take courses in science, art, philosophy and mystical practices. And naturally, they spend lots of time visiting the art gallery, the planetarium and the science museum. Most impressive is the Rosicrucian Egyptian Museum, which contains a large collection of ancient Egyptian artifacts. Incidentally, even if you aren't a Rosicrucian, these latter buildings are open to you. And the Rosicrusians strongly urge you to visit any or all of them if you are ever in San Jose.

Builders of The Adytum

Rosicrucians aren't the only ones who study ancient Egyptian and other Mediterranean mysteries. Another school that is deep into the Hermetic arts is called Builders of the Adytum. In fact, B.O.T.A. may even be deeper into the secrets. From the very beginning of B.O.T.A. instruction you are taught how to *experience* your inner powers. You are given intellectual instruction about laws that govern the universe too, but the main focus is on first-hand to experience.

Why such a weird name as Builders of the Adytum? It derives from antiquity. *Adytum* is Greek for "Inner Shrine" or "Holy of Holies" and "Builders" refers to emulation of the Carpenter from Nazareth, Jesus, whom many people believe was versed in traditions that were later to appear in the Kabbala. B.O.T.A. is not a strictly Christian organization. Nor is it Jewish, as the Kabbala is thought to be. B.O.T.A. accepts the Kabbala as the mystical root of both ancient Judaism and the original Christianity, but people of all faiths should have no difficulty accepting B.O.T.A. teachings if they are mystically inclined. The teachings include alchemy, mystical astrology and the Tarot—lots of Tarot.

That's as you would expect. B.O.T.A.'s founder was Dr. Paul Foster Case, a renowned expert on the Tarot. He is said to have received his instruction from a secret master who was himself one of a chain of mystery school masters dating back to before the rise of the pharaohs. Dr. Case's successor is Rev. Ann Davies, who in her youth was fortunate enough to meet him and be initiated into the wisdom of the Tarot. Rev. Davies is now the spiritual leader of what many believe to be one of the most outstanding metaphysical schools in the country.

Why so outstanding? Because of the way it approaches subjects that are mostly associated today with magic and the occult, but which were practiced by the ancients for spiritual unfoldment. Astrology was studied by Plato, by the neo-Platonists, by the Essenes, Christians, Gnostics, Kabbalists and even the relatively new Hasidists. But it isn't the type of fortune-telling you get in the daily horoscope of your newspaper. Esoteric astrology holds that nothing is separate. The entire universe works in concert with all its parts. All is one. So special patterns of energy that existed when you were born tend to stick with you. By understanding these patterns, you learn not so much how to predict the future as what the universe really is. You learn the relation of living things to the universe and how that delicate instrument called "you" will react to changing universal vibrations.

Then there is spiritual alchemy. B.O.T.A. claims to teach the secrets of alchemy as understood by the Fire Philosophers of old, an alchemy of the soul, not of chemicals. It's not much different from what the Rosicrucians teach except there's more meditation thrown in. Rev. Davies describes it this way:

> "It's a step by step meditational training. Our teachings integrate all methods of meditation in order to bring about a capacity for spiritual experience which must then be expressed on the physical plane. Otherwise meditation tends to become escapist in nature; especially if you are a natural mystic. You withdraw into a kind of trance, you might say. People who show this tendency usually don't stay with us long."

Rev. Davies says that B.O.T.A.'s teachings are for practical purposes. You learn how to bring about physical improvements in your health, income, environment and associates. You develop your mind by improving concentration, reason, memory, imagination and intuition. Your spiritual self benefits too through direct knowledge of yourself and the universe. You get the answer to "Who am I?" Above all, you learn to live life as it should be lived . . . with excitement . . . with joy . . . with love. And this you learn from the Kabbala.

The Kabbala teaches that everything that happens to you is created by you—that your mind has molded your environment. The basic principle of the Kabbala is that the whole universe is nothing more than consciousness. Consciousness is creator and created. Separateness is an illusion. Yet consciousness exists at different levels. The Kabbala symbolizes these levels with its sacred Tree of Life. The Tree of Life is illustrated by ten spheres, or levels of Being called Sephiroth. These are linked by twenty-two lines, or paths of progress. Mankind descended from the top one down through the others to the lowest level. Now it's your job to climb back up. The Kabbala tells you how. Thus, the Kabbala is not only a treatise on wisdom and philosophy, but is a guidebook like the Egyptian Book of the Dead.

The paths of the Tree of Life are used for meditation. Sometimes you meet strange creatures in your psychic explorations along these different paths. Often they are frightening. Could the ancients have known about archetypes long before Carl Jung brought them to the attention of modern psychology? Is this the reason many Orthodox Jews steer clear of the Kabbala, believing that it can drive you crazy? B.O.T.A. believes differently. To them the Kabbala clears your mind and makes it whole. As Rev. Davies points out:

> Kabbala is a system that doesn't separate itself from any portion of the personality. You know, it doesn't give one kind of method for the devotional nature and another method for the active nature. All of this is included. You can say that Kabbalistic training is a synthesis of every type of training that exists. There isn't a phase of training that doesn't integrate into the whole.

"Well," you might ask, "Where in this esoteric scheme of things does the Tarot fit? What does the Tarot have to do with the Kabbala?" That's not clear. No one knows for sure just how the Tarot came into being. No one can define where and how it developed; nor can anyone trace it beyond the late fourteenth century. It consists of two decks of cards comprising the Minor and Major Arcana, or mysteries. The Minor Arcana indicates that the Tarot might be linked with Hinduism and its caste system. The four suits of the Minor Arcana, chalices, swords, pentacles and wands, have been interpreted as symbolizing the priesthood, the nobles, merchants and peasants. Hearts, spades, diamonds and clubs of our modern-day playing cards evolved from these symbols. Or the Tarot may be rooted in alchemy because some people claim the symbols stand for water, air, earth and fire. But Tarot scholars and most enthusiasts will tell you the cards are founded in the Holy

Kabbala. The Major Arcana suggests this. It consists of twenty-two elaborate designs that are believed to symbolize the twenty-two paths of the Kabbalistic Tree of Life. Many Tarot decks have one of the twenty-two Hebrew letters on each of the cards. This is how Dr. Case equated the Tarot with the Kabbala. Jungian psychologists prefer to equate the Major Arcana with archetypes. Indeed, the designs depict personages, activities, situations and metaphysical principles in a strongly archetypal way. There are esoteric drawings of such things as a magician, an emperor, strength, justice, a hanged man, judgment and the wheel of fortune.

Most people think of the Tarot in terms of divination. They believe in the law of synchronicity, presuming that cosmic influences guide whoever deals the cards into laying out a pattern that can predict the future. In response to the question of whether this is true, Rev. Davies answered, "I know this is the idea that most people have, and certainly it lends itself to the promotion of supersensory awareness. This has made it popular. But, we do not encourage divination because that is not the purpose of the Tarot."

Builders of the Adytum use the Tarot as a psychoanalytic tool. More explicitly, it's a psychological purgative. In fact, the Tarot makes modern psychology's ink blot, or Rorschach, test look positively primitive. It contains archetypal symbols. When the cards are laid out, they have the makings of a story, just like a dream . . . just like "absurd statement" Gestalt therapy. It's up to you to put the story together. Do you remember that dream interpretation class where the students use other people's dreams to get at their own psychological hang-ups? The Tarot, like dreams, only comes up with symbols, infinite as the arrangements may be. You have to fill in the scenarios. You can do this by meditating on the symbols and on the pattern in which they were laid out. If you are schooled in the psychological use of Tarot, buried emotional experiences and even archetypes may be triggered. As they rise to consciousness, strong feelings rise with them. You live them in your imagination and, similar to *est*, then eliminate them.

Rev. Davies has more to say on the subject:

> "The Tarot basically is a pictorial representation of the principle of consciousness. According to Jungian psychology it stimulates the subconscious. Consciousness thinks with words; subconsciousness responds to pictures. You get more direct contact with

deeper parts of consciousness via image-pictures. In order to discover what you are, how to control your consciousness, how to express yourself in the most highly evolved manner possible, how to obtain all your various spiritual goals, it's absolutely essential to come up with subconscious images. That's why our meditational techniques are the opposite from that which lends itself to escapism—because they train people to become more and more aware of their images, to use their images consciously."

Like the Rosicrucians, B.O.T.A. uses the same bearer of knowledge. You get your esoteric wisdom via the postman. Members receive two correspondence lessons each two weeks. This costs $4 a month. The first seven weeks of lessons succinctly present metaphysical principles that would normally take reams of documents to cover. But even at this early stage you are shown how to delve into your subconscious through meditation. If you are serious and remain with B.O.T.A. for at least four and a half years, you will cover the complete spectrum of the basic teachings. These make up a practical inventory of esoteric psychological methods to develop your powers of consciousness through attunement with Divine Consciousness. In addition to lessons on the Tarot and its sacred meditations on archetypal symbols, and the study of the Kabbala with its paths of return to union with Divine Consciousness, there are also courses devoted to lesser mysteries such as Color and Sound, Spiritual Alchemy and Esoteric Astrology. Beyond these are still more studies—studies that enhance what has been already learned. Ann Davies says, "It's like travelling the pathways of consciousness to the infinite limits; there is no end." Each lesson is considered a spiritual communication. Each lesson links each member to the whole B.O.T.A. membership.

That membership is now changing. It used to be primarily middle-aged. In fact, the membership of *all* established esoteric societies used to be middle-aged. It was only these people who were interested in esoteric teachings until the drug culture burst on the scene in the 1960's. Now B.O.T.A.'s ranks, and those of other groups, are rapidly filling with younger people.

As far as centers are concerned, B.O.T.A. doesn't have many. Rev. Davies stresses, "We seek quality rather than quantity of membership." You will find one center each in France, New Zealand and Colombia. In North America they are more numerous. You could affiliate with one in Boston, New York, Tulsa,

Denver, San Francisco, Sacramento or Los Angeles. As you might guess, headquarters is in Los Angeles. And what a beautiful chapel they have there. It's a delightful shock to your nervous system when the lights in the sanctum go on. There in a cove all around the altar are exquisite oversized reproductions of the Tarot's Major Arcana, all authentically colored and glowing brilliantly in the radiance of ultraviolet light.

All B.O.T.A. centers conduct Sunday services. The public is invited. But in addition to services and the basic training, if you have completed the four and a half years of required correspondence work, you may be eligible for the Esoteric Training, depending on how diligent you have been. It's by invitation only and consists of direct personal instruction. Its teachings, ceremonies and rituals are secret. If you join this exclusive club you advance from Associate Member to Working Builder. Beyond that is the highest level of membership, the Stewards. The leaders of the organization are drawn from this group and they must all take vows of renunciation of life's luxuries, for they are Stewards of the Work. But they don't renounce life's joys. To B.O.T.A. life's joys *are* the work.

The Kabbala teaches that Cosmic Mind, or God, created the universe to experience it. It also teaches that man is a co-partner with God in creating the universe. Thus, man is a co-partner in experiencing it. Rev. Davies emphasized this point when she said, "We feel it's our responsibility to the Almighty, to our own higher souls, to heighten our awareness of what we see, what we hear, what we experience, so we appreciate and enjoy every last subtlety."

For true mystics, reality does not lie in philosophies, doctrines, creeds or dogmas. It resides in experience alone . . . experience through which Cosmic Consciousness manifests, and thus lives. The concept that you are one with a single Supreme Being and that your purpose for living is to be one of the organs through which this Being experiences the world is not impossible to envision. There was once a television commercial that opened with a father, mother, and child walking toward a city streetcorner. As they approached, the individuals were silhouetted against the background of the street. Slowly the street scene faded. Simultaneously within each silhouette appeared that aspect of the scene that most interested each of the separate people. The father saw a fancy sports car. Mother's concern centered on the laundromat. The child zoomed in on the toy store. Each had a separate interpretation of what the visual scene contained. The television viewer got all three combined.

Now multiply this three and a half billion times. This is how a Universal Consciousness would experience Earth through you and the rest of mankind. Add several billion more experiences and you have what might be God's impressions through animals, birds and fish. Throw in another trillion for all the insects, and another quadrillion for the amoeba, bacteria and viruses. Multiply this by ten quintillion other worlds and illuminate it all with the light from every blazing star in the Milky Way. Then expand all this grandeur to infinity. Try to conceive of having all these experiences at once. What an indescribable spectrum of experience you would have. A resonance of billions of impressions that range from serenely winking fireflies to the incredible violence of colliding galaxies. Yet the experience of Cosmic Being would exceed all you can ever imagine, and then an infinite times more. Still, the enlightened masters say, it is your duty to Universal Mind, no matter how limited you seem to be, to create as much harmony and joy in this Divine Experience as you can. Because the only pleasures Divine Consciousness experiences are through its creations. At least that's what they say.

Religious Science

One person who searched for harmony and joy in his life was the founder of one of America's fastest growing metaphysical schools. Ernest Holmes believed beauty is everywhere. That's why he saw it everywhere. To demonstrate this, he always carried a pocket knife. Whenever he saw a weed, he would pull out his well-used blade, cleanly sever the weed from its stem, then take it home with him. When he had gathered several different samples he would arrange them into intricate and beautiful patterns to demonstrate that beauty can be created and experienced from anything—that beauty and perfection are everywhere.

He made this philosophy a part of the school that he founded. He named the organization Church of Religious Science. And its teachings he called Science of Mind, a science of the Law of Mind. It is a law that is immutable, a law, when repeated in the same way, gives the same results over and over. It is a law that is logical. In fact, Holmes came on this law purely by intellect, by study, by reason: no revelations, no special masters, no secrets passed down from antiquity. Unlike the previously discussed metaphysical schools, Religious Science has no secrets. Dr. Holmes put it simply, "Religious Science is the correlation of the laws of science, the opinions of philosophy, and the revelations of religion applied to human needs and the aspirations of man."

Ernest Holmes never considered himself particularly unusual. He was born on a farm in Maine and as a youth he attended Gould Academy in Bethel nearly half a century before NTL Institute invented Sensitivity Training there. Shortly thereafter, while studying in Boston, he met a reader from the Mother Church of Christian Science. What he learned about Christian Science had a strong influence on his later thinking. Perhaps he was even more profoundly influenced by the writings of Ralph Waldo Emerson, especially those about transcendentalism and the imminence of Divinity permeating all life. Holmes said, "Studying Emerson was like drinking water to me." He was also swayed by the great metaphysical theorist, Judge Thomas Troward, who looked to nature rather than scripture for evidence of God. The judge's writings imbued in Holmes a synthesis of Eastern and Western mysticism. Added to the influence of these men were Holmes' studies of the world's religions. He later wrote, "Religious Science reads every man's Bible and gleans the truths therein contained."

The culmination of Holmes' metaphysical self-education occurred several years after he migrated to Southern California. In 1926 he published his most famous book *Science of Mind*. A year later he founded a corporation in Los Angeles which served as the basis for all future churches of Religious Science. Originally the idea was that all churches were to be separate entities with affiliated charters from the founding institute. It didn't quite work out that way. Instead, two basic movements emerged. Religious Science International is now headquartered in Fillmore, California. A very loosely structured organization, its member churches are autonomous in authority and somewhat so in what they teach. The other branch, the United Church of Religious Science, remains in Los Angeles. It claims to be the most valid successor of the original church and retains copyrights to many of Holmes writings. Certainly it preserves the teachings more precisely. The United Church of Religious Science is the one described here.

It now has 108 separate churches. As you might guess, California has the lion's share—73 to be exact. But most major cities throughout the Western states also host Religious Science denominations. So do cities in Alabama, Florida, Georgia, Ohio and Oklahoma. The lone one in Canada is in Vancouver. Naturally, Los Angeles has the most churches. Along with the headquarters are the educational arm, four separate churches and Founders Church which boasts of having the largest metaphysical congregation in the world.

Like Christian Science, Religious Science stresses healing. It has professional healing practitioners too. And like Christian Science, Dr. Holmes claimed that Religious Science is ". . . a vigorous gospel applicable to the everyday needs of our common life." Dr. Holmes also spoke of Oneness. He wrote, "The whole universe is the Manifestation of a Unity which men call God." To him everything physical is the result of thought patterns. It is only your belief in other forces, powers and individuals that makes them seem physical to you. To Holmes the Law of Minds holds center stage; it is the supreme law.

The Law of Mind is impersonal. Yet it can be personal to the degree that you use it personally. When making a prayer, or treatment, as Science of Mind refers to it, you the praying person must change before the prayer can work. A successful treatment of another person will change you as well as affect the person being treated. Holmes wrote, "In our practice, what the practitioner silently realizes for John Smith in his own mind is known in the medium of the One Mind, which is also operating through the patient's mind and, theoretically at least, rises to the same level of realization in his mind."

The clue to a treatment is to think in terms of perfection. According to Dr. Holmes, *real* life is perfect. But in individual minds it is not. Religious Science doesn't deny illness or pain. It just affirms that perfection is at the center of everything—because everything is God. So, perfection is in you right now—it just may not be manifesting. Prayer doesn't *create* this perfection, this God; it only reveals it. And God, once revealed, brings about the change desired. That doesn't mean you can turn God into your Cosmic bellhop. You don't bring God's thought to you—you have to go to the answer. To achieve wealth, companionship, good fortune, or health, you have to go where it is. You must mentally move from the level of the problem to the level of the answer. You have to think like Mohammed when he said, "If the mountain will not come to Mohammed, Mohammed will go to the mountain."

In the metaphysical tradition, Religious Science has its dramatic healing. In one instance during a church service, a member of the congregation fell over, seemingly dead. There was no physician present to certify that death had occurred, but the man had no detectable pulse and no respiration. He was carried outside and laid on the lawn. Then the fire department respirator team was called. The congregation prayed. As it turned out, the man was already sitting up and mumbling "What happened?" when the respirator arrived.

So you are probably asking, How does Religious Science differ from Christian Science? So far they both seem to be almost exactly the same. Essentially they are. But there are differences. The attitude toward physicians is one. Christian Science has an "either-or" attitude; that is, either have confidence in God *or* in physicians, whereas Religious Science believes a little bit of confidence in God is better than none. In fact, Religious Science acknowledges that all knowledge is God-given, therefore, medical knowledge is helpful. That's why the Church cooperates closely with physicians. Religious Science even claims to help them. Dr. Holmes wrote, "I have not known one single physician who would not have been glad to have had a spiritual practitioner working with his patient."

Religious Science seems to get deeper into meditative processes too. These spiritual treatments relieve guilts, tensions, insecurity, rejection syndromes, and other neuroses. But the process isn't like those therapies that drag up subconscious problems to be relived over and over until they are resolved. Religious Science treats problems on a subconscious basis. Occasionally the problems surface, but generally they just vanish without the person even knowing what they really were. This same method, when called meditation, often results in profound revelations and awesome mystical experiences. A few people report receiving cosmic enlightenment during the first church service they ever attend. Religious Science is truly a mystical church, but in the modern tradition.

A major difference between Religious Science and Christian Science is in the methods of instruction. Christian Science relies on church and testimony services. Religious Science does too, but considers them more inspirational than instructive. The core of Religious Science is contained in its numerous lessons. These are given in three separate year-long courses. Religious Science courses literally teach you to have faith. They teach you to reach a mental state without material concern. Every student learns the prayer treatment. You are taught the process of changing your thinking. The same basic technique is used to achieve enlightenment, or gain wealth, develop talent, get guidance or improve your health. The whole course of instruction slowly reprograms your mind-set from a consciousness of pain and lack to an awareness of joy and abundance. "When you treat, all you do is convince your own mind."

The basic text for all courses is Dr. Holmes' book *Science of Mind*. The courses involve theory, actual practice and even speculation on the nature of the universe and the realms beyond death. There is lots of Bible thrown in along with Eastern scripture. You can take the first-year course in two ways. One way uses that versatile teacher, the postman. This 48 week Extension Study course comes from Los Angeles. All weekly lessons, the text and monitoring of your progress can be had for $90. The other way to take the first-year course is by weekly attendance in class. These two- to three-hour sessions are held in every church by a minister and each lasts eight months. This way you get personalized instruction along with incentive to practice the lessons. The price is $105. The classroom is the only way you can take the second and third year courses, and the price is similar. If you have proven yourself with the first three courses, you may take the practitioner course, also 8 months, which qualifies you for licensing as a practitioner. From there you can go on to ministerial and doctorial training in Los Angeles.

What do you have to do to get the basic teachings? Are there special requirements or abstentions? Must you join the church? "No!" answers all these questions. Nothing is mandatory in Religious Science. There are no diets; no Masses; no required rituals; no affirmations; no specific religious beliefs. As one minister put it, "We don't have any rules for people to break at night or behind our back. We say 'do what you want to do.' If it is destructive, you're going to pay the price. As you get into this you will automatically change your ways. You will automatically discipline your thinking, your vocabulary and much other behavior as well." In fact, you aren't even expected to attend Sunday services while taking the courses. Nor do you have to take courses to attend church. Teachings and services are open to everyone, but are not interdependent.

In addition to lessons and services, the various churches offer Junior Church, Youth Groups, Mid-week Lectures, Discussion Groups, Practitioner Counseling, and the numerous social activities that all churches have. But to really learn Religious Science you have to take the courses, because the prayer treatment is the essence and artistry of spiritual discipline. It is the only way to *experience* Religious Science—and Religious Science *is* an experience: an experience of nature and of God. When you become a true mystic, nature ceases to be a collection of objects. It becomes God. Then God ceases to be an object. Both the world and God are experienced as being the same.

That's what Saint Paul meant when he referred to the *indwelling* Holy Spirit. That's what Hindus mean when they refer to mystical union with God. That's what they mean when they claim that all awareness of the material world must cease before this can really happen. Religious Science gives you bold hints of this union, and its courses are a good way to get you on the mystical path. But Religious Science is a new religion. Hinduism, the world's oldest living religion, offers many other methods of discovering this union. It should. It's had plenty of time to develop them. The next chapter describes some of what it has evolved over the last few millennia.

Chapter 6

TRADITIONS
OF INDIA

Hinduism is so ancient that some say it started before time began. Certainly the source of Hinduism dates from before recorded time. The oldest and most sacred scripture of this ancient creed, the Rig Veda, is said to have been divinely inspired. It speaks of philosophy, rituals and mythology. For centuries its couplets were chanted to the tune of primitive instruments and its one thousand hymns are so impressive that the ancients memorized them and passed them down through the centuries by word of mouth. Yet the Rig Veda does not portray Hinduism as the religion is known today. It was in the 10th Century B.C., after the Rig Veda was committed to writing and other vedas had followed, that the concept changed.

Modern Hinduism

Though the Rig Veda firmly expressed the concept of universal unity, the later Brahmana emphasized a single God. This emerged as the central theme of the religion. To modern Hindus, Brahman is the one God—the supreme Mind of the universe. Unlike Western concepts of God, Brahman is not personal. Nor is Brahman manlike. That's why Brahman is referred to as "That."

Brahman is all there is. All that is is Brahman: "I am That; thou art That; all this is That; That is alone, and there is nothing else but That."

Hindu scriptures also teach that all that exists is but the meditation of Brahman. Brahman is all because all is in Brahman's mind. This is *maya*, the world of appearances. The material world "emerges from Brahman as heat emerges from a fire." It is a paradox. The world radiates from Brahman, but is not Brahman. Maya is real . . . but real as in a dream.

The concepts of an impersonal God and that the world is just a dream are difficult for most Westerners to grasp. But this was also true for the uneducated masses of India centuries ago. So around the 5th Century A.D. a sage offered something easier to envision. He pointed out that nature seems to operate in three ways. There is a creative aspect, a preservative aspect and, finally, a destructive aspect. A wave as it forms on the ocean might symbolize creation. Its travel across the water's surface is preservation. Then it crashes on a rocky shore and is destroyed. The scholars reasoned that what man sees as creativity, preservation and destruction are only his imperfect understanding of the eternal and unchanging Brahman. Yet that is how things appear to be. So why not give them a place in the concept of Divinity? Thus, Brahman became a *trimutri* (three-in-one God). The aspect that creates the cosmos was called Brahmā; Vishnu was the sustainer of the cosmos; and Siva was the eventual destroyer of it. To wrap the idea all up logically the sages proclaimed the cosmic cycle to last 4,320,000,000 years. Then another one starts all over again . . . ad infinitum.

So from the One came three. Since these were represented as being human-like, they naturally had to have wives. Soon goddesses came into being. Then the human traits of these gods and goddesses had to be depicted as manifestations of the original gods. That meant more gods. Soon there were animal gods, nature gods, demon gods and hero gods. There were dancing-girl gods, benign spirits and evil spirits, beautiful and ugly gods. Long before Carl Jung ever thought up his archetypes, Hindu sages had securely inserted India's unique version of them into the religious pantheon. Today they can be personalized and worshiped to any degree that a devotee wishes.

Hindus are considered the most religious people on earth. They should be. They worship over 330 million divine manifestations of Brahman. That's one individual god looking over the shoulder of every living Hindu.

The degree of Pantheistic worship among Hindus varies greatly. Still, the most enlightened Hindus tolerate it among their fellows. "Why not?" they say. "Any form of worship is a stepping stone to real understanding." However, to all Hindus there is oneness; and they have devised an elaborate theology and complex mythology to explain the many sides of this oneness. These are supplemented with stirring rituals and rich symbolism, all with lots of emotion and color. Then there are the intricate carved temples, boisterous parades, glittering ceremonies and splendorous festivals, all designed to make religion exciting to the world of mankind.

One exciting, if not necessarily comforting, Hindu concept is that of *karma*. Karma means action. Every action you take has a reaction, a ramification in your future. Everything you have done affects you now, or soon will. But to enlightened Hindus, karma is not divine whim or punishment from heaven. It is retribution caused by you. It is created by what you do to others, by what you don't do and even by how you think. You must pay for past karma, especially if it's bad. Unfortunately, much of it is bad. And one lifetime usually isn't long enough to pay. Thus the concept of reincarnations. Thousands of them. These are repeating cycles of birth, death and rebirth that leave spiritual imprints called *samsaras*. To a Hindu the most important goal in life is to work toward release from the influence of past mistakes, from past lives, from samsaras. That means learning from them. In the Hindu tradition, life is the schoolhouse of mankind.

There are three ways to work off bad karma. The slowest and the one requiring the most lifetimes is through suffering. This route requires that you suffer equally for all the evil you have produced in all your different lives. A faster way is through service. By helping others, you counteract bad karma. But the fastest of all is by direct communion with the divine essence—with Brahman. Through mystical union and the ensuing enlightenment it produces, all bad karma is wiped off the slate. Why? Because karma, like the rest of the world, is maya. When you become enlightened, you see the world as Brahman sees it—as a dream—as an illusion. So you must know Brahman. The Vedas say, "He who knows *himself* will know Brahman." And to know yourself and Brahman, you must know the wholeness of life by direct experience.

One person who emphasizes experiencing the wholeness of life is Maharishi Mahesh Yogi. He's that gentle person with the beads, white robe and flowing beard who loves flowers and always wears a delightful smile whenever he talks. But what he talks about is profound. His message is the Science of Creative Intelligence (SCI), a science based in the ancient traditions of India. Today it is known throughout the world as Transcendental Meditation (TM).

Transcendental Meditation

Maharishi says that we all have within us an unlimited reservoir of energy, creativity and intelligence. Transcendental Meditation is a technique that lets you dive to the depths of that reservoir. TM taps into the source of thought itself. It is a means of shifting your awareness to numerous levels of consciousness that you never knew existed. Maharishi emphasizes that TM is not like Zen or Jnana yoga. It does not employ concentration and contemplation, but is just the opposite of these disciplines. That's what makes it so easy.

In TM you make no attempt to still your mind. No need to control your thoughts. TM uses the natural tendency of your mind to seek out fields of greater satisfaction. A restless mind is a mind in search of greater fulfillment, of less boredom, of greater happiness. If what you do is interesting, your mind won't wander. TM is a natural process of going to levels of your mind that are the most interesting and most pleasurable. These are deep within your psyche. The closer your awareness gets to the source of inner pleasure, the more automatically it goes even deeper inward. TM just aims your mind in the right direction. It's like diving from a high board. If your body hits the water at the right angle, it will go right to the bottom of the pool. TM sets your mind at the right angle. All the rest is automatic and natural.

With TM your mind transcends even the subtlest form of thought. It discovers the source of thought. It experiences the reservoir of creative intelligence. As Maharishi says, "The field of pure creative intelligence lies beyond all seeing, hearing, touching, smelling and tasting—beyond all thinking and beyond all feeling. This state of the unmanifested, absolute, pure consciousness of Being is the ultimate state of life."

According to Maharishi, this ultimate state of consciousness, this awareness of awareness itself, this being both the experience and the experiencer, can be a part of your daily activity. You can bring the source right into the mainstream of your life. Maharishi doesn't look on meditation as a technique to escape from life. Rather it helps you cope with life. That's why so many meditators seem healthier, happier and more alive. They claim TM increases their creativity. They seem to have greater perceptiveness. They exude self-confidence. They have more energy, higher efficiency and for once in their lives enjoy perpetual peace of mind. As one student put it, "There has been a quantum increase in the quality of my life since I started meditating."

Even big business has discovered TM's benefits. The Arthur D. Little Company discovered that TM increases individual productivity. It also helps supervisors get along better with their employees. So TM is now part of the training program for the company's top executives. The same, to some degree, goes for over sixty other large corporations.

But mental improvement isn't TM's only benefit. Kudos go to its health aspects too. Dr. Keith Wallace, a UCLA physiologist, found that the amount of relaxation you get in just a few minutes of meditating may exceed that of a full night's sleep. The average decrease in metabolic rate is 16 percent. During meditation your heart beat slows by 30 percent. This helps people with high blood pressure. Meditators with low blood pressure see benefits too. Their pressure tends to rise. TM seems to bring all body functions into balance and into a norm. All aspects of the body in disequilibrium eventually come into harmony. That's why so many meditators see postural changes over time. This is another way of accomplishing what Ida Rolf does with her vigorous massage. But that's not all. Drinkers seem to have less desire to drink. Smokers give up polluting their lungs. And even drug abusers are said to kick their habit.

But TM isn't just an efficiency trip, a blood-pressure trip or a habit-kicking trip. Its real purpose is to get you deep into your mind. This isn't a trance. It is expanded consciousness. It makes you aware of yourself. As so many other disciplines emphasize, mind and body are linked. TM releases your body tensions. The traumas associated with them come loose too. Yet at these deep levels of consciousness, at the source of thought, you don't suffer the pains of your traumas. Psychiatrist Bernard Glueck of the Institute of Living in Hartford says TM "allows unconscious material to come into awareness without intense emotion." In meditation you don't come to violent emotional grips with complexes as in some other methods; you just dissolve them in your new-found consciousness. You recognize your guilts and fears as unimportant fantasies.

As with all methods that resolve inner problems, TM can produce definite personality changes. The more you meditate, the more you recognize your inherent strengths. You recognize your individual differences from other people. Yet you also see your similarity to them. You become the master of your experiences while at the same time becoming more united with the human family. One TM instructor, Phil Anderson, summed it up this way:

> When we meditate, we begin to use more of our mind. We begin to expand more of our awareness. We begin to eliminate tension and stress. Then we are able to support life at a higher level. So that we reach with Transcendental Meditation a time in which we are using 100 percent of the mind. Now, when we are using 100 percent of the mind; that is when not only the mind is full, but the body is completely free of stress and strain; now that is the state we call Cosmic Consciousness. In the state of Cosmic Consciousness you are one with the nature of things. There is no separation. You are flowing in harmony with yourself and with nature. As Maharishi calls it, that's when you are normal—because you are experiencing fullness of life.

That's the philosophy most meditators develop—that we are here to enjoy life free from stress and strain. We are here to unfold . . . to expand. Above all, as Maharishi wrote, "Because of its own nature; perhaps for the sake of variety, expansion of happiness is the purpose of creation."

Maharishi sees his mission as the expansion of happiness. The best way he can do this is to help everyone discover his inner self and the source of his being. In fact, he has come up with what he calls a World Plan, to disseminate TM all around the world. Transcendental Meditation will someday be taught from numerous centers on all continents. Maharishi hopes to have one center for every million of the world's population. So far, the United States is the only country that has met its full quota of centers (330).

How come the United States? Why were Americans, and now Canadians, the chosen people? Because Maharishi had to move fast. He knew he couldn't teach the world all by himself. First he started training instructors in Southern India. Still, he calculated, even that way the task would consume the better part of 200 years. But, he reasoned, North America is dynamic. There people do things in a hurry. So he introduced TM to the United States in 1965. By 1974, 2,400 Americans and Canadians had been trained as instructors and there were student TM centers on numerous campuses along with adult centers in every major city. What once attracted mostly college students has now spread to engineers, scientists, businessmen, attorneys, housewives, bartenders and even Army generals. Today 400,000 Americans and Canadians practice TM, and 10,000 more join the ranks every month.

The whole operation goes under the general name of World Plan Executive Council. Within this is the International Meditation Society (IMS) and the Students International Meditation Society (SIMS). Both of these do the same thing, teach you TM. Then there is the American Foundation for the Science of Creative Intelligence (AFSCI). This branch concentrates on business firms. These three organizations are headquartered together in Los Angeles, just as their services are often combined at local TM centers. The larger local centers are called World Plan Centers. At these you will also find CHIMS (Children's International Meditation Society). This is designed for youngsters aged 4 to 9 and uses a special TM method appealing to children. Teenagers aren't forgotten either; at least not at the San Francisco Peninsula World Plan Center. This youth group ranges from age 10 to 17 and has lots of outings along with its TM practices. No ordinary name for them. They go by the acronym BATMAN—Bay Area Transcendental Meditators Above Nine.

Anyone can learn to meditate. In just a few sessions too. There are no special requirements to be a meditator. You certainly don't have to become a Hindu. In fact, Maharishi insists that TM is not a religion. It's just a technique. It will supplement any philosophy or faith. No abstentions either. Maharishi doesn't ask you to give up anything permanently. TM is so natural that with time, unnatural and unhealthy qualities should automatically fall away. Still, there are some requirements you must meet to get instruction. TM involves your mind. So you should have an alert mind. Maharishi insists that for fifteen days prior to initiation you refrain from what are known out West as California Recreational Chemicals. Liquor doesn't count. Also, you have to pay for what you get. Maharishi doesn't personally benefit from your donation because he has taken vows of poverty, but the expanding organization needs money. The important consideration, though, is you. Most people appreciate only what they pay for. So normally you would pay $125. The price is less if you are retired, unemployed or a student. The same for married couples. Their children taking TM at the same time get it free, except they are encouraged to donate two weeks' allowance. After the initial fee, all future services are free.

TM training is a program of several steps. After a couple of free introductory lectures, you participate in the one and only ritual in the program. This is somewhat unnerving to practical executives and rugged masculine types. You have to bring fruit, flowers and a white handkerchief. Then, to wafts of Oriental scents, you watch as your instructor performs a ceremony to the ancient Vedic teachers in gratitude for their having passed the knowledge of TM on to mankind.

Then you are given the key to TM. This is a mantra, a vocal sound that supposedly massages your nervous system. The resonances of the mantra are so subtle they are believed to create vibrations that affect various levels of your body, both physical and psychic. This is specially true if the sound is properly selected. So your mantra is the vehicle that gives you, the high diver, just the right angle that lets you reach the bottom of your psyche.

All individuals vary in their psychological, physical and spiritual constitution, so your mantra is specially selected just for you. Ancient tradition prescribes how that is done. This doesn't mean that no one else has your same mantra—there are only so many in the inventory. But it does mean your mantra is suited to you. It is considered your very personal property and shouldn't be shared with anyone else. So instead of speaking your mantra aloud, you use it silently. You are taught how to do this along with how to avoid concentration or contemplation. The results of TM are cumulative, so you have to be regular in your practice. Maharishi recommends fifteen to twenty minutes twice a day, preferably the same time each day.

Getting your mantra and learning how to use it doesn't end your instruction. You are expected to attend evening meetings for three consecutive days to discuss your progress and to verify the correctness of your practice. Still you aren't finished. Twice during the first month you are asked to come to the TM Center to have your technique checked. Then, for the next year you are asked to come in at least once a month for interview and updating to make sure you are advancing. Beyond this period you can go it alone.

There is more to TM if you want to participate more fully. Group meditations, advanced lectures, group checking—all are available along with fun things like local picnics, pot luck dinners, movies and other activities for those who enjoy this kind of camaraderie. Whatever way you participate, you are encouraged to visit a center *any* time to have your technique checked. All of this is free.

If you want to go further in TM, you can become an instructor. Maharishi now trains over 1,500 new teachers a year in Switzerland. The cost, including transportation, runs about $1,000. Also there is TM at the academic level. The student branch (SIMS) teaches courses for academic credit. This started at Stanford in 1970 and then spread to such academic giants as Harvard, Yale, UCLA and UC Berkeley. You can now take credit courses in TM theory and practice in over forty colleges and universities. Then, of course, there is M.I.U. That's Maharishi International University. It is a four-year college located in Fairfield, Iowa that emphasizes the Science of Creative Intelligence.

Who knows where TM will go from here? One thing is sure: Maharishi is confident there will be three and a half to four thousand centers around the world in the near future. To Maharishi and to TM meditators, TM is the gateway to fulfillment. It is considered mankind's easiest way to enjoy, en masse, spiritual enlightenment. It is a major step on the path of mysticism.

What is real mysticism? Swami Prabhavananda of the Vedanta Society came up with one answer. Echoing the opinion of most mystics, he said, "True mysticism is the conviction that God can be seen; that He can be directly known and realized; and that to have this realization is the only purpose in life. . . . Mysticism has no creed, no theory, no dogma. It says that you can see God, talk with Him, have a unitive knowledge of the Godhead."

That unitive knowledge of the Godhead, a merging with Cosmic Consciousness, a feeling of oneness with the universe is an experience reported by many mystics. It takes different forms and seemingly occurs in different degrees of awesome majesty. Some people experience what they best describe as exquisite pain, an outpouring of ecstasy that surpasses any earthly experience. It vibrates all your bodily cells until they are exhausted, yet you still cry out for more. Or ecstasy can be nonphysical. Saint Teresa of Avilla speaks of being immersed in the ocean of God, of bathing in a fluid of love. Some mystics describe their experience as one of sheer bliss, being enveloped in the deepest and darkest silence. Others have seen brilliant light. When the brilliance eclipses that of the sun, they spiritually merge with this Divine radiance. They are at one with all of creation, existing everywhere in the cosmos all at once, seeing reality as a space-time continuum of ecstasy and magnificence, understanding everything that is, was and will be. It is a return to the Beginning, to absolute Being, to changelessness and timelessness, back to the Father and Creator. This enlighten- ment, in the words of the Upanishads, is "infinite knowledge, infinite freedom, infinite peace." It is the return to infinite existence.

According to the Vedas, this return, this reunion of your individual self *(atman)* with the universal self *(Brahman)* can only occur when your individual self has been purified. For most people, say the Hindus, purification takes an eternity of lifetimes. But there are faster ways. And the ancient Indian sages, steeped in mystical tradition, devised many such ways. Many of these ways, including TM, are called yoga. Yoga is Sanskrit for "union"—union with God. It also refers to methods of achieving this union. It deals with the whole you—physical, mental and spiritual. And it is one of the most complete and refined set of disciplines ever devised to help you transcend your sense of personal identity.

Yoga

The form of yoga best known in the Western world, Hatha yoga, is extremely old. It probably came into being before the third millennium B.C., and is still the most commonly practiced. Actually, it isn't a true form of mysticism, but is a method of preparing you physically for the more advanced spiritual yogas. It is based on the principle that a healthy body means a healthy mind. Thus, its unusual postures and contortions *(asanas)* provide physical strength and stimulation. The breathing exercises *(pranayama)* increase energy and relaxation. There are other techniques used for cleansing the inner parts of your body, but few of these are emphasized in America.

Actually, the more advanced forms of yoga may be as old or older than Hatha yoga. But they weren't codified and organized until the Second Century B.C. when Rishi Pantanjali elaborated his famous step-by-step process for achieving *samadhi,* or mystical union. It is really a combination of what are now defined as separate yogic practices, each devised to produce different effects on different types of people. According to yogic theory, there are four basic types of personalities—inquisitive, reflective, active and emotional. Yoga today consists of four basic pathways to self-realization, each devised for one of these personality types.

The path most resembling Pantanjali's original yoga is called Raja, or "Royal" yoga. This is your path if you have a scientific bent, if you like to experiment, if you are searching for the truth. Really it's a combination of several yogas. Its primary purpose is to penetrate your psychic layers and expose the universal consciousness beneath. But it's not like TM. Raja is perfecting meditation *through* concentration and contemplation. This concentration is so intense it is claimed to be like focusing the rays of the sun through a magnifying glass. It literally blocks out all external stimuli. This way you can supposedly achieve union with whatever subject has your attention. For most yogis, this subject is God.

But some seekers approach enlightenment through self-knowledge. Hindus have a profound respect for wisdom. They say a person without wisdom is like a frog in a dry pond. So there is a yogic path just for those who seek wisdom, for those who want to know about themselves. It's called Jnana yoga, the path of self-knowledge. It is the path of self-analysis. Through it you recognize your various natures. You discover the functions and limitations of your body. You examine your reasoning and your intellect. In ways it's similar to gestalt therapy or *est.* You examine your gross body and lower mind. Then you explore higher minds. As you proceed to the most subtle aspects of your self, you break through all layers of your personality; you see your masks, your traumas and your archetypes. Eventually you must understand your true self. Then you merge with the Supreme Self. You arrive at the same destination as Raja yoga through a different combination of techniques and different types of understanding.

Then there is the pathway of action. This yogic road of service to other people is appropriately called Karma yoga. Its adherents claim that by willingly performing good deeds in life, especially if you expect no earthly reward, you rapidly free yourself from the wheel of karma. By looking upon all recipients of your deeds as manifestations of God, and upon your work as the will of God, you reduce your need for ego satisfaction. Then the barriers to Oneness collapse, and mystical union results. Karma yoga is for active people. But it is a labor of love.

Perhaps the most popular yoga in India is Bhakti yoga. It is said that a truly religious Hindu pants after Brahman as a miser after gold. Bhakti is the yoga of devotion. It is also the yoga of emotion. It involves lots of prayer, chanting, praising and devotion. Through it you evolve from devotion to your loved ones, to adoration of your guru, to worship of a personal divinity, to devotion to an ideal and finally to the ultimate recognition of the Supreme Oneness. If you are familiar with Christian mysticism, you probably recognize many similarities between Bhakti yoga and fervent worship of Christ.

Seldom are any of the four basic paths used totally to the exclusion of the others. All yogas combine to some degree the pathways of the others, and different gurus create different combinations. But yogic *pathways* are really just philosophies and attitudes. There are other specific practices, or techniques, that are also called yoga. These are the real meat (pith, if you're vegetarian) of Oriental mysticism. These are the specific methods you use when following the basic paths. They can be likened to the separate cars, buses, trucks, and motorcycles on any highway. The road leads in the direction you want to go, but the vehicles get you there. There are many of these yoga vehicles. Some are similar, some overlap and a few are the same things going under different names. The following yoga techniques are a few of the vehicles you may wind up using on the road to self-realization:

Asana—postures and physical exercise
Pranayama—adaptation of breathing to body and mind
Kundalini—awakening psychic energy in the spine
Nada—concentration on sound and its source

Tantra—uniting male and female polarities within the body and psyche

Mantra—concentrating on a sacred formula of sound

Japa—repetition of spiritual thoughts or phrases

Yantra—meditation on a spiritual form

Mudra—gestures used in meditative practice

Mandalla—concentration on complex psychometric designs

Laya—mastery of will power and psychic energy

Shakti—working with Divine feminine forces

Siddha—enlightenment through absorbing the guru's psychic energy

But just because there are several pathways to enlightenment and lots of vehicles to travel these pathways doesn't mean you can just start practicing yoga any time you want. Yogic practices have no inherent power of themselves; they are not magical devices or formulas. They are merely tools, or channels, that guide and concentrate your mind and emotions. It is your mind that contains all the magic and power, not the techniques. So you have to understand the nature of yourself and your relation to an even higher self. And you have to understand the many strange phenomena you will experience as you progress. This, it is claimed, can only be revealed to you through the lips of a teacher; through someone who has traveled the road before and is wise enough to understand how you and your specific personality should travel it. The mystical practice of yoga is very personal and different for each individual. Only a master teacher who has become enlightened himself and has been trained to guide others can guide you. Fortunately, many such teachers exist in North America. Among the most renowned and most qualified are the Vedanta swamis.

Swami translates as "he who is one with the higher self." It also means "master teacher." To Hindus it indicates a member of one of the most venerated organizations in India. The holy Swami Order has existed from time immemorial, though its present organization dates from the 9th Century A.D. Its more than one million monks have all received a powerful spiritual initiation that permits them to go by the title of Swami. This training often includes use of numerous yogic techniques and how they should be applied to different individual personalities. It also includes vows of poverty, chastity and obedience to spiritual authority.

In the 19th century one of these swamis, a Bengali saint who so venerated the earthly incarnations of Vishnu the Preserver that he took the name Ramakrishna, made a startling discovery. He, like many others, was convinced that true religion is not belief or dogma, but experience. So he decided to experience himself. First he did this through love and devotion to God which he conceived of as being a Divine Mother. Then he developed an intense love of Krishna, Hinduism's youthful manifestation of Godhead. After he had achieved union of his atman with Brahman by practicing these Hindu versions of Bhakti yoga, he spent the next twelve years trying other religions. He had the satori of a Buddha. He followed the teachings of Mohammed. He worshipped Christ. All of these experiences resulted in mystical union. So Ramakrishna declared that all religions lead to the same ultimate destination—that the goal of all religions is the same. And this he passed on to his followers, whom he then ordained as swamis.

This great teacher's legacy was organized by his followers into what they named the Ramakrishna Order of India. In 1893 one of the brighter of these young monks, Vivekananda, was selected to represent Hinduism at the World's Fair Parliament in Chicago. Once in the United States he became an instant hit. When the Parliament was over, many Americans invited him to remain and tour the country. For the next three years, Vivekananda lectured and held classes. He taught what the Vedas taught and that Christians and Jews and all the other devout in the West can achieve mystical enlightenment right here and now. He was so encouraged by the way he was received that he founded the Vedanta Society in New York City. From this beginning other Vedanta Societies spread around the country. Each is a separate entity, but all are linked under the spiritual guidance of the Ramakrishna Order in India. Today you can find a Vedanta Society in Boston, Chicago, St. Louis, Providence, Seattle, Portland, Ore. and two in New York. The biggest are the Northern California one with temples in San Francisco, Berkeley and near Sacramento, and the Southern California Society located in both Hollywood and Santa Barbara. All the Vedanta teachers are swamis as well as being monks of the Ramakrishna Order. In Canada, another organization, the International Sivananda Yoga and Vedanta Society, is quite prominent.

Vedanta Societies

What is Vedanta? And what do its teachers teach? The word *Vedanta* means literally, "the end of the Vedas." Actually the Upanishads *are* the Vedanta because they are the substances of the Vedas. Thus, Vedanta is a summary of spiritual knowledge. Vivekananda put it this way: "The whole world is full of the Lord. Open your eyes and see Him. This is what Vedanta teaches." That means renunciation. Not renunciation of the world, but renunciation of your concept of it. Vedanta deifies the world. To Vedantists all that exists is God. To Vedantists, "Thou art That."

Vedanta is a philosophy and a way of life, not a religion. Its instruction is open to people of all creeds who are seriously seeking the truth. If you are one of these, you are welcome at any Vedanta temple, though Vedantists do not try to convert you since they abhor proselytism. However, Vedanta does deepen your understanding of your own religious conviction, but you have to discover that for yourself. It is a strong Vedanta belief that when you are ready for spiritual enlightenment, you will automatically find your teacher.

Vedantists believe you *must* have a teacher . . . a living teacher. To them interpretations of scripture must come directly from someone who understands scripture. The teacher should be so wise that he can teach you those scriptural truths that you, with your specific knowledge and personality, should know. And he must be there to answer your questions. This is why Vedanta places strong emphasis on a close relationship between teacher and disciple. In fact, the word *Upanishad* means "being near your guru in a mood of devotion." But such devotion isn't a prerequisite to your being welcome at a Vedanta center.

Each Vedanta Society center offers at least one lecture open to the public, usually on Sunday. Whether these are presented from a large altar emblazoned with the Sanskrit symbol for Om or from a simple lectern, whether the temple is a gleaming white mosquelike structure or a low Chinese-style hall, the lectures around the country are similar. They tell you what Vedanta is. They teach how you, your beliefs and Vedanta are mutually supporting. For those with greater interest each temple conducts classes in the Upanishads, Bhagavad-Gita and the aphorisms of Pantanjali. These too are open to the public. And most temple doors remain unlocked during daylight hours to provide a sanctuary to all seekers for meditation.

For serious seekers membership in one of the Vedanta Societies is only possible if you live near a Vedanta temple. That's because Vedanta is a very personal thing. Prior to being accepted as a member you must attend lectures and classes for several months. To be admitted to membership, you have to be personally sponsored by a swami who is willing to give you instruction. As a member you may participate in all activities and religious festivals, and you have complete access to the temple's library. Most important, you now have a close association with your swami.

Your teacher is your very own personal guide. He meets with you privately where you tell him of your experiences and your troubles and your doubts. You hear the scriptures interpreted from his lips. And he trains you in the various yoga techniques most suited to your personality and to what he considers your ability to realize God. Even private rituals are devised if your temperament demands it. Vivekananda, like most good gurus, believed many yogas should be combined.

What does this all cost? Very little—just enough for the various Societies to get by. There is no charge for any lectures, classes or private instruction. But, as with any church, donations at services are welcome. If you are a member, you are encouraged to meet a monthly pledge if you can afford it. One dollar to ten dollars is average; generous or well-to-do members pledge more.

Who are the members? Almost every type of person: doctors, lawyers, factory workers and housewives. Vedanta is an excellent way for ordinary people caught up in the workaday world to get the very personal and private instruction so often reserved for renunciants living in distant monasteries. The small membership is mostly middle-aged, but is now growing with younger people attracted to Indian mysticism. The Vedanta Society of Southern California serves 700 members, along with many non-members who attend lectures and classes. The other Vedanta Societies, though having similar types of members, vary considerably in size of membership.

If you are really serious about Vedanta, you can eventually become a swami. That's not easy. Americans are slow in adapting to the attitudes and privation required. That's why all the swamis so far have come from India. Still, the Societies provide a life-style which allows you to devote full time to spiritual development. There are several monasteries where resident students live under the supervision of a swami. As renunciants they refrain from liquor and smoking. After taking certain monastic vows of chastity, love for God and service to others, they also assume Sanskrit names with spiritual meanings to remind themselves of their goal in life. And they work at this goal without ceasing. Their training is really a form of conditioning—so much so that Ramakrishna had only to hear the name of The Divine Mother to be transported into the rapture of samadhi.

Swami Prabhavananda, in describing the effort needed to achieve salvation, put it this way: "My Master used to teach us to practice recollectedness of God while eating, walking or sitting. His one insistence was to practice, practice, practice! Thus, through practice and dedicated struggle we will at last know and experience God, who is none other than our very Self."

Ananda Marga

From Hindu teachings it would appear that duty to God is also duty to yourself. And "practice, practice, practice" is Vedanta's way of fulfilling this duty. To an extent that is also the philosophy of Ananda Marga. But to Margiis the word "practice" has a different connotation. Though *repetition* is a part of their methods, the main thrust in Ananda Marga is *applied action*. The main goal of Ananda Marga is to raise the spiritual level of the whole world society. Margiis are dedicated to uplifting all people—no one should be left behind.

The maxim "To a starving man, a piece of bread is God" makes a lot of sense to the hungry. The poor, the uneducated, the imprisoned and the infirm look upon their wants with a similar view. Therefore, a major part of Ananda Marga activity is to relieve the world's unfortunates of the mundane cares that inhibit their spiritual growth. Margiis believe everyone should be free of earthly survival problems so they can devote some time to self-realization. So to Margiis, Karma yoga is one of the major pathways to fulfillment and to salvation.

Ananda Marga's founder, Shrii Anandamurtijii, states that the duty of all who seek true enlightenment is to go out and work for society. That's why the Margii motto is "Salvation to Self—Service to Humanity." As Anandamurtijii told his followers, "The marching together of all in unison is society. Instead of despising those who have lagged behind, help them to advance. This alone will be your social duty. It is action that makes a man great. Be great by your sadhana (meditation), by your service, by your sacrifice."

Anandamurtijii made quite a sacrifice himself: he's in prison. Not that he chose to be, but India is full of religious-political strife. So when a spiritual leader with a large following is critical of the nation's distribution of resources and preaches that all of society should be responsible for each individual, that in a nation where famine is commonplace it is evil if even one person starves, some politicians may feel threatened.

Anandamurtijii's followers claim he was framed. Certainly, appearances suggest that. One of his disciples, after being charged with another crime, accused Anandamurtijii of conspiring to kill six former students. The disciple was pardoned with amazing speed. The government locked up Anandamurtijii equally fast. The courts since threw out the disciple's testimony, but they also denied his former guru bail. So Anandamurtijii remained incarcerated without bail and without resolution of his case.

Anandamurtijii's imprisonment certainly doesn't deter his followers. They are devoted to him. One young Margii could hardly contain himself as he said, "Baba—we call him Baba [beloved father]. I went to India and I saw Baba. I can't really say anything about Baba, you know, except that I realize, thinking back, that when I saw Baba, I just felt emotions and things that I have never felt in my whole life. You know, it's that presence; he just brought this stuff out of me. There was this beautiful man, and he just brought all of this stuff out of me. It's like his divinity just produces divinity in other people. His whole being, you know, that's what it does. Wow, here is this guy and I'm getting so high just looking at him. It's not idolatry, it's just—Wow!"

Anandamurtijii was born unusual. As a young child of seven he engaged in learned debates with holy men, and exposed many of them as charlatans more interested in alms than in service. He was so harmonious with nature that his parents were afraid to let him go into the forest because he liked to ride on the back of a tiger he had befriended. He so loved that tiger that when, years later, after he had become an adult and the tiger died, Anandamurtijii considered that he too might give up his body. But some of his disciples begged him to remain incarnate and to teach. Fortunately, they prevailed.

So in 1955 Ananda Marga was born. The name means "path of eternal bliss." Anandamurtijii called hundreds of adepts and yogis from the professions, universities, caves and forests. Then he sent them around the world as *acaryas,* or teachers, to give his teachings to all who asked—all of this to be without charge. Margiis say, "These priceless teachings can never be sold and are being offered to all as free as sunlight, air and water." So if you become a Margii, there will be no fixed fee, just whatever you care to donate.

Baba has personally trained over two thousand men and women to be acaryas. Each of these teachers learned how to discriminate between different personalities and each has the gift of sensing the truth. Thus, they know what type of instruction you personally need. In North America seven of these acaryas circulate among the two thousand Canadian, American and Latin members of Ananda Marga providing instruction all over the continent.

Ananda Marga is not a religion, or even a philosophy. It is a way of life . . . a life dedicated as intensely to serving mankind as it is to seeking enlightenment. That's why Margiis come from all religious faiths, including atheism. In India most Margiis are older family people, but in America the majority are young, since the activities of Ananda Marga appeal to idealistic youth. Some are in high school. Many aren't yet out of their twenties, though recently the ranks of middle-aged enthusiasts have grown. If they aren't in school, the vast majority of members hold down a job. That's in addition to performing social work.

Margii social participation is counseling delinquents. It's distributing free food to the poor. It's providing yoga classes and entertainment for the handicapped. All over the country Margiis conduct inmate meditation groups in prisons or tutor disadvantaged children. And for the environment, Ananda Marga has ecology projects like recycling centers. The Educational Relief and Welfare Section puts volunteers in schools, children's homes and hospitals. Ananda Marga Universal Relief Teams provide help during floods, fires, and other disasters. Margiis who can't personally participate on a national scale are encouraged to perform services locally. They hold banquets and rummage sales, then send the proceeds to the newly renovated Victorian house in Denver that serves as Ananda Marga headquarters and distributes these monies where needed.

The basis of Ananda Marga is the local unit, or chapter, where the members meet on a weekly basis. Over 100 of these units dot America in every state and in most large cities. There are also 10 in Canada. Units differ slightly in their activities, depending on the participants. All have some form of social, recreational, and spiritual get-togethers. Some units are structured formally, others very loosely. But the similarities of the units are much stronger than the differences.

Some units hold philosophy classes or workshops conducted by qualified instructors. These may be in the form of lectures or group discussions. They often occur in conjunction with the weekly *dharmachakra*, or "circle of people whose goal is self-realization." These latter ceremonies are powerful collective meditations. All are open to the public, so you are welcome. It's a good way to see what Ananda Marga is all about and to experience the collective spiritual vibrations. As Baba said, "Good company is conducive to liberation." In addition to instruction and meditation, the dharma-chakras have lots of Sanskrit chanting. By far the most impressive is the Kiirtan, a powerful group activity. It's a rich and rhythmic clapping, knee-bending motion during which the mantra *Baba Nam Kevalam* ("Beloved Father, I see you in everything") is intoned over and over. It is a combination of moving asanas that balance your glandular system and soothing chanting that dissolves your ego, thus generating a collective spiritual flow among all persons present.

Aside from participating in social service programs and attending weekly unit meetings and dharmachakras, Margiis can attend mass get-togethers. In many regions of the continent Ananda Marga holds quarterly weekend retreats. Costs vary, but the accommodations are usually good because so many families bring children. There are national and international get-togethers too. In December of 1973, seven hundred Margiis from North and South America, Europe and the Far East descended on Tahlequah, Oklahoma for a biannual gathering.

Most Margiis meet once a week at their training center. But if you want to spend all your time with fellow Margiis, you can become a member of a *jagriti*, or communal house. These aren't monasteries since most members hold regular jobs. But they do provide camaraderie and a chance to serve alongside fellow members of the society. Ananda Marga is meant for people who want to belong. But as one Margii put it, "The major attraction for each individual is as different as the individual. Some are attracted to the solutions of social problems which Ananda Marga presents, some to the spiritual philosophy, some are attracted by the selfless dedication they see in some Margiis and acaryas. For me it was the joy that I saw in the faces of the Margiis I met."

Still, camaraderie, service, philosophy and chanting alone don't necessarily lead to enlightenment. And enlightenment for everyone is Anandamurtijii's goal. He claims a person seeking liberation from "maya" needs a liberator just as a prisoner in shackles must be freed by someone with a key. Acaryas, the teachers, are the keys to Ananda Marga training. The crux of the training is private individual instruction. Every Margii gets it. It is claimed that through the acaryas Anandamurtijii is able to project knowledge and meditation techniques directly to you.

It starts with your initiation where you receive your own special mantra. From there you work closely with your acarya. These teachers are trained to be sensitive to you and your unique personality. They know exactly which techniques are best for you and when you are ready for them. They don't spend much time with you because each acarya must travel all over the region teaching other Margiis, but they do periodically check your progress. Meanwhile you are expected to practice twice a day the techniques you have learned. Hatha asanas are prescribed, depending on your specific needs, to balance your metabolism and glandular system. Diet isn't of concern initially, but as you progress in Ananda Marga you will probably become a vegetarian. *Yama* (abstentions) and *Niyama* (observances), the spiritual attitudes of Pantanjali's eight-fold path, are the basic moral foundation of Ananda Marga meditation. Anandamurtijii has said that without morality true meditation is an impossibility.

Ananda Marga training comes in six lessons, each specifically geared to you. The first is where you get your basic meditation technique. Successive lessons build on this with different techniques that teach you one-pointed concentration and help you see everything as a manifestation of Supreme Consciousness in your everyday life. But this can't be hurried. Your acarya will return and give you further lessons only when you have the capacity to receive them. For some Margiis the process takes a long time. But for the diligent and sincere, time is unimportant.

Many Margiis have visited the society's monasteries in India to experience the life-style. Those who wish and are deemed qualified can spend even longer periods in special training at these monasteries to become monks or acaryas. Most Margiis don't do that. They don't believe that they must be in a holy place in order to be spiritual, and are quite content with the improvements they already see in their lives. Most have gone far beyond what they had imagined as their physical, moral, and spiritual goals. Most, indeed, feel that they have been reborn.

Other Yogic Schools

People all over North America are becoming reborn through Indian methods. Not just Margiis, or Vedantists, or Transcendental Meditators, but students of literally hundreds of yoga teachers are making the same discovery. Yoga instruction is so prevalent and growing so rapidly across the land that it is impossible to keep track of all new schools and teachers. There are some large organizations, like that of the audacious teenage guru, Sri Maharaji, who claims to be more important than God because he introduces you to God. He established the Divine Light Mission with centers that are now mushrooming all over the continent. Sri Chinoy centers and his campus meditation groups are prominent on the Eastern seaboard and in Canada. Chicago and Minneapolis have their Himalayan International Institute of Yoga Science and Philosophy, and there are local schools like the International School of Yoga and Vedanta Philosophy in Miami and similar organizations which were founded by missionary Hindus. Others like the East West Yoga Center in Boston and New York's Yoga Therapy Center are American products.

In addition to yoga centers you will find many individuals who teach yoga privately or to classes. A few of these are genuinely adept Oriental masters. Others from the Far East seem to be adept primarily in their financial judgment, namely that guruing in North America is more profitable than in the Orient. Many Americans and Canadians also teach yoga. These latter tend to concentrate on postures and breathing because this doesn't require much insight into individual personalities. The same is true for the now-popular adult education and church yoga courses.

How do you find a local guru? Some are listed in the yellow pages under "yoga." A few may advertise in your newspaper. Better yet, check with your local college bulletin board. That's always a natural sounding board for the latest in esoteric goings-on. Some locales have formed societies of yoga teachers to provide a central directory like the Bay Area Yoga Teachers Association in San Francisco.

Is it really important to have a teacher? Can't you learn equally well from a book or from correspondence lessons? Many people say no. Certainly, if you have a well-trained teacher who understands personality differences and can devise a spiritual growth program just for you, logic would say this is the best approach. Also, a personal guru who is truly interested in your development gives you someone to focus your affection on. It's a form of Bhakti yoga. However, in many cases personal relationships are more of an ideal than a reality. Only the best-trained teachers have experienced enough of the numerous yoga techniques to properly apply them specifically to you. The same with understanding personality types.

Most individual yoga teachers have to charge for their instruction because they don't have large followings or organizations to support them. That's why many teach classes rather than personally. It is difficult, in a class situation, to develop the rapport you can when an instructor works privately with you. Also class instruction teaches mostly techniques. It can't devise special development programs just for you. Few class instructors even specify a program for the group. However, don't knock class instruction. It is beneficial, a lot of fun, and often reasonably priced. Professional teachers charge $25 to $50 for six to twelve lessons, and adult education or church classes cost considerably less. Certainly, yoga class instruction can give you an insight into what is possible with your mind and body. Often personal instruction under a true master just is not available, so classes are all you can get.

In fact, in many locations even class instruction isn't available. Some people live in parts of the country where the yogic movement just hasn't made inroads yet. That shouldn't bother you. Remember, there is still that bearer of wisdom of all sorts, your postman.

His pouch can hold instruction for you in yoga too. The Self-Realization Fellowship takes advantage of this.

Self-Realization Fellowship

SRF's concept is that most people *do* need a guru, a very personal guru along with a strong guru-disciple relationship. But to SRF the guru need not exist in the flesh. To SRF, a guru is not a teacher. He is considered a divine channel to attract and guide seekers to God. A true guru is God-realized, one whose consciousness is omnipresent. Thus, your true guru may reside on this earth or can just as easily be discarnate. He can guide you in the spirit or through the truth inherent in his written teachings. The guiding spirit of SRF is Paramahansa Yogananda. Before he died he told his followers: "To those who think me near, I *am* near." That's why Yogananda's teachings are available by mail.

Yogananda considered his primary mission was to show the similarity between the ancient science of yoga and the original teachings of Christ. Therefore, he didn't think of himself as the only SRF guru. Jesus holds a special place as an SRF teacher too. At all SRF shrines you will find the pictures of six holy men—Jesus, Yogananda, Krishna, Sri Yukteswar (Yogananda's guru), Sri Yukteswar's guru, and the guru before him. The purpose of emphasizing these teachers is more than just to show similarities between Eastern and Western mysticism. It is to provide a focus for concentration and devotion. By loving Yogananda, Christ and the others, you love certain aspects of God. You get practice in loving someone in the spirit. This eventually expands your love to everything and everyone.

Yogananda was both a graduate of Calcutta University and an ordained swami. Though not of the Ramakrishna Order, he was a member of the same ancient order to which all swamis trace their lineage. Like Vivekananda, he came to the United States to represent Hinduism at a religious conference, though it was twenty-seven years later. Americans liked what they heard, so Yogananda stayed on to lecture and give classes. In 1925 he established the Self-Realization Fellowship in Los Angeles expressly to adapt yoga and its philosophy to Americans. Yogananda ministered for over thirty years. During that time he personally wrote or recorded what is now included in the correspondence lessons for which SRF is famous. He also wrote the book *Autobiography of a Yogi*, which has sold over half a million copies to date. Many devotees are drawn to SRF just by reading this fascinating work. By the time Yogananda entered *mahasamadhi* (conscious exit from his physical body) he had gathered an American following in the hundreds of thousands. The same thing happened all over the world. SRF has monasteries and meditation groups in India, Europe, Africa, Australia and Latin America. The international headquarters and main monastery is in the United States. It occupies beautiful facilities of what, at the turn of the century, made up the fashionable Mount Washington Hotel in Los Angeles.

From here Yogananda's teachings flow to all parts of the world through weekly correspondence lessons. Though they can't be designed for your specific personality, they do lay out a comprehensive three-and-a-half-year program. This is a well-defined series of steps to spiritual development. Your progress is monitored too, albeit for most by correspondence. The cost? Amazingly, during the thirty-two years since this instruction started the fee has remained $2.50 per month.

The present teachings descend from antiquity but have been modified for Western tastes. They provide a balanced program to develop your three-fold being—body, mind, and soul. This method can also be defined as Raja yoga. First you are taught how to attune your body, mind, and soul to the cosmic laws of life. Then comes a special form of Hatha yoga devised by Yogananda which charges your body with life force *(prana)* through energization exercises. There is also a simple but scientific technique of one-pointed concentration, and you are encouraged to meditate twice a day—the longer the better. As Yogananda once said, "You might think that after two hours of meditation I would be bored to death. No, I couldn't find anything in the world as intoxicating as this God of mine. When I drink that aged wine of my soul, a skyfull of happiness throbs in my heart."

Also included in the instructions are explanations of creation, death, karma and cause-and-effect. Very important are the comparisons of philosophies of the different religions. SRF's present leader, Daya Mata, explained, "This really is what religion is, the discovery of those universal laws that the followers of all religions seek and attempt to live in their own lives." You also learn many practical things, like how to deal with nervousness and health, or how to bring about success. You are encouraged to abstain from meat, alcohol, smoking and, of course, nonmedicinal drugs. Most important of the teachings is SRF's highest formal instruction—Kriya yoga—the technique of blocking out all external sensations so you can go from ego awareness to soul awareness. You are not given this treasure automatically, but only after you master the basics and demonstrate complete devotion to and acceptance of Yogananda and his teachings.

To supplement your lessons you may subscribe to the quarterly magazine, *Self-Realization.* Then there are numerous books and records for sale. Yogananda was well aware that the lessons would raise questions that didn't have universal answers. And he knew that individuals differ in how they progress. So he encouraged personal inquiry about spiritual problems and use of the techniques. Any questions you mail in are answered by an SRF minister. And if you live near one of the temples you can meet a minister personally during classes and services. Even remote chapters are often visited by a minister several times a month, while most centers are included in yearly tours during which members can review their meditation techniques and get personal counseling from ministers. There are also meditation groups around the country where lay members conduct services that include discussions, chanting and, of course, extensive meditation. For those who like to travel, there is the annual get-together in Los Angeles where members receive class instruction and can meet the SRF leadership. It is during these sessions and when ministers visit the centers, that you receive your personal initiation into Kriya yoga. And if you want to get away from it all for a while, a quiet facility near San Diego overlooking the Pacific is available to all members for brief meditation retreats.

If you want to get away from it permanently, there are the monasteries. These are for members who believe in Yogananda's dictum, "Work, eat, walk, laugh, cry, meditate—only for Him." Over 150 men and women have chosen to live this way at the Mount Washington headquarters. There are smaller monasteries in other cities. To become a member of this Self-Realization Monastic Order you must have had one year of study, have been initiated into Kriya yoga, and you must renounce your personal family for the world family. Chastity is required, but married couples may join a similar order. Final vows of renunciation don't come for at least another ten years. At that time, as in many other orders, you assume a Sanskrit spiritual name. Right now membership is limited by the available accommodations. SRF monastic life is so popular that there is a waiting list.

But that shouldn't bother you. After they have been in SRF awhile, most members develop patience and serenity. This is perhaps best symbolized by the SRF Lake Shrine. Its ten acres snuggle tranquilly in a huge U-turn of Sunset Boulevard, right on the coast near Santa Monica. Because its gardens are open to the public it has become a national landmark. As its name indicates, the central feature is a small lake teeming with ducks and swans. On its shore quaint structures like the windmill, chapel, houseboat, Golden Lotus Archway and the Gandhi World Peace Memorial nestle among exotic plants and trees from around the world. SRF's link with the past and its universality with other creeds is best symbolized by the most unique of these trees. This aristocrat is directly descended from cuttings of the famous Bodhi Tree that sheltered Gautama Buddha when he achieved enlightenment 2,500 years ago.

So the SRF Shrine not only reminds you of Hindu traditions, but symbolizes most other faiths, especially those of the East, both Near and Far. These other faiths have developed mystical teachings equally as fine as those in the best of Hindu schools. Some are severe; others dynamic; and a few downright exotic. Most are well-devised methods of in-depth psychology. These other pathways of the East are discussed in the next chapter.

Chapter 7

OTHER PATHWAYS OF THE EAST

Throughout the entire Near East and Pakistan, along all the Indonesian Archipelago, and in many regions of India you will hear the words *"La ilaha illa Allah, Mohammeda Rasul Allah!*—There is no god but Allah, and Mohammed is the Prophet of Allah!" These summarize the beliefs of Islam, the world's second largest religion. It is a faith that proclaims but one god—one god to such a degree that it considers even Christianity's Trinity polytheistic. And Mohammed is recognized as God's last and most special prophet. Legend has it that when the camel driver Mohammed was born, idols of false gods all over the world shook and crashed to the ground.

Islam

Years later Mohammed actually brought this about in his native land. As a young man he became disturbed with the life-style of his own people, the Arabs. He abhorred their tribal conflicts, the gambling, drunkenness and idolatry that permeated their culture. As a student of both the Old and New Testaments, he believed debauchery to be sacrilegious. So he brooded about it. Then one day in 611 A.D. while contemplating in a cave in the barren hills outside Mecca, Mohammed had an awesome revelation. The angel Gabriel is supposed to have appeared to him bearing golden tablets inscribed with a profound message. The world, this message said, was created by one god. All living things from the biggest to the lowest are the work of a single mind. Mankind is the highest creation of this mind—of this god. Thus, man is of divine origin. And it is a sin to forget this divine nature and follow impulses lower in the cosmic order than man's true nature. The tablets instructed Mohammed to raise his people from their abomination and lead them from their idols to the one god—Allah.

This Mohammed tried to do. He even tried to convert Jews and Christians to the new-found faith. His early efforts failed, but he persevered, eventually converting most of the Arab world to his new-found religion. Though Mohammed's original desire was to have his own people submit to Allah, his successors were equally enthusiastic that the rest of the world should submit. In fact, for several centuries Moslem armies swept through Africa, Europe, and India, spreading the gospel to the infidels, often with the sword. Within fifty years of Mohammed's death half the known world's population had become followers of Islam. "Islam" means to submit to the will of Allah, and "Moslem" translates as "submitter."

Islam's gospel is contained in the Koran. This sacred text was compiled twenty years after Mohammed's death and contains his major sermons, not only those about the relationship of man to Allah, but rules and religious duties and practices for every situation. Islam is strongly oriented toward Do's and Don't's. The future consequences of these are clearly specified in the Koran. The sinner can expect a hell of demons, drinks of boiling water and baths in molten brass. For the sinless heaven offers beautiful gardens, palaces, fountains, abundant fruit trees and youths or maidens to satisfy every want. Though it is said in the Koran that God is closer than your jugular vein, most Moslems concentrate more on an afterlife, and are inspired less by spiritualistic idealism than by concern for the consequences of their deeds. Few Moslems practice mysticism and experiencing God in the here and now.

However, in the eleventh century a school of Persian Moslems rejected the authority of theologians. Nor did they accept the prevalent methods of preserving the teachings by means of schools and rituals. These mystics were not inspired by mere philosophy and bowing to Mecca by rote five times a day. They wanted to experience God personally. These early ascetics, whose clothes were of undyed wool, became known by their garments. The Men of Wool were called Sufis.

Sufism

Sufism is an intense form of *living* Islam, living in the sense of "Peace of God." The goal of Sufism is union with God in this life. That's why the Sufi dictum is "Say Allah, and Allah thou shalt become." Sufis emphasize "*Anui Hak*—I am He." To a Sufi, you are a scaled-down version of the Divine Unity.

Sufism is a mystical school that evolved from the teachings of ancient Zoroastrian Magi. It also picked up a little Egyptian lore, and, according to Gurdjieff, the dances for which Sufism is so famous were originally practices the Christians had abandoned in the first few centuries of Christianity.

Sufis developed the dance into a profound and elaborate mystical tool. Its practitioners are often called Dervishes, a Persian term for mendicants. The slow Dervish gyrations are not performed as an art. They are actually a type of prayer. They help you think about God. The whirling dance, the one that makes you so breathless, is a way to ecstasy and enlightenment. Yet dancing is even more than that. Since it is always performed by groups, it demonstrates the brotherhood of mankind. As Pir-O-Murshid Hazrat Inayat Khan, founder of Western Sufism said, "If anybody asks what Sufism is, what kind of religion it is, the answer is that Sufism is the religion of the heart, the religion in which the thing of primary importance is to seek God in the heart of mankind."

From its inception Sufism had lots of popular appeal. During the fifteenth century it reached such a pinnacle of acceptance that it enjoyed prestige throughout the entire Moslem world. It developed into many separate orders and brotherhoods. During its heyday its authors created the most beautiful philosophical poetry that Islam ever achieved and Sufi scholars wielded tremendous influence in the court of the sultan.

Its political and theological power declined and rose again several times, its last bastion of strength being in Turkey during the nineteenth and early twentieth centuries. That was abruptly halted in 1925 during the Turkish revolution when strongman Kemel

Ataturk, determined to stamp out all religious power, closed the Sufi Tekkes (convents) and turned them into museums. Today Turkish Sufis are forbidden to assemble except for the annual Dervish dance—and that's to satisfy the tourists, not the Sufis.

But long before Sufism's demise in Turkey, it had found another home in India, a land more hospitable to mysticism. From there, after absorbing a little Vedanta and Buddhism, this active form of worship was brought across the sea and established in the United States by Hazrat Inayat Khan. What he founded was called the Sufi Order.

Sufi Order

Today the spiritual leader of the Order is a man of regal quality, Pir Vilayat Khan, son of the founder. The Order functions in Europe and all over North America. Its seventeen *khankahs* (teaching and retreat centers) dot the country from Northern and Southern California through the Southwest and Midwest to New York, and from New Orleans to Massachusetts.

The Sufi Order's dances, though based on tradition, were created by an American for Americans. Samuel Lewis, or Murshid Sufi Ahmed Murad Chisti, a Zen master as well as a Sufi, was a disciple of Hazrat Inayat Khan. He spent many years in San Francisco devising dances and chants, based on his master's teaching, which are now used throughout the Order. That's why the city by the Golden Gate is headquarters and still the main center for training in the Spiritual Dance and chanting.

Lewis created many dances. Some are Dervish and include chanting the Divine name in the many different Sufi ways. Some are mantric dances borrowed from India, which include chanting Rama, Om and other Sanskrit words. The repertoire also includes astrological dances, Tarot dances, Christian and Hebrew dances, Universal Peace dances and the dances of the five elements, all to well-prescribed formulas of rhythm and motion.

American Sufis differ considerably from their Turkish counterparts. For one thing, all Turkish Dervish dancers are male. In America both sexes enjoy the rapture of the dancing prayer. In Turkey it is mostly the elders who keep and pass on the traditions. American Sufis range in age from twenty to thirty with only a few older members. Actually, there aren't many members of any age. The Sufi Order isn't concerned with building its membership. What it wants is excellence in its practices and thoroughness in its teachings.

The Sufi Order discourages your joining without some preparation. You have to attend several open meetings first. These include lectures, instruction in meditation, dance training and chanting. Their purpose is to give you a feeling for Sufism before you commit yourself. Along with the open meetings you are encouraged to read Sufi literature which can be purchased from the Order. And also available to the public is a $10 subscription course by Pir Vilayat Khan on various methods of meditation.

After you attend several open meetings, you may be qualified for full membership. But you must be deemed a sincere seeker and you have to be accepted by a teacher. These teachers come with all kinds of titles like Pir, Murshid, Sheikh, or Khalif. They don't consider themselves so much instructors as matchmakers. They look upon themselves as cupids between you and God. You will discover that what they teach is not necessarily Islam. Modern Sufism is a universal creed. There is no dogma since Sufis don't quibble about the nature of God, reincarnation, heaven, hell and all the other philosophical problems that so vex orthodox religion. Sufism is experiential. It's a *feeling* religion.

Like most organizations that must sustain themselves, the Order has membership fees. They vary around the country. There is usually a registration fee and $5 a month dues is about average. Of course, any alms for the love of Allah will be appreciated. Your first official ceremony is your initiation. It is a simple one. There are a few candles, readings from scripture and acceptance of God in your lifestyle. The initiation is your link, or attunement, with all illuminated souls. Along with this you may be given a special spiritual name. It can be in English, Persian, Arabic, Hebrew or Sanskrit. Then your obligations begin—to yourself in the form of diligence in seeking God and learning the techniques to foster this: and to mankind in the form of service. It's not organized service, but personal, a commitment of individual love.

Your own personal progress depends on both your own effort and how you are taught. The Order has developed numerous techniques to help you to experience Divine consciousness. Your master will decide which methods are best suited to you. They are all very personal and all specially adapted just for you. Some techniques may take you into terrifying traumas that resurrect your negative archetypes. Sufis call this going to hell in order to get to heaven. But most techniques are not designed for emotional purging of your subconscious. Nor do Sufis use will power to overcome faults. That gives too much validity to the faults. Sufis prefer to think in terms of perfection. Sounds a little like Christian Science and Religious Science, doesn't it? Mostly you will learn the mysticism of breath, the power of chanting, the vibratory force of repeating the name of God. Of course, you will learn the deep inner penetration of meditation. And in addition to your individual devotion and practices, you will learn Sufism's most powerful tool of all. This is the group practice that makes Sufism a true brotherhood. This is the weekly dance.

To Sufis, your body is the temple of God. Thus, they emphasize rhythm, posture and breathing to develop body attunement. Joy of the dance is most important; skill is only secondary. Sacred dancing is designed to take you into the universe of feeling. It's an inner feeling in which a current of life-force builds among all participants, and the ecstasy of it remains long after the dancing is finished.

In the San Francisco area members from all the nearby khankahs gather at a large college gymnasium. The walls are hung with oriental rugs and the bearded dance leader, Wali Ali, has donned his ceremonial beads and yellow robe. The dancers surround him and with joined hands move in a circle to the rhythmic beat of guitars, drums and flutes. Arms are raised, then lowered. The dancers all face outwards, then inwards. They make a full turn, then two full turns, then three, and then they spin—all the time chanting a sacred phrase, or *wazifa*.

The most exciting and dynamic dance of all is the Whirling Ecstasy. The group moves in a circle chanting over and over "Allah Hu." Then one member is selected to whirl in the center of the group. He whirls round and round with his arms stretched out to the side, and tries to feel his heart radiate outward as he spins. The dance continues unabated while the first dancer is replaced by another to star in the center; then another and another until all have spun separately. Then they all spin together, all hoping that during the whirl their ego will vanish and they will *become* the whole circle. The joy of this dance springs directly from the light of their souls. True adepts feel nothing but the music and God. And during those precious whirling moments they often become one with each other and one with God.

Of course, there are many ways of experiencing this oneness with God. The Sufi way is very active. Others are equally passive. One of the best known of these was discovered 2,500 years ago by a young man named Siddhartha Gautama, born around 563 B.C. in Nepal. Unlike the camel driver, Mohammed, Siddhartha was of noble birth. Legend has it that when this infant prince took his first steps, lotus blossoms sprang up wherever his feet touched the ground in tribute to his innocence. Twenty-eight years later he was still just as innocent. Surrounded by luxury, a lovely wife and beautiful baby son, he had never seen the hardships of the workaday world. But one day while hunting he noticed a diseased man suffering great pain. Later he spied a trembling old man, toothless and bent. Next he saw a corpse. These sights shocked him. They were things he never knew of inside his sheltered palace. Then he briefly witnessed a monk wearing a saffron robe whose face radiated serenity and contentment. He was a man at peace with the world.

"How come?" Siddhartha asked, "What causes suffering? What brings contentment and peace?"

Soon after, with these questions burning in his mind, he reluctantly renounced his family and princely life to enter the outside world as a mendicant. For years he wandered throughout Northern India, undergoing privation, along with diligent religious study and many other ascetic practices. Yet with all these observances, he did not find the answers to his questions. "Enough is enough" he reasoned. So he sat down under a fig tree to contemplate, vowing not to get up until he solved the riddle of why unhappiness exists and how it can be overcome. He secretly believed this wisdom was already within himself. His intuition paid off, for the next morning he had his answer. What he discovered led to his eventually becoming a Buddha, an enlightened one. And from that time on, in tribute to his momentous discovery, the tree that sheltered him was called the Bodhi (wisdom) Tree.

Buddhism

What Gautama Buddha discovered was awesome in its simplicity. He reasoned that when you are unhappy, it is because you aren't living harmoniously. You don't live harmoniously because you won't accept the world as it is. You cling too much to the separate elements in life and lose sight of the world as a whole. In reality, the things you experience in life are neither good nor bad; it's your attitude toward experiences that makes them appear good or bad. Usually, that attitude is a craving for something or other. So if you stop craving, you will no longer experience good and bad. Just as a fire dies and is finally extinguished when its fuel is gone, so too will your unhappiness cease when you stop feeding yourself desires.

That's the crux of Buddhism: stop craving. You can accomplish that if you follow what Buddha called the Noble Eight-Fold Path. It's a "right" way of outlook and of living. The eight elements that must be approached in a "right" manner are Viewpoint, Aspiration, Speech, Behavior, Livelihood, Effort, Mindfulness and Contemplation. All the schools of Buddhism pivot around these principles of living.

Gautama Buddha never thought he was establishing a new religion. He believed he was merely correcting misconceptions and abuses of Hinduism. He abhorred the unjustness of the caste system. He disapproved of the extremes of Hindu debaucheries on the one hand and privation on the other. He didn't accept a god that creates in the manner of Hinduism's permanent Brahman. Nor did he believe in an individual self (atma). Instead, he thought of the world as just existing and of the self as *not* being a part of Brahman, but as an impermanent state of mind and matter. Yet he accepted karma and the cycles of birth and death. He saw the world as ignorance and sorrow. But he saw eventual release from this in the renunciation of worldly things. All of karma, he believed, can be resolved if you stop uncontrolled craving; if you experience the world without good or bad. When you can do this, you achieve Nirvana, a mental state of "absence of subject-object relationship." It's a state beyond the flux of "ever-changingness." Nirvana is the ultimate ineffable selfless reality.

Though Buddhism originated in India, its existence there was precarious. During the last century B.C. the powerful Brahmin class of Hindus began to persecute Buddhists because of their opposition to the caste system. This continued off and on until the 12th Century A.D. when the Moslem conquest finally dealt Buddhism a deathblow in the land of its birth. But Buddhism blossomed in other parts of Asia, eventually developing into two major schools of philosophy.

Today the oldest of these, and the one most nearly approximating the original teachings of the Buddha, flourishes in Thailand, Vietnam, Burma and Ceylon. It's called *Theravada,* the "teachings of the elders." The concept of this Buddhist philosophy is that all people are responsible for their own spiritual development.

The other basic Buddhist school developed later. It is the path of faith and good works, the path of *mutual* help to enlightenment. Thus, it is called *Mahayana*—"The Greater Vehicle." That's also why Mahayanists gave Theravada and other schools of Buddhism the name *Hinayana*—"The Lesser Vehicle." It was in Mahayana Buddhism that the concept of Bodhisattvas achieved prominence. These are enlightened priests, masters or lamas who forgo the perpetual state of Nirvana, and remain incarnate to guide all of mankind toward self-realization.

Mahayana is the largest branch of Buddhism and became prevalent in China, Korea, Japan and to some extent in Tibet. It is also the most prominent branch to spread to the United States. And its most popular form is well known to thousands of Americans and Canadians. That, of course, is Zen.

Zen

Zen stems from the Buddha's admonition that to understand a flower, you must contemplate it, not just talk about it. So Zen is not a theory. Zen is a practice, a practice of observing. It even has elaborate rules about observing. These apply to eating, tea drinking, gardening, depicting nature and many other aspects of life. Yet all these things must be done with nonattachment. This practice is based on the Buddha's statement, "Let no man ever cling to what is pleasant, or to what is unpleasant. Not to see what is pleasant is pain, and it is pain to see what is unpleasant. Let therefore no man be attached to anything."

That is the essence of Zen. You live your life without attachment. Life is seen as an experience, neither good nor bad, just interesting. It is observed like a wave that comes in and goes out. It might be likened to the experience you live when you watch a movie. The only difference is that in your life you are the star.

Even with Zen you can't transcend unpleasant experiences. But you can learn to live with them. You can change your reactions to problems. You can develop nonattachment. This leads to the next step, a step of learning about your true nature which occurs only after your mind has become open to every experience and reflects each experience like a mirror and doesn't absorb it. Zen is a state of mind when your thoughts move without leaving a trace, without any attachment—not even attachment to Buddhism. Some Zen masters believe that if you mention the word "Buddha", you should wash out your mouth. One teacher, when the room was chilly, added all the wooden statues of Buddha to the fire. He said they were cluttering up the place anyway. Thus, while warming the room he also demonstrated that you should beware of clinging even to ideas; they shouldn't be allowed to clutter your mind. There is a famous Zen saying, "I owe everything to my teacher because he taught me nothing."

Zen is a route that transcends the intellect. That doesn't mean profound philosophy or enlightening scripture. It means mind busting. Zen's attitudes are so intentionally confusing that they drive your reason beyond the limits of understanding. Your intellect breaks. It dies. Then in a flash of intuition, in an instant of direct insight, you understand your real nature. You become enlightened. You are intellectually reborn. You achieve what Zen calls *satori*. You are totally aware of everything, without and within.

The basic practice of Zen is sitting. Just sitting. It's called *zazen*, or "wall gazing." It's an eyes-open form of meditation which you should practice one or more times a day, sitting twenty to forty minutes each time. But it's not like Yoga meditation in which you are oblivious to everything around you. During zazen you are aware of everything that happens; all aromas, noises, sights, and thoughts. Yet you must learn not to have any mental response. This way you learn to see situations or concepts in their true essence— as neither good nor bad, but rather as yang and yin, as the synthesis and resolution of paradoxes. Zazen also brings up subconscious images, complexes, traumas and archetypes. Yet you are not supposed to see these as good or bad either. You just experience them. Your thoughts should come and go, eliciting no more emotional response than you would give the chirp of a bird.

That's hard to do. You learn slowly. Ten years is considered rapid advancement. But over time, as you follow the Zen approach of nonattachment to the world, of not seeing good or bad, you become less emotional. You calm down. Your inner yin and yang merge. That's when you become serene enough to have that sudden flash of satori, when you get the "big mind." That's the purpose of all Zen training. Your zazen, your chanting, your breath training, your ritual dining—all of these are designed for just one thing: to demonstrate your true nature, to let you understand all, to give you "big mind."

Zen comes in two varieties, rough and easygoing. The most prominent is the Rinzai approach. It emphasizes strict obedience to the dictates of a master and strict adherence to the practices. You've probably heard of that custom that when a sitter moves during zazen or, worse, goes to sleep, the master whacks him with a flat stick. That is Rinzai discipline. Rinzai also has koans. These are questions put by the master to his student. They are sublime paradoxes with no intellectual solution. You are supposed to spend days, even weeks, concentrating on these riddles. Eventually, your mind tires. Then intuition gives you the answer and you are one step more enlightened. Buddha came up with the first koan when he asked, "What would you see through a window in the middle of nowhere?" Since then koans have been meticulously collected as powerful tools of the Buddhist tradition. They vary in subject matter and difficulty:

"What were you like before you were born?"

"When you are working, where is your true self?"

"What is the sound of a single hand clapping?"

These and others are your main contact with a Rinzai master. You have periodic interviews *(sanzens)* with him to answer koans he has previously given you. The way you answer shows whether your Zen (feeling) or intellect holds sway. Really, there are no specific milestones in Rinzai—only receiving of more difficult koans.

Where Rinzai stresses *attaining* enlightenment, Zen's other major school, Soto, claims you are already enlightened. You just have to become aware of it. So where the Rinzai master tests his students and tells them when they have advanced, Soto teachers encourage self-discovery. Soto doesn't have koans, and may not use severe rituals or discipline. A Soto master will accept almost anything a student does so long as the student is trying to find his *own* nature. That gives some students the excuse to be sloppy in their dress, or not to be regular in the practices. But that's OK if you continue to advance. The Soto teacher is there to give advice and encouragement. He doesn't test, and he doesn't browbeat. He just tries to guide you in balancing all aspects of your Zen experience—physical, mental and spiritual.

Those are supposed to be the differences between Rinzai and Soto Zen. At least that's the popular conception of them. But most Zen students will tell you that the schools have far more similarities than differences. In fact, Zen practitioners don't even like to discuss the differences.

Zen Centers

Zen has been in North America since the late 1800's. But it wasn't well known until the 1960's when Alan Watts and other authors intrigued lots of Americans through their writings. Soon it became an intellectual fad to toss around words like *sensei* (teacher), *roshi* (master) and *zengi* (dead great master) along with quoting a koan or two. With that, for most people, their interest in Zen was exhausted. But a large number stuck with it. Today hundreds of serious students practice Zen throughout the United States and Canada. They come in all descriptions—from gold miners to psychologists. They are teachers, students, writers, painters, housewives and businessmen—and 99 percent of them are non-Oriental. At first they recruited their teachers directly from Japan. But now many native-born North Americans are teachers. A few are masters. You will find Zen centers in Honolulu, San Francisco, Los Angeles, San Diego, Philadelphia, New York City, Rochester, Boston and other cities as well as in some small communities. They are even on farms. Unfortunately, they are all independent organizations, so there is no central headquarters to write for information about the nearest one to you. However, if you live out

West, the Zen Center in San Francisco can tell you about many of them. Send a stamped self-addressed envelope with your inquiry.

If you are in the Northeast, contact the Zen Center in Rochester. It's the largest in the nation and, in addition to being a live-in center, has several affiliates in the East. These affiliates are *zendos* (meditation halls or temples) like the main center, and many have their own teachers. The Rochester group also gives lectures and classes to various colleges and other organizations. If you are interested in a practical introduction to Zen, you may wish to attend one of the Center's full-day workshops some Saturday in Rochester. These are given during the warmer half of the year, and for a modest fee you get lectures on all aspects of Zen plus practice in postures, breathing, and mental control along with several guided zazens.

But, as you might expect, California has the broadest spectrum of Zen activities in the country. An outstanding example of a Rinzai group is the Cimarron Zen Center in Los Angeles. Inside this high-walled compound you find young people doing walking zazens every day. Also, twice daily there are sitting zazens conducted in the narrow wood-beamed zendo which once served as a Catholic chapel. These are open to the public, to resident roomers, and to affiliated outside members. The twenty-five who live in are mostly in their twenties and pay around $125 a month for room, board, and the teachings. Nonresident students pay only $10 a month. Most students, resident and non-resident, have regular jobs such as clerks, construction workers and secretaries. But Zen is the major influence in their lives, and work is a major part of the practice.

The Cimarron Center was started by Joshu Roshi, a stern, no-nonsense Japanese master. He coaches his students in chanting, postures, breathing, sitting and walking,—and he isn't stingy with koans. He'll toss one at you practically on impulse. But he expects you to meditate diligently on it. And he expects you to be prepared when he calls you up for the sanzen interviews about your koans. When he's not teaching at the Center, the roshi is often out visiting other religious groups or is busy taking care of the six zendos associated with Cimarron as part of the Rinzai-Ji sect. And then there is the monastic Zen Center on Mount Baldy just outside Los Angeles for advanced students.

If you are in Los Angeles and are interested in Cimarron, the roshi's shaven-headed assistant, Gentei, says you are welcome to the Saturday morning beginners classes and to the daily zazen meeting. He also cordially invites you to dinner. But, he says, "Please bring fifty cents." And if you ask him what the Zen philosophy of life is, he'll probably answer, "That's almost a koan itself."

On the Soto side is the Zen Center in San Francisco. It too was founded by a Japanese master, Suzuki Roshi. But now his outstanding student, Richard Baker, is roshi. Inside the Center's large brick residence hall the sparse zendo reflects the Zen life-style. It contains nothing more than tatami mats, cushions and a lone altar supporting several statues of bodhisattvas. It's called the Great Bodhisattva Zendo.

Zen Center can accommodate up to fifty-five resident students who pay $125 a month. It can also take twenty guests at $5 a day including room, meals and instruction. If you want to try this lifestyle, write or visit first. Most of the Center's members live out however and drop in periodically for instruction and zazen. This allows participation without requiring them to follow residency restrictions. For the interested public, instruction in zazen as well as lectures about Zen are free. Potential members are urged to attend these sessions first before applying for membership.

Not all the San Francisco members participate at the city facility. There are affiliated zendos around the Bay Area that provide lectures, breakfasts, zazens and the intense meditations called *sesshins*. These are zazens that last from a full day up to a full week. Every Zen organization has something like this periodically during the year. Even more sesshins are conducted at the affiliated Green Gulch Farm seventeen miles north of San Francisco. More than just a farm, this is really an exquisite community of twenty-five serious students who participate in their Zen as a total community, with visitors welcome on weekends. For Zen students it's a great place to do zazen. Though you are supposed to have unattached experiences, what could be better than the aroma of fresh alfalfa? Even more, the white stucco zendo is within earshot of roosters, lowing cattle and an occasional boom from the Pacific surf not far away.

Another affiliate of San Francisco's group is its nationally renowned Zen Mountain Center 150 miles to the south. It's really a 160-acre monastery at 2,500 feet altitude in the narrow Tassajara Valley, and can only be reached by a tortuous dirt road that twists and turns for 14 miles through precipitous mountains of the Los Padres National Forest and Wilderness Area. During the summer, when the road is passable, paying guests are welcome to spend a few days at this former resort. Here they can enjoy views of ridges and meadows, and can use the trails, fishing streams, swimming pools, and hot springs like those at Esalen Institute located only a few miles away by crow. Unlike Esalen practices, the Tassajara baths are segregated by sex. Living accommodations are spartan but adequate, and the food is delicious. Added to this is the charm of seeing Zen students pad around in their sandals and black robes. At night flickering path lamps heighten the Oriental mood. For the visitor, the Zen Mountain Center is a delightful way to relax and become one with nature in a truly spiritual atmosphere.

For Zen students it is much more. Those who have successfully completed a preliminary period of introspection and testing called *Tanganyo* are qualified to participate in long sesshins of meditation, ritualistic meals and work. You can see their sandals lined up in neat rows outside the zendo. Inside meditators spend hours sitting on cushions staring at a blank wall. Or they may be chanting in Japanese, "Form is emptiness, emptiness is form." There are other activities too, all in accordance with a strict schedule that is guided by the sound of a drum, or a bell, or a gong. The meal ceremony—*oriyaki*, it's called—is a very important and special ritual all in itself. The diners sit on cushions and must unwrap their three bowls in a specific way. When each portion is served, they and those who serve them bow to each other, not to be polite, but to honor the Buddha essence in each other. The meal is eaten in silence so each person can totally experience the act of eating. One newcomer thought this was too austere and complained about the rigidity of the ritual. His master was surprised and reminded him that he could eat from the three bowls in any order he wished.

Every activity in Zen has equal importance. Doing zazen, eating or scrubbing the floor—each is an experience. None is better or worse, than another. Everything just is. And since satori is an abrupt, illogical experience, it can occur under any circumstance. One master experienced satori when he was told to wash the dishes. So Zen Mountain Center participants work as well as meditate. They keep the place clean. They cook and wash dishes. They wait on tables of the guests. They serve one another—all with equal serenity and inner joy.

To some outsiders, the practice of Zen may sound austere and downright boring. Yet those who persist in it find a peace and contentment they can't explain. Nor can they describe the intense experience of the eating ritual, or how they feel while sitting in zazen. Most will agree that you can't just plunge into the full Zen ritual all at once. That's why you can't attend a Tassajara sesshin until you have had adequate practice first. Full-time residence requires not only previous experience in Zen, but dedication too. Still, there is a waiting list of those wanting to join the sixty priests and students in residence. So Zen obviously has appeal for the right people. You may be one of them.

Or you may be interested in another form of Mahayana Buddhism. Some people call it a separate school. It's called Vajrayana, the Diamond Vehicle. It was named this because it is both precious and because its methods are so keen they can cut through any psychic barrier. It was the most advanced form of Buddhism to develop in India, and in 770 A.D. Guru Padmasambhava introduced it to Tibet. That was fortunate. All other traces of Vajrayana were later destroyed when the Hindus and Moslems wiped out Buddhism in India. The remote Himalayan state of Tibet remained sole custodian of this precious jewel until 1959, when Mao Tse Tung's armies destroyed it there too. Fortunately there was the United States. America may prove to be the perfect setting for this most brilliant diamond of all the mystical arts. At least that's what a couple of lamas who escaped the Chinese conquerors hope. Both have set up shop here, and seem to be doing well.

Tibetan Buddhism

There is a reason Vajrayana appeals to many Westerners. It doesn't demand that you eliminate desire. In Hinayana you must completely give up all satisfactions; in Mahayana you must transform them; in Vajrayana you just understand them. Another appeal of Vajrayana is that it has the greatest variety of techniques in Buddhism. It is really a fantastic science of psychology. It includes the complete inventory of Indian yoga and then lots more.

It has something for each type of personality and for each set of personal goals. It is said that all these *yanas* (techniques) attest to the compassion of Buddha because they show his love in creating so many ways to help people.

Vajrayana seems to have helped Tibetans. Many of them develop outstanding mental powers—miracles some say. There are tales of lamas who see at night through their feet; of orange trees being created out of thin air; of electricity generated solely by mind power; and of psychic trips out of the body. Reliable witnesses report psychic healings, super-fast runners gliding along for hundreds of miles without stopping and naked monks melting snow with extreme heat from their bodies. Tibetan mysticism has been called the most advanced spiritual and psychological system mankind has yet seen.

What accounts for this? Perhaps Buddha's view of the world as being impermanent. Instead of the I-view he took the non-I-view. By overcoming egohood, he taught, you can eliminate the source of hate and greed and thus eliminate the source of suffering. Tibetan Buddhists emphasize that all experiences in the material and psychic world are nonsubstantial; they are a wakeful dream. When you are freed of the idea that the world is self-existing, you then realize that your worldly experiences result from your own actions and that these originate in your own mind. The world may not be an illusion, but it is *like* an illusion. The tiger that threatens you is very real and can kill you. Yet your mind created and can control all the action as it does in your nightly dreams. Tibetan Buddhism teaches you how to control the action of your waking dream.

Your individuality is also thought to be an illusion. By becoming *dis*illusioned with the material world, you eventually become *dis*illusioned with your ego. You lose your individuality. Successive births are just as illusory as your individuality. Tibetan Buddhists claim that karma evaporates in the light of true knowledge because you are freed from consciousness of the past.

Most yogic practices emphasize disillusionment with one aspect of worldly life at a time. Vajrayana deals with *balanced* disillusion—all aspects simultaneously. That's why it is also called the Short Path. Being based on Buddhist (not Hindu) Tantrism, it is the yoga of resolving your inner polarities through meditation on archetypal images. It's also known as Lamaism, and is perhaps the most hazardous mystic path of them all.

The preliminaries of Vajrayana are similar to some Encounter techniques of inner observation. Also there are practices not unlike Bioenergetics and Rolfing that date back 1,200 years. Tibetan formless meditations are similar to Zen's mental observation without thought. But what Tibetan mysticism is best known for is its stress on image-type meditation. This is the practice of creating mental images in detailed form, color and sound. You learn to crystalize these forms, and then to dissolve them. This is supposed to demonstrate the unsubstantive nature of the world. It also develops in you nonattachment to your creative experiences and achievements. Lamaist students learn to hallucinate at will and can create, sustain and destroy their hallucinations. They become something like earthly Brahmas, Vishnus and Sivas.

Since Tibetan Buddhism absorbed lots of Chinese Taoism, it places considerable emphasis on deities, spirits and demons. These symbolize the duality of human nature like *good* and *evil* and are the subject matter of most meditations. It is common Tibetan practice for neophytes to isolate themselves in *tsams* (quiet retreats), sometimes for years, and mentally create various divine and demoniac images. This is a practice that, if continued long enough, ultimately leads the student to enlightenment. These deities and demons are not *real* entities to knowledgable Tibetans. They are practical meditative tools. Carl Jung would say they are resurrections of eternal archetypes. They create a schematic map of the consciousness of man. There are so many that only a few of them can be discussed here.

The ones called Dakinis are female embodiments of knowledge and power. They are subconscious impulses that lead to understanding. They can be divine or demoniacal, angry or compassionate, loving or hostile, violent or serene. They depict all aspects of human nature. The male archetypes are called Herukas. These symbolize the dynamic aspects of the Buddha nature, the inner violence and power that all enlightened persons must endure to break through to Buddhahood. They are called the "blood-drinking deities." Here's how Lama Govinda in his book, *Foundations of Tibetan Mysticism*, describes the Vajrayana path:

> This is not merely a path of mild virtue, benevolent feelings and tame renunciation, but a path of "frightful abysses," a path which forces us to face the bottomless abyss of our own being, of our

passions and sufferings, a path of heroic struggles and ecstatic liberations, in which not only the peaceful, but also the heroic and the "blood-drinking deities" are our companions. And if we do not sacrifice to them the blood of our own heart, we shall never reach the end of this way and realize the mystery of Body, Speech and Mind.

All divinities and demons are defined in detail by Tibetan literature, even to their colors and how they relate to one another. Tibetans have translated these descriptions graphically into pictorial displays called *thankas*. These designs are full of psychological symbolism ranging from commonplace emotional experiences all the way to archetypal divinities. As uniquely Tibetan art forms, they integrate exquisite images into complex dynamic patterns. The figures range from the serene seated Medicine Buddha to fanged demons garlanded in human skulls and carrying red-hot tongs. These thankas aren't just objects of art. They are to be meditated on and their symbolism is designed to penetrate your psychic barriers, to force you to confront the buried concepts and forces they symbolize. They might be likened to sophisticated Tarot symbols. Other psychological art forms are the mandalas. These intricate and colorful geometric designs show the sequence of your potential psychic unfoldment. You identify with figures and patterns of the mandalas, and in time you hopefully attain advanced states of awareness depicted by them.

The heart of Vajrayana Buddhism, though, is its special form of Tantric yoga. This is the path of creative energy, the way of yab-yum, the way of inner sex, the way of mentally uniting the male and female within you. Unlike the normal concept of sex, it includes complex breathing, dream control, mystical syllables and meditation. Tibetans consider these to be advanced practices that convert sexual energy into inner creativity. And it psychically unites your inner Dakinis and Herukas in a permanent embrace.

Tantrism is based on the theory of *chakras*. These are psychic centers in your body that supposedly collect, transform and distribute your creative energy. Depending on their school, Buddhists claim there are four, five or seven of these centers, and believe that each of them operates at a different level of vibration and energy. Each chakra is a center for a different dimension of consciousness. In most people only the root chakra is active. This is the sex center, the source of blindly creative vital forces. The objective of Tantrism is to sequentially experience all centers and activate them with the vital energy. In so doing you achieve a multidimensional awareness of yourself. Potentially the entire universe is accessible through your higher chakras. Through full awareness of them you can achieve spiritual enlightenment.

Whereas you create mental Dakinis and Herukas to break through psychic barriers to become aware of your chakras, you also create other symbolic deities to activate the chakras. These are the five Dhyani-Buddhas. They typify desirable qualities and forces with which you saturate and activate the chakras. Unlike the other divinities, they are not dynamic. They are passive, and represent the final ideals of Buddhahood. Each possesses different qualities for its specific chakra. Dhyani-Buddhas, like the others, must be created mentally over and over until you have psychically infused the five-storied temple of your psyche, with their refined and powerful creative energy. Only then will you know the truth about your real being and find the treasure called enlightenment. And for this treasure, Tibetans are willing to spend years in total isolation with only their demons and gods as companions—because to Tibetans these are the only companions who can lead them to Buddhahood.

Now Tibetan mysticism is available in America. Both of the sources of this wisdom are lamas (superiors) who came here on direct charter from the Dalai Lama himself. One of these is Chögyam Trungpa, former Supreme Abbot of the Surmang Monasteries. After leading 200 refugees out of Tibet during the Chinese invasion, he established Tibetan centers in India and Scotland. Then in 1970 he found his way to the United States. Ever since he has been like a dynamo, creating a large and complex organization.

Vajradhatu Association

Chögyam Trungpa's organization has a split personality. One half is called the Vajradhatu Association of Buddhist Churches. This is the lama's religious arm. It has Tibetan study centers in eleven American cities and two in Canada. More are on the way. They are called Dharmadhatus and all conduct seminars and meditation instruction. Periodically they are visited by Chögyam Trungpa who is also called *Rinpoche,* or "Precious Master." This provides members with some exposure to Tibetan mysticism. But the real Tibetan practices occur at one of the four retreat centers, three in Colorado and one in Vermont. These retreats all emphasize integrating daily life and the spiritual path through work, study and meditation. They even have small huts that allow total isolation for brief periods. Most of these self-sustaining retreats conduct seminars, study groups, and occasional all-day meditations called *nyin thun.* Visitors are invited to participate in all activities for a modest fee.

The nonreligious side of Trungpa, Rinpoche's operation is called Nalanda. It too is split into several separate organizations. One helps the mentally distressed in New York state; the Maine branch rehabilitates alienated teen-agers; and Padma Jong is a community of artists, craftsmen and musicians on 275 acres of California wilderness.

But what you are probably interested in is the Naropa Institute in Boulder, Colorado. It was created as an environment for the interaction of Eastern and Western intellectual traditions. It's really a college. Its courses include intellectual and experiential disciplines. Every summer it conducts two series of courses, each five weeks long. The numerous courses range through the arts, Buddhist studies, culture and society, modes of self-exploration and philosophy of science. They are taught Esalen style—that is, by well-known guest instructors from all across the country. Each course costs $65 a college credit or $55 without credit. Different types of housing for each five-week period can be arranged in nearby facilities. The Naropa Institute also offers full-time instruction leading to B.A. and M.A. degrees in "Buddhist Studies" and "Self and Society." Students claim Chögyam Trungpa has fully adapted his Tibetan Buddhism to suit American tastes and needs.

The other American school of Tibetan mysticism is more traditional. That's because its founder wants to preserve and disseminate Tibetan teachings in their pure form. He is Tarthang Tulku, a high lama of Nyingma Buddhism, the oldest and most revered of the Vajrayana Schools. The word *Tulku* indicates he is considered a reincarnated, enlightened master—a bodhisattva. His followers prefer to call him Rinpoche.

Tarthang Rinpoche's organization is also diverse. He started it in an old fraternity house purchased near the University of California in Berkeley. That is still his headquarters and, despite a punishing schedule, you'll always find him in the living room every Wednesday morning where he conducts personal counseling and interviews. The walls are covered with colorful thankas, and the lama, seated formally on a bright quilted couch and wearing an embroidered jacket over his orange robe, epitomizes Oriental dignity. In front of him on a large table burns a coil of incense. Yet whatever awe you may have had when you first glimpsed him vanishes the moment he speaks. His eyes sparkle, his body vibrates, and every aspect of his being communicates with you. You feel completely welcome. Yet there is something, perhaps the aura of the land of his origin, that adds a little mystery. One of his students put it this way: "Probably the first time I saw him was one of the most intense, one of the nicest experiences I have ever had. Part of it was just the realization of ideas I had. I had read lots of stuff about Tibet. Now here was an honest-to-God Tibetan lama right in front of me."

He's there for you too, if you can visit in Berkeley. But you can meet other honest to goodness lamas too—if not in person, at least by mail. Someday Tarthang Tulku hopes to bring refugee lamas to this country as teachers. Meanwhile they are struggling to survive in India. Tarthang Rinpoche's Pen Friend Program allows you to correspond with these lamas, and by enclosing $10 a month or more you can free them from working in the fields so they can teach other Tibetan refugees in India. For details write to the Nyingma Institute in Berkeley.

Also part of Tarthang Rinpoche's dream is the Nyingma Country Center located on 1,700 acres of wooded countryside in Northern California. It is patterned after a Tibetan monastery-college and will eventually grow to a community of 1,000 permanent residents engaged in farming, the arts, study and psychological research. The hope is to bring thirty lamas and their families to the Center where they will teach and be free to translate rare texts covering all forms of Tibetan life and history.

Nyingma Institute and Center

Right now Tarthang Rinpoche has two main interests. One is the Nyingma Institute. It is an educational facility housed in another fraternity house, a huge four-story, sand-colored building accented with bright red decorations reminiscent of the Dalai Lama's palace in Lhasa. But it's what goes on inside the Nyingma Institute that is important. Its purpose is to disseminate teachings in the old tradition, yet couple these to advanced Western psychology. So the faculty, in addition to Tarthang Rinpoche, includes prominent American psychologists, psychiatrists, philosophers and linguists.

Despite the wonders of Tibetan mysticism, you don't learn magic here. It's not a school that teaches about potions and incantations or lets you shoot sparks three feet across the room. But you do learn some of the most advanced psychology, philosophy and metaphysics now available in the Western world. There are courses in Tibetan psychological theory, Kum Nye relaxation, Nyingma meditation, Upa (emotional) yoga, Vajrayana visualization, Buddhist philosophy, and training in Sanskrit and Tibetan language. Some of the more exotic practices are also taught, like *tumo* (body heat) and a Tibetan form of Rolfing to release emotions and relieve tension.

The Nyingma Institute offers three basic programs in Tibetan culture which lead to an M.A. degree in either Tibetan art, psychology, or philosophy. Because of the lama's interest in translating ancient scriptures and texts, every M.A. candidate must develop a reading knowledge of Tibetan and Sanskrit. But most of the instruction is oriented toward your own personal growth. If you are a full-time student in an M.A. program you can expect to spend at least two years and pay $1,800 for this education. There is some housing at additional cost.

But you don't have to be an M.A. candidate to attend classes. If you aren't, the curriculum is up to you and many other institutions will accept some of the courses for credit. There are also weekend seminars that introduce you to various aspects of Vajrayana. These run $45 and up. Advanced students can arrange for three-week to two-month isolated retreats. Then there are the summer programs. The five-week Buddhist Philosophy program is geared to educators and other interested people. It runs $350 and up, depending if you live out or in. The eight-week Human Development course is for practitioners of mental therapy. This costs $700 and up. Both summer programs include instruction in visualization, philosophy, physical yoga and meditation. With this variety of programs it's not hard to understand why people from all over the country visit the Nyingma Institute. So far over 4,000 have participated in some form of Nyingma education since 1969.

Then there's the religious side of the operation. This is the Tibetan Nyingmapa Meditation Center. It's housed in the original fraternity house which the lama named Padma Ling, or Lotus Ground. Padma Ling is for students who wish to pursue Buddhism as a life-style in a master-disciple environment. The discipline is rigorous and the demands for effort great. The program is open only to those who have had personal contact with Rinpoche. They must be sincere in their wish to accept his guidance and diligently practice what he teaches. They must have also completed an initial probationary period of meditation, self-examination and hard work. That's why only about 100 students participate in this form of religious activity. Most of them are in their early twenties.

In addition to ritual ceremonies that Padma Ling disciples must observe regularly, there are the five *Bum Nga,* practices that must be performed 100,000 times each. The first are prostrations. It takes a healthy young person three months at least to get through them. Then for the next two or three years the students practice specific ways to meditate, visualize, pray and chant complex mantras. These exercises are also repeated 100,000 times each. Concurrently the students receive individualized instruction from Tarthang Rinpoche in all the nine yanas (ways of liberation) and in the higher Vajrayana practices that must eventually be mastered. Then they are ready for their final gigantic step.

The Tibetan Nyingmapa Meditation Center has now reached the stage where it is ready to launch several disciples into their tsams, those lengthy retreats where for three years, three months and three days the students will meditate in isolation. Here they will create and dissolve Dakinis, Herukas and Dhyani-Buddhas until they have dredged the depths of their psyches and finally learned the true meaning of Buddhahood. When they emerge, the disciples will be masters of their own psychology, and they will be qualified to pass on to others the esoteric methods they learned.

They will be teachers who can preserve Tibetan traditions for future generations, and for what may be an emerging new humanity. They will be lamas—the first lamas ever produced in the Western world.

Chapter 8

BLENDING EAST
AND WEST

Most growth methods of both the East and of the West were created for specific cultures at different times and in unique climes. Though each may have been designed for its own people and times, most strip away false beliefs, they expose phoney attitudes and they shatter hampering inner discord. Each may have its limitations when used by other cultures in these modern times, but they all can change people into whole new persons, into beings who are bright and alive. But, now there are ways of getting the best from both East and West. And one of these ways is literally bright and alive in itself. It's bright and alive in a physical way; it's bright and alive with color. That bright and alive way is called the Arica Institute.

Arica Institute

When you enter this unique organization's New York head-quarters, an escalator carries you through a many-hued tunnel and deposits you in a bright-carpeted suite of rooms. The walls vibrate in reds, yellows, blues, and greens. The colors alone make you feel lively, while the Tarot cards and dramatic symbols of yin and yang on the walls arouse your intense interest. All around you, enthusiastic bright-eyed trainees perform vigorous exercises or meditate or chant or perhaps engage in something similar to an encounter session.

Three thousand miles away in San Francisco other trainees are doing similar things amid multicolored cushions, esoteric wall charts, and exotic Oriental symbols on the walls. Cheerful young instructors constantly shuttle between the ringing phone in a bright reception area and their students practicing in different colored rooms throughout the building. These same surroundings exist in nearly all the numerous Arica Teaching Houses in the United States and Canada. A colorful, bright, lively environment is the trademark of Arica.

There is nothing quite like Arica in the world and in many ways Arica seems symbolic of the destiny of mysticism. For, despite its antiquity, mysticism is now very modern and is destined to be a new science. That's what Arica is, a new science, a technology in human consciousness. Yet it is also very old. Its founder synthesized in a modern way the numerous ancient teachings of both the West and the Orient.

That founder is Oscar Ichazo, a Bolivian whose dark, thinning hair and mod, dapper clothes make him look like anything but a guru. But his experiences testify otherwise. And so do his devoted followers, who wouldn't think of calling him anything but plain Oscar. Oscar truly is different. Even as a child he felt different. He had out-of-body experiences. He was seized by epileptic-like attacks that took him through an inner heaven and hell. As he grew older, he was strangely drawn to the martial arts, to hypnosis and yoga. He even experimented with psychedelic plants given him by Indians who worked on his father's ranch. But at nineteen his planless experimentation stopped. An elderly man took him under his wing and introduced him to an esoteric school deep into Zen, Kabbala and Sufism. Oscar worked as coffee boy for the group while he was initiated into their practices. Then the members sent him to several schools in the Orient. Thus began a twenty-year exposure to numerous theories and yogic and mystical practices. He shuttled back and forth between South America and Afghanistan, or Hong Kong, India, Tibet and China. And from what he learned, a new concept slowly evolved in Oscar's mind—a modern concept that one Arica graduate explained this way: "What he has done is consolidate many different theories and practices. He has stripped away the religious dogmas and given us what is functional, what is essential from these practices. We use only the most functional techniques."

One of the first things Oscar discovered is that most psychological problems are produced by civilization. Arica is based on the concept that as each culture evolves, its social development disrupts inner human harmony. Today the pressures of modern society have caused an imbalance of your physical, emotional and intellectual selves. Society has conditioned you to behavior patterns that distort your basic instincts so that you lose your harmony with your inner being. You don't trust it. Instead, you seek harmony and balance in the outer world. You imitate others. You accept their values rather than your own. Yet you subconsciously fear the outer world.

But, to Arica, the outer world, though illusory, is precious and beneficial. You aren't taught to reject it, or even to make yourself independent of it. You are simply shown how to become independent of the illusion and artificiality of the world created by society and your own ego. As Arica instructor John Miranda pointed out, "The point of Arica is enlightenment, man's transcending from the state of ego into what's known as the Void. This is a state of consciousness. The state of Essence is the same thing. It's not God. It's God Consciousness."

Arica is one of the few schools that actually measures God Consciousness. In fact, it has assigned numbers to all levels of waking consciousness. To Aricans consciousness is a spectrum that can be broken down into three basic classes. They claim 99 percent of us operate in the lowest class. We are in some form of waking sleep. We work, play, fight and love in a sleep state, in a state of ego. There are several degrees of this. Then there are levels of transitional consciousness that only a few people experience. They are the prelude to truly waking up. Finally Arica defines several degrees of wakefulness, or satori.

The lowest level of consciousness is called Pure Belief and is the deepest level of waking sleep. But you can begin to arouse by awakening from Pure Belief through five higher levels of sleep. You really start waking up in the levels called Karma, Empty-Mind and Wisdom. Then, with increasing enlightenment, you climb through the five satoris to arrive at the ultimate consciousness, that which Tibetans call Buddhahood and which Aricans call simply Unity.

However, it's the second satori, the level called Divine-Life, which Aricans consider to be a reasonable level of consciousness that can be achieved with their form of training. Others are possible, but this one is the target. The number assigned to this level is 24. Ideally an Arica graduate should be able to remain in this level of consciousness all the time. So the goal of Arica training is Permanent 24. It is a state of impartiality without expectations or prejudice. It is a feeling of oceanic peace, of harmony, of love. It is a state that is completely natural, but experienced rarely by most people. You may have been in it at times for just an instant when you were totally living in the moment. It's the state of experiencing your Real Self. And it comes to you permanently when your ego games are exposed and understood.

To Aricans your ego results primarily from society and your attempt to exist in society. In growing up in society your reasoning mind took over the functions of your instincts. This threw them out of balance, thus interfering with your natural perception of reality. Without proper balance of your instincts you have ego. John Miranda explained the Arican concept of instincts this way: "What Oscar has found in his study of man is that we, each of us, men and women, have three instincts—Conservation, Relation and Syntony. Conservation is the question of how am I?—how do I exist?—what do I need for my survival? Relation goes into what others need—who am I with?—the sense of how I relate to others. And syntony goes into how I am balanced in the universe—how do I maintain with my total environment?—what's going on? Most of us are out of balance. We need to balance our Conservation, our Relations and our Syntony so that all three function together—so that we as an individual unit are flowing harmoniously with ourselves, with others and with the total environment. In ego we aren't doing that. The purpose is to get into the state of Essence where we are doing those things."

Then John explained Arica's view of an ancient Oriental concept. "Karma," he said, "is accumulated imbalance of the instincts. Karma is really, as far as I know, our degree of imbalance. It manifests in terms of fear, in terms of psychic pain, in terms of mental contradiction, in terms of physical contradiction. Our karma is our imbalance with the universe, and with ourselves and with others. Whatever keeps you out of positive spaces, out of enlightenment, out of satori is ego, and is karma."

So how does Arica balance the instincts? By blending and harmonizing all aspects of your psyche and body. Arica teaches that you have three basic centers in your body. The intellectual center is in your head; the emotional center rests near your heart; and the vital center, the area where your instincts reside, is located just below your navel. This is theoretically the center that should be master of your life. But in modern society the center in your head has control, and is completely oblivious to how its actions affect the rest of you. So the methods of Arica aim at blending all of your three centers. The main emphasis, however, is to transfer your awareness to your vital center, and thus to your instincts. When this happens, they will become balanced. But this can't be done intellectually. You have to perform exercises and experience the results.

That's the theme of Arica: experience. You don't teach mature people on the basis of faith, only through experience. And in Arica you don't need an enlighted master to teach you. You just perform the exercises according to direction. And Oscar has trained lots of people how to direct you.

Oscar discovered he was destined to teach through a revelation he had during a seven-day Divine coma. After this he stopped his travels and retired to the small Chilean town of Arica perched right on the Pacific shore. There he started teaching small groups. Unbeknown to him, his fame spread. Then, practically without warning, fifty Americans descended upon him. They were Gestaltists, psychedelic drug experimenters, bioenergetics teachers and encounter leaders. After spending ten months with Oscar learning his methods, most of them joined him in forming an institute to pass their valuable experiences on to the world. Oscar's institute appropriately took the name of the town of its birth, Arica which, in the Quecha Indian tongue means "Open Door."

Oscar decided to introduce Arica to America in New York City where, he reasoned, could be found the entire spectrum of humanity. And there the social environment couldn't be much rougher. Oscar wanted to make a go of it in the most difficult place in the world. In the fall of 1971 he did.

The growth of Arica was spectacular. By 1974 graduates from the basic training course numbered over 2,500 and 10,000 others had participated in some Arica programs. All age groups have benefited, but most graduates have been in their twenties. 1974 also saw over 700 fully and partially qualified Arica teachers. More than half are college graduates, and several have advanced degrees in psychology. They are concentrated in Teaching Houses across the land. You'll find them in New York State, Massachusetts, Pennsylvania, the District of Columbia, Georgia, Florida, Louisiana, Michigan, Wisconsin, Colorado, Texas, Arizona, California, Hawaii and British Columbia. More are on the way. The Teaching Houses, though they coordinate with New York, are really independent and self-sufficient. So you will discover that while the training follows a similar format, prices may vary to some degree.

One thing the Teaching Houses have in common is that at least once a week each holds a free open house of lectures and demonstrations. They all conduct 16-hour introductory courses called Open Path Weekends too. These include examples of breathing, physical exercises, diet, movement, chanting and meditation, and cost from $20 to $50. You can get more extensive introductions to Arica with the five- and nine-day Open Path Workshops which are priced in the $100 to $200 range. And special Open Path Workshops can be arranged that are geared specifically to businessmen, women, mental health professionals, the clergy, hospital staffers and even prison inmates.

But the core of Arica is the intensive 40-day training. It's a strenuous 400-hour program that compresses many of Oscar's techniques into the minimum time possible for you to assimilate them. The 40-day training comes in two types of package. Both are group affairs with the number of participants ranging up to 100. For those who can take off for the full time, there is the 40-Day Intensive, a seven-week marathon going from 10 a.m. to 7 p.m. six days a week. However, if you are like most people, your job won't permit that much time off in one stretch. So there is the three-month 40-Day Extended program. But it is still intensive. You attend several nights each week along with all weekends during the period. In both programs the results are the same. Depending on the Teaching House, the prices range from $350 to $650.

With each 40-Day Intensive you get a whole battery of instructors. That's the way instructors get trained. Sometimes there are more teachers than students, so you get plenty of attention. As a group experience, the training isn't specifically addressed to you as an individual, but the group experience helps you as an individual. Instructor George Garvin explained it this way: "Just the very fact that we work in a group for a goodly period of time makes it in effect a minisociety, and it has all the problems that normally occur in the field of relations and all the blocks that people have with one another on all levels."

Everyone goes through the same set of exercises that make up the course. These comprehensive deconditioning and reconditioning procedures were drawn from everything from Tai Chi to yoga, from Gestalt to meditation. During certain periods of the training a high-protein diet is important too, and for the entire forty days alcohol and drugs are No-No's.

Since your physical well-being is an extremely important aspect of Arica enlightenment, you do psycho-calisthenics, or what is called Arica Gym, every day. These are 26 physical exercises to release tension in all parts of your musculature and to break down fear patterns in your body. The gym exercises often arouse negative feelings and thoughts until your body becomes tuned and flexible. Then it becomes a joy. The physical side of Arica also includes breathing to stimulate your glands, and lots of African dance and eurythmics to develop grace and break habitual body patterns.

Naturally there are mental exercises. Aricans meditate on all kinds of things. They meditate on sound, on symbols, on movement and even on silence. There is one-pointed meditation and many-pointed meditation. You meditate with visualization and without. Each meditation has a specific purpose and each helps you eliminate your mind chatter. In addition there is traspaso, the practice of sitting motionless and staring into another's eyes. Its objective? To break through ego barriers so you will experience the essence of another being. By switching partners often you develop rapport with the whole group.

The heart of all mysticism is getting deep within yourself. To many mystics that means getting at your karma. John Miranda explains how Arica does it: "We use other techniques in our 40-day training to trace back certain action patterns, to find roots of them and to break the charge that we carry to free ourselves of that karma. It's a matter of clearly observing without judgment what actually that emotional charge was and releasing it so it is no longer an attachment. The lower awareness levels are dealt with, and some people even experience bad trips. But these are experiences on the path to the Void that must be dealt with."

Then there are those instincts. Your nervous system extends to every cell in your body. Aricans claim all the organs in your body can pick up things about you. They sense situations and display them in unique ways you aren't normally aware of. You can learn to become aware of this. You learn to feel with your whole body. And you can learn to allow your whole body to think. The Arica *Mentations* do this for you by getting your awareness into all your body. Through these exercises you learn to hear music with various parts of your body. You learn to think intuitively with your body by observing how it feels. Your knees, elbows, liver, bladder and stomach—all respond in certain ways to situations and to your emotions, and you can become aware of all this.

Ancient esoteric techniques of inner awareness aren't forgotten either. There is Tarot, Kabbala and spiritual alchemy. Also lots of laughter and humor. They are combined into what is called Protoanalysis, a procedure that helps you recognize the difference between essential elements of your personality and conditioned behavior patterns. It's a process to reduce your ego. With it you demolish the mechanical structure that hides your instinctual self-expression. You experience a psychic transformation. You literally reshape your consciousness, and you are then able to use the high levels of energy that become available to you.

What are Arica graduates like? They are like graduates of so many other types of spiritual training. Some have experienced their *real* selves; others, not quite that much. There is no guarantee that you will reach Permanent 24. During Oscar's 10-month program in Chile many of the participants did achieve what they believed to be Permanent 24. But 40 days is a lot shorter period than 10 months. However, many people do reach *plus* 24. That is the same mental level of satori, but it's not permanent. Oscar says that once you achieve level 24, it never completely goes away. It's always there, even if it isn't permanent. With a little effort you can always bring it back on a temporary basis.

But the 40-Day Intensive isn't the end of the Arica road. For serious students and those who want to become permanent members of the Arica Institute and teach its methods, there is an advanced training course in New York. It is directly under Oscar himself and lasts three weeks. The cost is $300. After that you can join a Teaching House for practical experience in teaching and in further developing yourself. Or you may elect to be a member at large. In either case your world will have become Arica and you will be on your way to Permanent 24.

Arica leans heavily on group participation in its training. It also relies on your continuing to work with groups in furthering your development. But, that's not what you would expect a psychiatrist to believe. You'd think he would prefer individual guidance. And that's exactly how Dr. Roberto Assagioli did feel. He believed individual attention is very important. But he also advocated that you develop yourself on your own, and often by yourself. These philosophies, especially the latter, were prompted by no less a person than Benito Mussolini.

During World War II Dr. Assagioli was a gentle man with strong convictions about the universality of all mankind. He believed in the commonality of all peoples and in internationalism. In fascist Italy those ideas weren't too popular. So Mussolini sent Assagioli to jail. As a political prisoner he got solitary confinement. Since he was forced to abandon his busy practice in Rome, the kind doctor naturally worried about his patients. But being curious, he soon started to observe his worry. He asked himself, "What good can I get from worry? What can I do that is more useful?" Then he was hit with the answer from his Higher Self. "Meditate," it said, "You've always wanted to, but were always too busy." So he did.

In solitary confinement nobody bothered him. He meditated for hours every day. The result surprised him. He never felt such peace. He never had such high experiences. He recalled later that never in his life had he so enjoyed being alive. Never had he been happier. It was such a refreshing experience that when not meditating, he started to write a book to be called, "Freedom Behind Bars." He never completed it. The Fascists played dirty. After two months they released him. Then his conscience forced him to return to his patients and the helter-skelter of the workaday world.

Psychosynthesis

That was fortunate for many people. Dr. Assagioli was able to bring them the benefits of his experience. These he integrated into an inventory of analytical and growth techniques called Psychosynthesis. Actually he had been developing Psychosynthesis since 1910 when, in studying Freud, he concluded psychoanalysis was missing something. That led him into other methods of psychology. He even learned Sanskrit so he could read Oriental mystical texts in their original form. From this he synthesized Eastern and Western psychology, and developed many new concepts on his own. He first founded the Instituto di Psicosintesi in Rome in 1926. After the war it was moved to Florence where Dr. Assagioli continued to develop new aspects of the method until his death in 1974. In addition he wrote two books and taught therapists and educators from around the world how to apply psychosynthesis to their patients and clients.

Though psychosynthesis is used with some emotionally disturbed people, it is primarily geared to "normals" who want personal growth. And it will give them all the growth they want. According to Assagioli, "The scope of the psychosynthetic approach ranges from the personal, through the interpersonal, to the universal, and includes the transpersonal dimension and superconscious process." Thus, Assagioli not only accepted Freud's conscious, unconscious and preconscious, but added another realm normally beyond your awareness. He called it the superconscious or higher unconscious. Outside of all this, he said, lies Jung's collective unconscious. And, he believed, there are two aspects of your being. Your personal self, or little self, is your worldly one. It is a reflection of the second self, your Higher Self, which is transpersonal and resides in your superconscious. So there are really two dimensions to psychosynthesis—personal and transpersonal. If you are concerned primarily with how to be more together and effective in society, you can achieve this through personal psychosynthesis. If you are concerned with questions of meaning, with spiritual experiences, with higher values and with being all you can be, then both the personal and transpersonal aspects of psychosynthesis will help.

Psychosynthesis is individual and orderly. Usually you start by considering what you want to do in life. Then you focus on what has held you back and what you have to develop in yourself to move ahead. Your specific needs determine what you do in psychosynthesis. Assagioli drew on Freud, Jung, existential and humanistic psychology, yoga, Christian mysticism and spiritual alchemy to make his process active and all inclusive. You may get into meditation, encounter, psychoanalysis, body awareness, Gestalt, aikido, transactional analysis or rational-emotive therapy. Assagioli listed over 60 different techniques, many of which include more than one exercise.

The concept behind psychosynthesis is that each person is

unique. Programs vary for each individual, and techniques are specially selected depending on your goals, age, constitution and psychological development. Other influences would be whether it is a therapist working with you as a client, an educator with you as a student, a clergyman with you as a parishioner or you working with yourself. If there are no appropriate techniques in the inventory, psychosynthesis practitioners—or guides as they prefer to be called—invent them.

In 1957 psychosynthesis came to the United States when a student trained by Assagioli started the Psychosynthesis Research Foundation in New York City. Since then other Assagioli graduates have established the Institut de Psychosynthèse in Montreal and the Psychosynthesis Institute in Palo Alto near San Francisco. The latter is presently the largest. It has over two dozen fully qualified practitioners, along with an ongoing professional training program. All centers are independent, so their methods may vary slightly. Still they follow the same basic guidelines. Besides Canada, New York and California, psychosynthesis is available in New Hampshire, Massachusetts, Kentucky and New Mexico from nearly 40 qualified psychosynthesis practitioners with the numbers growing each year. In addition about 200 more do excellent work by incorporating some psychosynthesis techniques with other growth methods. Where there aren't psychosynthesis guides, the Palo Alto institute will send them. So far their practitioners have ranged to New York State, New Jersey, Colorado, Kansas, Texas, Iowa, Washington, and Florida. These traveling guides do individual psychosynthesis and train professionals in the methods. They also hold workshops which can be arranged in many locations for groups of 10 to 25 people. Write any of the three centers for information.

Psychosynthesis comes in several packages. There are group workshops, individual guidance and you can even get special group work for a single family. A workshop is considered a good way to get into psychosynthesis. For around $50 each, you and ten to twenty-five others of all ages spend 12 to 15 hours using many techniques to look at yourselves. During this time most people can get in touch with major psychological blocks as well as establish basic goals. Then they learn techniques to overcome the blocks and advance toward their goals. A few people have major breakthroughs that keep them busy for several months assimilating and integrating. That's why so many people are willing to travel thousands of miles to attend workshops at one of the centers.

Many psychosynthesis practitioners recommend that you have one individual session some time after a workshop. The $45 to $60 you spend for the 1½ to 2 private hours with a guide is more than paid for by the additional guidance you receive in applying psychosynthesis to yourself. If you then want to continue regular individual sessions, they can be scheduled once every two weeks or so. During these you are given reading and writing assignments as homework. Most important, you learn the essence of psychosynthesis, the techniques for exploring and improving yourself. These you are expected to practice at home until the next session, usually two weeks away. After six sessions you will be well into your psychosynthesis. After twelve sessions your guide may start easing you on your own by reducing the sessions to one a month. In a year you are likely to be well on your way to understanding yourself and to having your growth process solidly in your own hands. Total cost—about $1,200. Then, armed with an arsenal of methods, you can continue on your own except for an occasional checkup.

Of course, if you want to be a practitioner, there is more. An extensive training program leads to full qualification in psychosynthesis. This includes individual in-depth work, observing experienced practitioners in their work, field practice, theoretical seminars and satisfactory completion of your own project.

Assagioli-trained practitioners staunchly uphold the high quality of psychosynthesis everywhere in the world. That's why everywhere in the world psychosynthesis is based on the same fundamental principles. First you must discover what your own unique situation is. From there you develop your potential and strengthen your weakest functions. Gradually you integrate these functions into a harmonized whole. Some time during the process you learn to contact your transpersonal nature and utilize the energy of your superconscious.

You will probably begin with a personally written assessment for both your own and your guide's information. Also you start a running journal that you keep up-dated during the whole program. One experienced practitioner says, "When people write this way, the guide can go through the material in ten minutes at the beginning of the session and get as much information as if they talked for an hour. This is one way our sessions are so effective, because through writing we save a great deal of time. This writing also teaches you which of your feelings have value and which are garbage." Then he emphasized: "We can't write all that's in our minds. We have to make a decision to put down only what's important. That's very hard; but very productive."

One beginning technique is called "Verbal Who Am I?" Each day you ask yourself, "Who am I?" Then you write down your answer. Over time you get deeper and deeper into your psyche and gain increased self-awareness and insight.

Lots of effort is devoted to harmonizing your subpersonalities. These are semi-independent personages, or psychological formations, often in conflict with each other. They can act alternately or simultaneously and are tied to your unconscious role playing. Through them you can be several different selves. It's like the boss who is tough at work but meekly "Yes dear's" his wife at home. By learning to recognize your subpersonalities you not only understand what they are but learn to become detached from them. Then, most important, you recognize the *real* you is not any of them, but something deeper.

In this process of disidentification and self-identification you discover that your thoughts, feelings, sensations, wants and roles are constantly in flux. They change. Your real self doesn't. So with the process you regulate and harmonize the many changing elements within you. During this process you may reach critical stages where critical problems emerge. These problems and the feelings involved with them must be experienced. They must be understood and dealt with in the most appropriate way. But psychosynthesis doesn't go looking for bad trips. Let sleeping dogs lie, say the practitioners, but at the same time be ready to deal with them if they wake up.

One of the basic tools for getting you into yourself is the guided daydream. This is valuable in the early stages of psychosynthesis because visualization can be such a powerful link between your subconscious and your conscious awareness. Your guide may suggest you are in a meadow, or climbing a mountain, or beside a stream. From this setting you are encouraged to let your subconscious roam, hopefully, to come up with insights for conscious analysis. The insights may appear in the form of dragons, swords, fountains, bright suns, wise old men or other symbolic images. With your guide's help you interact with the images and then interpret what they mean to you. Or your guide may suggest a specific image to meditate on: an abstract symbol, a mythological or religious figure, or one of the many mental images that evoke inner experiences. There are also image-producing techniques that use all the senses—those of hearing, taste, touch, and smell. Another powerful technique is the "Ideal Model." It's really a synthetic experience, a mental image of the way you would like yourself to be. And this ties in with training of your will.

Will is an area most psychiatrists have ignored. Not Assagioli. He considered developing your will to be extremely important—but not developing it as you might expect. A psychosynthesis guide illustrates: "We find that some people are a great deal more effective than average, yet are always very relaxed, always centered, always on top of what's going on. They can take time off, go on vacation, and yet achieve much more than most. If you look at the way these people use their will, you see there is a great deal of *skill* involved. Not so much strength, though that's there too, but skill." The practitioner continues: "Then there is another aspect. Not only how to use the will skillfully, but *what to use it for*. It's very important that we look to the consequences of our actions because, if our will is good, that is in tune with what's going on around us, we find that truly it is much more effective. Psychosynthesis uses several techniques to develop and harmonize all three aspects of our will: its skill, its goodness and its strength."

What Maslow calls Self-Actualization corresponds to Assagioli's personal psychosynthesis. It provides relief from your hang-ups, but it doesn't deny the reality of the problems. It isn't a state of total harmony where you no longer have problems. It's not a transcendental state of ecstasy. But it is a transition from dealing with neurotic, infantile, fantasized problems to dealing with *real* problems in the real world.

Many people reach their personal goal and stop there. Others continue to grow beyond the boundaries of their personality. Psychosynthesis recognizes the spiritual dimension as being fundamental—in fact, just as fundamental as any other dimension. Assagioli wrote about it this way: "From this region we receive our higher intuitions and aspirations—artistic, philosophical or scientific, ethical 'imperatives' and urges to humanitarian and heroic action. It is the source of the higher feelings, such as altruistic love;

of genius and the states of contemplation, illumination, and ecstasy. In this realm are latent the higher psychological functions and spiritual energies."

According to psychosynthesis there are two basic ways, or paths, through which you can experience and use your transpersonal nature. One way is like Beethoven did when he wrote his best music. According to psychosynthesis theory he would psychically rise to his transpersonal level while remaining totally aware all the time of exactly what he was doing. Then he would bring his inspired results down to his personal level for use on the worldly plane. Mozart's music also seems to have been transpersonally inspired. But he stayed at his personal level and "received" from above. Things would come down to him and he would transcribe them almost automatically. People can either rise to the transpersonal level or let it come down to them. The two are actually complementary. An experienced person may rise to as high a transpersonal level as he can, then become silent and receptive so inspiration can come down from even higher levels.

Dr. Assagioli and his coworkers devised several techniques to help you do these things as well as to develop transpersonal qualities like peace, joy, serenity, courage and other high feelings. You use meditation; you recall the energy of previous high experiences; you surround yourself with pictures and objects that evoke these high qualities. And there is the old psychosynthesis standby, writing. A practitioner describes what it does: "We often find that if we start writing about some insight, more of it comes down. So writing can be a very useful technique to get in touch with the superconscious. In a way it aligns the mind with the transpersonal dimension. It makes a channel to its mode of peace and calm. For example, somebody meditates and has a flash of intuition, or he's thinking of a difficult problem and a partial answer comes. In many cases this initial insight is the tip of the iceberg. There is a great deal more that wants to emerge. People who have experiences like this try to hang on to the initial part. But that blocks the flow. By writing you unburden your mind of the experience and really let go of it. This makes room for the next insight to come down."

The guided daydream is another useful tool for getting in touch with superconscious wisdom. Archetypes are quite common in transpersonal psychosynthesis. By envisioning a wise old man or woman, many people are able to talk to them and get advice. Other symbols such as angels, Christ, the Buddha, or an unfolding rose are meditated on. This is where truly mystical experiences occur. There are techniques for developing your intuition and for dealing with other people from a transpersonal viewpoint. Dr. Assagioli was a firm believer that music can have a direct influence on your body and emotions; that its rhythm, vibration, melody, timbre and harmony all affect you. Some types of music can evoke archetypes. Others will bring up joy or pain. And some will elicit your highest spiritual qualities. These techniques and many more tend to align your personal will and personal self with your transpersonal will and self. In transpersonal psychosynthesis you will discover that in reality these are not separate from one another—they are one and the same. They are your real Self.

So what do you learn from psychosynthesis? You learn that you can develop on at least two levels. You can achieve a synthesis of your personality and you can go beyond to discover and really *use* your transpersonal nature. The process eventually culminates in the experience of universality—of unity with the cosmic process of manifestation. As a practitioner put it, "I would say that we very definitely have a basic assumption in psychosynthesis that there is a universal principle from which emanates everything we are dealing with—manifestation in the broadest sense of the word. That's what you might call the Universal Self."

This level of awareness is beyond the reach of most people. Psychosynthesis certainly doesn't promise that you will reach it. But, with determination and perseverence you can rise to your higher nature. You can increasingly realize who you really are. Dr. Assagioli described what it's like:

> A harmonious inner awakening is characterized by a sense of joy and mental illumination that brings with it an insight into the meaning and purpose of life; it dispels many doubts, offers the solution of many problems, and gives a sense of security. At the same time there wells up a realization that life is one, and an outpouring of love flows through the awakening individual towards his fellow beings and the whole of creation.

Chapter 9

THE ASHRAMS

So far you have read about many different ways to self-aware-ness. The number of paths to enlightenment appears unlimited and there seems to be something for everybody. Yet a major question remains unanswered: Why are so few people enlightened?

The answer may lie in something more than mere technique. It's one thing to know *how* to go deep within your psyche to discover its treasures. It's something else entirely to be able to *do* it. Likewise for having momentary *flashes* of illumination and being able to *stay* at higher levels of awareness all the time. It's true that most schools of mysticism teach practices and techniques which, in theory, can reveal your innermost mysteries and ecstasies. But is there some-thing unique that must occur to turn theory into reality?

You may have concluded by now that if your awareness is to reach beyond certain levels of consciousness, you have to lose your sense of identity. Your individuality, your ego, must vanish, if but for an instant. You must become like a raindrop that falls into the sea. Your individuality must merge with the cosmic ocean. Thus, you have to trade pride in your finite personality for the bliss of an infinite consciousness. Many people can temporarily lose their egos in the quiet of meditation.

Serious and sophisticated students of mysticism have learned that to achieve a permanent higher state of consciousness they must sacrifice. That usually means a lot of effort and time. But there is another type of sacrifice—the ultimate sacrifice. They know they must sacrifice their individuality. They must strive to give up on a permanent basis their ego—their finite personality.

Your finite personality is merely the reflection of those things you identify with. The stronger your identifications, the stronger your individuality and your ego. You identify with and are dominated by possessions and by possessiveness. As Swami Satchidananda said, "To measure your distance from God, list all the things you call 'mine.' " Your possessiveness seeks material objects; it encompasses loved ones; it is directed toward pride, power and even sacrifice. Possessiveness is the attachment to worldly things. And most of us moderns live in environments that foster possessiveness.

The Buddha admonished his followers to live a simple life. He suggested they have minimal possessions. He believed their abode should be aloof from worldly problems. And he strongly recommended they should surround themselves with spiritually minded people. Ashram living is designed to do just these things.

An ashram is a spiritual retreat centered around a teacher. In America most of these are also the permanent residence of their members. This type of communal living, with its sharing of material things and spiritual subordination to a teacher, requires personal surrender. It forces you to grow. It teaches you to relate with others minute by minute. If you get out of line, pressure from the group quickly steers you back to the path of humility. It allows you to observe how you interact. It is sensitivity training and encounter all rolled into one and served up 24 hours a day. Each ashram is really a form of family whose basic purpose is to serve each other . . . to help all members surrender their egos.

There are hundreds of ashrams, or ashramlike communes, throughout the United States and Canada. Many consist of small groups of people who, having been drawn to a specific teacher, live with him. Others, like the Lama Foundation in San Cristobal, New Mexico, invite teachers of different disciplines to visit them. Some, such as the Yasodhara Ashram at Kootenay Bay, British Columbia, consist of a small core of permanent ashramites who conduct spiritual retreats and workshops for limited numbers of guests. Larger organizations like San Francisco's Zen Center maintain one or more communal houses for small permanent groups, but make the facilities available for limited stays by other members or guests. A few organizations believe in both communal living and the diversification necessary to spread their teachings. So they have many ashrams and are literally families within a family. Most of their members live in one of their many ashrams. Some of these organizations, like the Children of God, follow Western philosophical paths, but most subscribe to Eastern traditions. So you will find the atmospheres of their ashrams reflect Oriental simplicity.

Integral Yoga Institute

One of these organizations in the Hindu tradition is the Integral Yoga Institute, or IYI. One of its advanced teachers, a young man who was given the name Jivakan, describes the life-style this way: "Integral Yoga is an approach toward harmonizing the mind and the body and the emotions and the spirit into a total well being. We learn from each other and from finding ourselves in the milieu of ashram life. When someone tells me I haven't washed a dish well, I look at myself and question why I didn't. The whole idea of living with other ashramites is that you can't fool yourself. One of the real benefits is that you get a reflection of your motivations, your drives that cause you to do a particular thing. And you are seeing yourself in different postures, and also understanding some of the things that make you tick. This is the yogic approach brought to us by Swami Satchidananda."

Two hundred of Swami Satchidananda's disciples around the country live like Brother Jivakan. They get up early in the morning to meditate. They end the day the same way. In between is a schedule of work and worship. Often you will find guests living in IYI's nineteen ashrams following the same schedule as the members. Several thousand more people take advantage of the yoga classes that are taught at all IYI facilities. Of those people who spend full time in the ashrams, the majority fit into the twenty to thirty-five age bracket, with both men and women sharing the same buildings. Though a few married couples live in, most participants are single, living segregated according to sex. They share their minimal possessions with each other and often sleep on nothing more than a pad on the floor. And individual ashrams—also called centers or IYIs—though somewhat different in their makeup and way of life, all share in common specific religious symbols to remind the ashramites of their guru. Each has a prominent altar on which rests a picture of Swami Satchidananda, an incense burner and one of the Swami's mementos.

Most of the IYI centers are in cities. They aren't there because cities are the most conducive places for self-awareness, but because they are where the opportunity to serve is greatest. You will find IYI urban centers in California, Colorado, Texas, Missouri, Iowa, Michigan, Massachusetts, Connecticut, New Jersey, New York, Washington, D.C. and Montreal. Only the main ashram and headquarters in Pomfret Center, Connecticut, also known as Yogaville East, and the center outside Santa Cruz, California are rural.

Ashram life isn't just communal living. Brother Jivakan, who once lived in a college fraternity, sees ashram life as being quite different. He said, "Where you talk of fraternities, there you're talking camaraderie. Here we use the ashram as a sounding board for your psyche; how you react to other people; sort of take yourself apart. Whereas you use the fraternity to build your ego up; you see, you pat each other on the back. In ashram living we remind each other of the very high goals we are seeking. At the same time we are analyzing ourselves, which at times can be very painful. So to go through this kind of analysis you need a place where you can be stable and at peace. Here the idea is a peaceful, gentle atmosphere. Then you can begin to peel off the layers that you mesh yourself with during your life."

IYI has several ways to peel off those layers. They are all aimed at putting you back together as a whole human being, as an integrated person. Essentially, Integral Yoga is the integration of your various physical, intellectual, emotional, and spiritual aspects. It is very much like psychosynthesis, but on a group and full-time basis.

The postures of hatha yoga are your starting point in IYI, and are continued throughout your training. They increase your physical fitness, they straighten your spine for a good sitting pose, and they calm your body to permit a peaceful mind. Pranayama breathing exercises are a major part of the training too. Then there is kirtan, the group chanting that harmonizes the vibrations of all present. Meditation is also a regular practice for IYI ashramites.

For those who have the temperament, Swami Satchidananda's teachings include Jnana yoga, the yoga of self-inquiry. This consists of observing yourself and asking yourself "Who is the witness? Who is the experiencer of what I am observing?" It is asking "Who am I?"

To round off the training a few members take up vegetarian cooking. However, most are content just to eat it. All ashram members stick to vegetarian diets. They steer clear of drugs; don't smoke; and are off liquor. Until they accept monkhood or become married, they all take the vow of Brahmacharya, a vow of celibacy and other abstentions. After a time, each new member receives a Sanskrit name from Swami Satchidananda and those who are premonastics studying for monkhood take the title of Brother or Sister. Beyond this stage is monkhood and the monastic life. At this level you may not have burned up all worldly attractions, but you have decided to be free of personal attachments and to lead a dedicated life of public spiritual service. This is when you receive the Sannyas initiation and become a swami in the Sannyas Order. So far only one Westerner, a Frenchman, has received this initiation from Swami Satchidananda. But several people are now well on the way to it.

Swami Satchidananda does not push his disciples. He sets no schedule for an individual's spiritual development, saying all people should progress at their own pace. But every ashram member gets individual attention. Mostly the senior members teach the newer ones. Advanced instructors learn from one another. But Swami continually checks on each center to see how the routine and training is going. In addition his wisdom circulates among all ashrams by means of videotapes of his numerous lectures. Not only does Swami Satchidananda regularly appear on each center's TV set, but other spiritual luminaries are invited to tape messages too; Rabbi Shlomo Carlebach and Baba Ram Das, to name a couple. Then there are the ten-day summer retreats. They too feature not only Swami Satchidananda, but leaders of other sects like Rabbi Joseph Gelberman, Swami Nirmalananda, and Brother David, a Zen-oriented Benedictine monk. Up to 500 participants from all over North America attend these retreats to meditate, chant and otherwise get deep within themselves. During this period they maintain communicative silence, a practice that helps them harmonize with the group vibrations and become aware of their oneness with all.

But that's not all there is to IYI life. Brother Jivakan explains: "The idea of Integral Yoga should permeate all your living. You should be able to relate to people, not just live in a cave. You should be able to do service. The watchword of our activity is 'service' . . . to do Karma yoga . . . to do selfless meditative action. It's done as worship. That way your worship doesn't come on just one day of the week or in the privacy of your room. We see your life pretty much as a celebration on earth; as an altar of God's presence. So selfless service of Karma yoga is a major part of our practice." With this attitude, any work you do—gardening, cleaning up, helping others, cooking or working in an IYI business to support the ashram—can become a whole day of spiritual practice.

IYI ashramites are readily identifiable in their simple spotless clothes. They all wear white pajamalike garments, and premonastics add saffron scarves as extra symbols of renunciation. Why the special garb? To make other people aware of the yogic life and to always remind the members that they have chosen a life-style dedicated to God.

So what does this Karma yoga provide? Teaching primarily. All ashrams hold classes for the public on the premises. Usually there is a charge for these classes that helps pay for food and rent. Fifteen dollars will give you a one-evening-a-week course in yoga that lasts eight weeks. The teachers, members certified to instruct, try to keep the classes small, about ten students per group, so you can get individual instruction. Also there are open classes at all the ashrams where you pay at the door. The public instruction ranges from basic Hatha yoga through advanced postures into Raja and Jnana yoga and even vegetarian cooking.

The centers vary in the other services they perform. The Montreal people are into drug rehabilitation and teaching at hospitals and at the YMCA. The New Jersey group is also concerned with drug problems along with teaching daily at Norris county jail. In Uptown New York City they serve vegetarian meals. Downtown in Greenwich Village is IYI's largest teaching center where over 100 students attend classes available throughout the day. This center also runs a natural food store. Out in California at Santa Cruz they have a similar food store. In San Francisco they process olives and produce puddings, oils and nut butter, while at the other end of the state in Los Angeles the emphasis is on teaching philosophy and yoga to housewives. The other IYIs have similar activities, and at Yogaville East, in addition to conducting classes, they produce organic food and publish and distribute their founder's teachings. And IYI is always anxious to demonstrate its way of life. Once a whole ashram visited a Catholic seminary in Los Angeles and prepared such a delightful vegetarian meal that the future priests voted to go vegetarian permanently. So all over the land IYI members practice Karma yoga. This, Swami Satchidananda reminds his followers, really turns out to be a form of Bhakti yoga, the yoga of worship.

IYI facilities are open to anyone at any time. In fact you are heartily welcomed. Ashramites will spend all the time you want discussing yoga, IYI, and anything else you'd like. The Santa Cruz food store was once visited by a soldier on pass from Fort Ord. He was of East Indian descent and missed his native foods. So when he spoke nostalgically about Indian delicacies, he was invited to spend the evening at the ashram where he not only got all the Indian food he wanted, but reciprocated by preparing his own spicy dish that had the ashramites drinking water for hours afterward.

Not only are you welcome to drop by the ashram, you can even live there temporarily. Anybody can visit an ashram to see if they like the life. Or they can use the ashram as a retreat. Cost varies from $5 to $7.50 a day. If you are serious about IYI you can stay on a monthly basis. After three months, if you want to settle in permanently, you can participate as a member by sharing with money or through work. The only prerequisites: you must be compatible with the group, you must observe the abstentions and you must want to practice yoga.

Members say that taking the first step, the vows of a Brahmacharya, are the hardest. And though it may be hard on you to give up all your pleasures and accept the discipline of Karma yoga, it can be hard on your parents too. Many parents are apprehensive about their children disavowing what seems like a perfectly good life to follow a strange swami from India. That's why Swami Satchidananda encourages parents to visit him. He is a gentle person and is especially loving with the mothers. He likes to give them flowers. After they learn what IYI is all about, the Swami says, "Sometimes the parents turn out to be better disciples than the children."

IYI's guru has a winning way with everybody. When in his mid-thirties, he met Sri Swami Sivananda Maharaj, the founder of the Divine Life Society (not Divine Light Mission). Sivananda was so impressed with this gentle man that he took him under his wing. After only two years, Satchidananda had learned so well that he was initiated as a swami into the Holy Order of Sannyas. During this ceremony in the Himalayan foothills he also received the title of Yogiraj because he had mastered so many yogic techniques. From then on he worked diligently for Sivananda organizing new branches of the Divine Life Society until 1966 when he came to the United States for a two-day visit. His sincerity again changed his life. He so captivated the students he met that he was practically mobbed by young enthusiasts seeking guidance. He decided to remain in America, and in August of that year founded IYI's first ashram in New York City. Now he spends most of his time visiting ashrams across the continent as well as filling a busy schedule of lectures in cities all over the country. Because of his charm and love of people and his great sense of humor, he is always welcome wherever he goes. And many of his hosts, in fact, are founders of other spiritual groups.

One of these contrasts sharply with the quiet lean swami. He is Yogi Bhajan. His 6 foot 2 inch frame supports 215 pounds of robust health that exude strength and force wherever he goes, and his flashing dark eyes tell you he knows how to use that power. Within a few short years this dynamic East Indian became the spiritual leader of over a quarter million young Americans and Canadians.

Yogi Bhajan's spiritual career began in earnest shortly after he graduated from Punjab University when for the next twenty-two years he sought out esoteric wisdom. He searched all over India for it. But he was unorthodox in how he went about finding it. You see, he was a cop. As an officer of Interpol he traveled all over India seeking out smugglers and other international villains. Lots of the time he used a helicopter in his work. So it wasn't difficult, once he heard of a guru in a remote cave somewhere, to go a hundred miles out of the way and literally drop in for a visit. Some of these holy men weren't overly pleased with his noisy unannounced visits. Others were reluctant to pass out their secrets to a total stranger. But Yogi Bhajan was persistent. Even saints are sometimes awed by the law, and it is rumored that he even did a little arm twisting. In any event the secrets eventually became known to him in bits and pieces.

What Yogi Bhajan finally pieced together from his numerous treks to the hinterlands turned out to be kundalini yoga, a mystic science said to be over 26,000 years old. But his version is claimed to be more advanced than anyone ever taught before. One student explained it this way: "There used to be intense taboos against teaching kundalini yoga. It always had to be for somebody who had been through Hatha yoga, and Jnana yoga, and Raja yoga and got devoted enough that he would go to a Kundalini yoga teacher and say, 'Oh master, I am so humble and would you please teach me?' Yogi-ji—that's what we call Yogi Bhajan—broke all kinds of these taboos. Yogi-ji didn't worry. The age is changing, he said. We are moving from the Piscean Age to the Aquarian Age. So Yogi-ji used his devotion to revered gurus and the changing of the planets to break old patterns and to bring Kundalini yoga here to be taught."

Kundalini yoga in some respects is similar to the Tantrism of Vajrayana Buddhism, but without the symbolic demons and gods. It also recognizes a total of seven spinal chakras. Kundalini is thought of as being a vast reservoir of psychic energy at the base of your spine. The word literally means "That which is coiled." Some people refer to it as serpent power, but Yogi Bhajan thinks of it as the basic power of awareness. He envisions it as a spiritual or soul nerve curled and trapped below the lowest or root chakra of your spine. With positive effort you can energize it and eventually raise it through all chakras. The chakras are not physical organs and Yogi Bhajan doesn't look upon them as psychic either. They are purely imaginary. They are the focal points where physical and psychic energy interpenetrate. It is said that as you learn to raise your kundalini to higher chakras you will have fantastic mystical experiences. More important, as the kundalini force is unleashed, you become aware of your Real Self. You become self-actualized. You become integrated and creative. You have little time or inclination for conflict and the petty games of normal society.

Sikhism

Kundalini yoga isn't the only thing that Yogi Bhajan brought to America. He brought his birthright. He was born into Sikhism, a creed that isn't well known in the West. It was started in the 16th century in India by Guru Nanak. Sikhism recognizes but One God who is considered both finite and infinite. And Sikhism sees all races, all levels on the social ladder, and both sexes as being equal. So Sikhism was conceived as the vehicle to unite all religions into a single brotherhood, with Hinduism and Islam as its immediate targets. Guru Nanak was followed by nine more pontiffs, but none of them was able to consummate the union with Hinduism and Islam. Though Sikhism was rejected by both camps, still it grew. Its first five gurus showed the followers how to live creatively by building great cities and stimulating the arts and sciences. Guru Ram Das was the greatest of these creators. Unfortunately, the next five gurus had to show the faithful how to die. By then the other religions were persecuting the Sikhs, and it is said that by the time of the tenth guru, Gobind Singh, the Saint Soldier, there were only four Sikhs left in the world. At this time the bearing of arms had become an integral part of Sikh tradition. In fact, during the persecutions Sikhs became so fond of the sword they nearly forgot the real purpose of Sikhism. The military prowess of the Saint Soldier saved Sikhism from extinction, and to this day his respect for power, weapons and the martial arts are an everyday part of Sikh life.

Guru Gobind Singh left another legacy: no more gurus. It had become the custom in India for people to give themselves primarily to their gurus. Gobind Singh believed you should give yourself only to God. So Gobind Singh declared himself the last guru. Today Sikhism has no living gurus, only teachers. But one student, in referring to Yogi Bhajan, remarked, "We don't usually call Yogi-ji 'guru', but that's the position he holds."

Healthy Happy Holy Organization

Yogi Bhajan's American ministry began in 1969 when he decided your lifestyle should be healthy, happy and holy. So he founded the Healthy, Happy Holy Organization. Everybody calls it 3HO for short. He selected the United States as its launch site because he believed it could mature best in the nation with the most material power. He must have been right. His numerous followers now live all over America and Canada in well over 100 ashrams and teaching centers. The headquarters in Los Angeles is so big it is not only an ashram but actually a small community of several hundred people living in clusters of communal buildings and private apartments.

Yogi Bhajan didn't come to America to gather disciples—he came to train teachers. Kundalini yoga can't be learned from a book, he says, but must come from an instructor. His training in economics led him to conclude that the most efficient way to disseminate the teachings would be to have lots of teachers—a form of educational compound interest. So 3HO is really a huge continentwide academy for teachers, and also a huge society of American Sikhs.

One of Yogi Bhajan's advanced teachers who goes by the spiritual name of Gurucharan Singh looks on the Sikh aspect of 3HO this way: "To be a Sikh means to be a student. Sometimes this is translated to be a disciple, but that has the wrong connotation. Disciple means 'Ah, I am *your* disciple.' If you are a Sikh, you are a student of God, of the cosmos, of infinity. You also accept as a Sikh certain structures to work that out in. Now Sikhs don't call it the Sikh religion, they call it Sikh Dharma. Sikh Dharma means a path or way of living, a way of righteousness. In the end that's what it's all about."

The Sikh way of life also is synonymous with truth. Guru Ram Das admonished his followers: "Ever speak the Truth, than which there is nothing more meritorious. The true Guru will assist him who speaketh the Truth. God is Truth, and he who speaketh Truth shall be absorbed in Him." That's why 3HO's motto is *"Sat Nam"*—"Truth is God's name." And that's why you can trust a real Sikh with anything. Sikhs do not lie. They do not cheat. They do not steal. And they do not cry. They earn their own way. They share with their brothers. And they meditate on God.

Because of its Sikh heritage, 3HO is not completely in line with current trends of women's liberation. Not that 3HO doesn't believe in liberation for women, but theirs is a different kind—it is liberation to be feminine—liberation to not be like a man. 3HO sees men and women as quite different. Men are considered steady and constant like the sun. Women are seen as emotional, changing like the moon. Thus, they have their separate roles. As Yogi Bhajan said, "It is through woman that man is born, and it is her Divine obligation to maintain her identity as the sustainer of mankind, the symbol and the ideal toward whom mankind can look for inspiration and renewal."

So men and women of 3HO take on different labels. All men add to their Western names the Punjabi word "Singh," meaning lion, and the ladies add "Kaur" meaning princess. Disciples who wish may also assume a spiritual name to signify and remind themselves of their total change in life. These are assigned personally by Yogi Bhajan, and are usually Sanskrit, Hindi, or Punjabi holy words. Both men and women wear a thin steel bracelet to symbolize strength. They go even further. They study the martial arts of Karate, Kung Fu and Aikido for self-protection and to defend the weak. Each member has a small dagger which is used for ritual eating and cutting holy food. And these daggers have the same curvature as weapons, so in an extreme emergency, they can protect their bearers from an attacker. Modern Sikhs are still warriors.

3HO is rife with other Sikh customs. One member, Baba Singh, describes a major rule the Sikh must obey: "He should not cut any hair from his body or otherwise alter his natural physical form. Exactly as God made him—that is how he should live." Sikhs also believe your hair absorbs energy from the sun, and thus is associated with strength. Maybe the myth of Samson isn't so mythical after all. Anyway, all 3HO men wear beards. Hairs are considered as antennas carrying solar energy to the body's magnetic field and dirt fouls up this function. So the hair on your head must be covered. Sikh men wrap the hair in a bundle on top of their heads and some wrap the tips of long beards up there too. All this goes into a carefully wrapped turban. So in a 3HO community you see lots of turbans. They can be blue, green and red for little boys; the men wear mostly white. And the women and girls—they wear delicate scarves called *chunis* to cover their uncut locks.

Members are like their Indian counterparts in other ways too. Most men wear those thin pants that tighten down at the calf. Along with these they wear nearly knee-length shirts, all in white, of course. And the ladies wear white too, shirts and pants informally and long white silk dresses and shawls when out in public. Why? Because the clothes attract attention to the movement. And it makes the wearers see themselves as a family. As the very feminine instructor Akasha Kaur says, "I feel that we're representatives of Yogi Bhajan's teachings and of 3HO, and that the community should know that I believe I am different from women on the street in miniskirts or in blue jeans. I would consider it an insult to my image of myself as a graceful lady to be wearing blue jeans and to be giving that external appearance to people."

Gurucharan Singh says the same thing in a different way: "It's not really that we wear the garb of a Sikh to look like a Sikh. It helps us to act as a Sikh. And to act as a Sikh is to act as a student of infinity."

Most Sikhs are not vegetarians. However, Yogi Bhajan strongly endorses such a diet, not only from a moral viewpoint, but because he believes it is more healthy. It's not a requirement for membership in 3HO, but if you live in an ashram, that's the only diet you will get. Among Yogi Bhajan's strong taboos are liquor, smoking, drugs and illicit sex. But 3HO stresses marriage and family life. In fact, procreation is considered a Divine goal in life. So you will find many married couples with their progeny living in 3HO ashrams.

A typical ashram is the large three-story redwood house in a fashionable neighborhood of San Rafael, California. Its thirty members all share the swimming pool and the spacious though furniture-sparse rooms, and take their meals lotus-style on a huge ornate carpet in the gaily painted dining room. Sometimes in the evenings you will find the members seated in a circle around the fireplace chanting to the strum of a guitar and the beat of gongs. When they aren't meditating or practicing Kundalini yoga, there is lots of camaraderie, singing and games. As one member put it, "It's like being in love without a love object. You love everything. It's a very blissful feeling." Many of 3HO's centers are not ashrams in the sense of communal living, but rather are teaching centers. They are usually the home of a teacher, and are open daily to members living nearby and also for conducting public classes. But 3HO teachings stress that real enlightenment evolves from personal consciousness through group consciousness to cosmic consciousness. That's why the main thrust of 3HO is on communal living—on ashrams that develop group consciousness.

Not everyone can join an ashram. You have to be accepted. This usually occurs after you have spent a brief period in an ashram and if it is determined that you will grow from the experience. Both singles and marrieds live in 3HO ashrams along with children. Since the purpose is personal growth, members have group discussions, encounter-style, to get things off their chests. They change roommates; they experiment with voluntary work scheduling; and they have glorious outings to nearby parks, beaches and festivals. To supplement the members' attempts at growth, Yogi Bhajan travels constantly to meet all the members he can.

3HO ashrams are training environments. That requires discipline. The daily routine starts $2\frac{1}{2}$ hours before sunrise with yoga exercises, chanting, prayer and meditation. After breakfast members spend most of the day at work since self-support is a major aspect of Sikh life, then classes are conducted in the evening after dinner. For this life-style you will pay from $100 to $200 a month plus a tithe of 10 percent of your income. In fact, all 3HO members are expected to tithe.

If there is any motto reflecting the Sikh way of life, it would be, "Work, work, work." All the men have a job or join together in business partnerships. Married women take care of their families, but single women also hold down jobs. All members do this in addition to chores around the ashram and teaching classes for the public. The businesses 3HO members have formed among themselves are legion. These are all supposed to make a profit for their participants and include graineries, import shops, health bars, candle shops, bookstores, bakeries, gem stores, construction companies, tree services, scent manufacturers and even a brass bed company. Naturally, there are organic food stores and restaurants. Sat Nam Products distributes natural foods through many outlets and the Golden Temple Conscious Cookery in Washington, D.C. always has long lines of people waiting for its vegetarian meals. Some ashrams have opened schools for tots based on a combination of 3HO methods and the Montessori spiritual techniques of awakening inner wisdom in children. Author Baba Singh summed up ashram life this way: "People live together, study together, form businesses to support themselves, and learn to become teachers to further spread our way of life. If you participate in the way of life, you belong to 3HO; if you don't, you don't."

All 3HO ashrams teach Kundalini yoga, both to the public and to the membership. The members get the lion's share of attention because each is expected to become a teacher. The more advanced members teach the newer ones, and if you have unique hang-ups or crises, you may get special treatment, like a specific private mantra, from Yogi Bhajan.

Though several yogas are taught, Kundalini is emphasized, and is usually taught on a daily basis. Watching a training session you may see all the members sitting on the floor bowing their heads rapidly, taking fast short breaths, bending over backward, stretching or rolling their necks around. Or they may be in one of many other postures. Lots of this is similar to the feverish exercise of bioenergetics. There is also heavy panting as in the "Breath of Fire" with its powerful exhalations. Controlled hyperventilation is considered a key to Kundalini yoga since it permits combining breathing patterns with concentration on your chakras. This produces different types of inner feelings. Many people report upwellings of buried psychic problems—fears, traumas and even archetypes. The objective? To clear each chakra before going to the next; to peel off the layers of your psyche one at a time; to reach the inner light. This is interspersed with chanting, sometimes $2\frac{1}{2}$ hours at a crack of repeating a sacred eight-word mantra.

But ashram training isn't the only 3HO way of learning. Twice a year at the solstices up to 1,500 members gather for ten-day periods during which Yogi Bhajan and his advanced teachers provide instruction. This is the only place that members can learn 3HO's version of Tantric Yoga. It is considered so powerful and makes such dramatic changes in you that you aren't allowed to practice it except in the presence of a Mahan Tantric, or master teacher of Tantric yoga. Members consider Yogi Bhajan to be the only living one on earth in this age, though Lama Tharthang might disagree.

There are some differences between Buddhist and Yogi Bhajan's Tantrism. Buddhists emphasize knowledge and understanding; 3HO concentrates on power, on controlling your inner psychic energy. Still, both have the basic goal of uniting the polarities in your body, of combining your male and female aspects. In Yogi Bhajan's method the exercises require mental, not sexual teamwork between a man and woman. A couple sits staring into each other's eyes. Through different intensive exercises involving asanas, gestures, breathing and visual imagery they delve deep within their individual psyches to raise and transmute lower passions into higher Divine vibrations. The practice involves Carl Jung's male and female anima-animus which is brought to awareness when the participants see in the opposite sex's eyes a reflection of that sex within themselves. In this symbolic union they discover true love instead of the lust most people know. Some participants eventually experience the sacred union of male and female principles of the entire universe and realize there is but one energy of the universe, the energy of female creativity, the energy of love.

3HO has its karma yoga too. Like so many other spiritual groups, 3HO is into drug rehabilitation, and through its yogic techniques claims to have gotten over 150,000 young people off drugs. There are also free kitchens for the needy, and members spend many hours each week taking the teachings to inmates throughout the nation's prisons. But the main thrust is to teach Kundalini yoga and expose the Sikh life-style to the general public. This is done for young people in high-school sociology classes or in teen yoga clubs where rudimentary Kundalini yoga is taught. It is also taught in YMCAs and on many university campuses. Yogi Bhajan himself gives two of these classes at UCLA, and many other colleges offer 3HO courses for academic credit. All ashrams and teaching centers provide hour-long classes for the public every day and many ashrams offer month-long intensives to nonmembers once a year. Hundreds of thousands of people have taken some form of 3HO training.

Yogi Bhajan encourages his protégés to teach whenever and wherever they can. 3HO members will travel almost anywhere within reason to give lectures, demonstrations and yoga classes whenever they are asked. Just call your nearest teaching center or ashram. Akasha Kaur said, "Our people basically have to start their own classes."

"As soon as they are able," she added.

With that she turned to an interested spectator, Daniel Singh, a six-year-old whose colored turban matched the sky blue of his eyes. She posed a problem for him.

"All right, you're a teacher, Daniel," she said. "Where would you go to find a place to teach and convince somebody they'll want a class?"

"Well, I guess," Daniel Singh answered, "I guess I'd like to teach my friends in nursery school some yoga."

"I bet they would like it too. Have any of your friends tried turbans yet?"

"All of them have tried them a little. Even some of the teachers come and ask me to tie them a turban. At least teach them how."

"How to put on a turban?"

"Yes."

"You had a friend who bought a turban, didn't you?"

"Lots of them did."

"Lots of them bought turbans already?"

"Yeah, even Charlotte, Jimmy, Germaine and Tilky and Jacob and Beth and Charlie and all of them."

Then the young lion tugged at the blond hairs poking from under his own turban. "And guess what?" he giggled. "Some even want a Sikh bracelet to wear with their turbans."

Evangelists seem to come in all ages and appearances. So it's not surprising to find in contrast to that six-year-old with his bundled golden locks, a 78-year-old teacher who hasn't a single hair on his head. This latter is His Divine Grace A. C. Bhaktivedanta Swami Prabhupāda, the latest guru in a direct line of teachers that is centuries old. What he teaches follows doctrines of the Gaudiya Vaisnava School of India. Contrary to common Hindu belief that Brahman and nature are One, this small sect speaks of God as being a real and separate personality. It's a concept not much different from the Judeo-Christian idea.

On orders from his own guru to go West, Srila, as they call him, Pradhupāda arrived in New York City in 1965 with just $7 in his pocket. Every day he went to a small park and chanted. In time people began to listen. From this humble beginning the movement he founded grew to over seventy spiritual centers throughout the world. There are few big-city residents who haven't heard the chant that he made famous—*"Hare Krishna Hare Krishna Krishna Krishna Hare Hare Hare Rama Hare Rama Rama Rama Hare Hare."*

International Society for Krishna Consciousness

The organization he founded, though officially the International Society for Krishna Consciousness—ISKCON, is also known as the Hare Krishna Movement. It doesn't follow the ancient tradition requiring that secrets of the Bhagavad-Gita and the sacred Hare Krishna mantra be given only to the most pious and devout. According to the Swami, in this modern age of Kali, this age of insincerity when man is farthest from God, the Lord in his mercy now wants the great secrets made available to all.

And the secrets are spreading rapidly.

There are now 35 ISKCON temples in the United States and Canada. You'll find most of them in large cities because that's where the people who need them most are living. The three-hundred-person community known as the Hare Krishna Quarter in Los Angeles is the world headquarters. Srila Pradhupāda spends three months in residence there every year. The rest of the time he is airplane hopping to other temples where each maintains quarters and even a throne for him.

When Swami Prabhupāda's plane arrives at an airport, his fellow passengers are treated to quite a display. As they disembark, they see the saffron-robed guru being joyfully and noisily greeted by a hundred or more shaven-headed young men in orange robes and by girls wearing many-hued saris. All are shaking finger cymbals or beating drums. The first thing the devotees do is shelter their master with a huge Indian parasol garlanded with colorful flowers, and as he walks to a waiting limousine they toss petals in his path to the joyous chanting of the Hare Krishna mantra.

To ISKCON, a bona fide guru is a link with God. Your guru is considered the ambassador of God who knows what God wants of you. So the guru should be treated as a jewel as precious as God himself. The president of the Los Angeles temple, Tulasi Das, explained it like this: "The guru—we give him all the respect we give God because he can introduce us to the Lord—he is the confidential servant of the Lord. Actually, this pleases the Lord. Just like a rich man. What can you give a rich man? But if you please the rich man's kid with a candy bar, you've really made a hit."

So by serving the Swami, ISKCON members serve God. And their god is called Krishna.

Krishna Consciousness comes straight from the Bhagavad-Gita, the most widely translated Vedic text and considered the essence of Vedic knowledge. Hare Krishna devotees accept it literally without interpretation. In it the Lord Krishna is described as being Absolute Truth and the Supreme Personality of Godhead. Krishna is said to be a real person, and at times has manifested on earth in different incarnations as real persons with the names of Rama, or Lord Caitanya. Yet Krishna is the source of all, the source of Brahma, of Siva and of Vishnu. But Krishna manifests through Vishnu the Preserver. This delightful god doesn't follow the Western image of an old man with a beard. He is depicted as an eternal youth—clean-shaven and with beautiful blue skin. Krishna is All-Attractive and the source of All Pleasure. And Krishna enjoys being surrounded and worshipped by devotees.

To ISKCON, Krishna is considered the *Creator* and the *Enjoyer*. *You* are the created and the enjoyed. According to the Bhagavad-Gita, Krishna enjoys you most when you are devoting your every thought to Him. ISKCON members do that. ISKCON is the ultimate in Bhakti Yoga. Swami Prabhupāda explains how, "One cannot understand Kṛṣṇa by sensual perception or by speculation. It is not possible, for Kṛṣṇa is so great that He is not within our sensual range. But He can be understood by surrender. Kṛṣṇa therefore recommends this process, 'Give up all other processes of religion and simply surrender unto Me.'"

That means giving up your ego. And Krishna Consciousness requires that you do this 24 hours a day. If you are really devoted to Krishna, all you can do is think of Him. Tulasi Das points out, "Just like if you love some girl friend, then you say over and over, 'Oh, Lucy, Lucy, wow that Lucy.' If someone loves God, you know, then he chants the names of the Lord. Also he talks about the Lord's forms, the Lord's pastimes, the Lord's paraphernalia. Just like people are enthusiastic about talking about their families. It's who you love. That's your interest. God is our interest."

ISKCON's most powerful way of talking about their Supreme Love is through the *maha-mantra,* the "great chanting." *"Hare* is the sound for addressing the Lord through love. Krishna and Rama are his names. By vibrating the names of God endlessly you associate with God. By repeating this mantra, first consciously and purposefully during your daily activity, later by rote, you open up your natural love of God, and Krishna becomes your sole thought. This is helped by a special ritual. Each devotee carries a rosary of 108 beads which are counted one at a time whenever the 16-word mantra is repeated. 108 repetitions constitutes a round. Every day the devotees chant 16 rounds, or 1,728 repetitions of the holy mantra. They do it while working, while meditating, even while eating. They can do it any time. And it can be done aloud or in silence. But its most powerful form is when it is combined with another spiritual practice. This happens at all ISKCON temples six times every day.

The greatest treasures in the temples are symbols of the Lord called Deities. Krishna is a transcendental being with a normally transcendental body whom you can't see. But vision is a strong way to fix your mind on something. So, through the Bhagavad-Gita Krishna authorized special visual forms to be worshipped in his place. Worshipping them is the same as worshipping him—just as putting a letter in a mailbox is as good as taking it to the post office. The Deities consist of six statues that represent different manifestations of Krishna and His consort. The Gita spells out exactly how they should look and what they should wear. That's why three times a day they are bathed and given a change of clothes—one for morning, one for evening and one for bedtime. And every day they are given new garlands of flowers.

To house the deities, ISKCON created temples worthy of them. Though the ashram buildings themselves may vary esthetically, the actual temple halls where ceremonies occur are all magnificent. The huge marble-floored hall in Los Angeles is the grandest, but the exquisite opulence in of San Francisco's temple is more typical. It is a columned atrium with illumination coming through a huge skylight. The gilded capitols on polished white columns support a golden frieze wrapping completely around the room. On the pale yellow walls hang ornately framed paintings depicting events from the life of the blue-skinned god. A blue brocade dais in the rear is reserved for the guru, and when he isn't in residence it bears his portrait. Up front a marble balustrade protects three closed doors of white and gold. As the time for each ceremony approaches, one side of the hall fills with orange-robed men while on the opposite side gather children and women in gay saris. All quietly chant the Hare Krishna mantra.

Then, to the beat of gongs, the three doors in front open to display a brilliant setting of light, form and color. On three marble platforms stand the six deities, all clothed in velvet and silk brocades of magenta, orange and purple. They wear elaborate headdresses and jewelled medallions, rings, bracelets and necklaces. Around them candles glow amid flowers and silver bowls brimming with milk and sweets. As three attendants gently wave silklike fans of bleached yak tail, the Hare Krishna mantra rises in tempo, all the while accompanied by sacred music from India. The devotees make ritual offerings of food. They water a sacred tulasi plant. They wave their hands through candle flames out of respect to fire. And they strew flower petals around the guru's picture on the dais. Then the Hare Krishna communal chanting, the *samkirtan,* starts in earnest. Voices rise even louder; mardunga drums beat; cymbals crash; and a harmonium organ picks up the rhythm: all into a microphone that amplifies the sound to a crescendo of sensory bombardment. The devotees wave their arms; they sway; they jump up and down; they prostrate themselves; they go into rapture. All to the reverberating chant of *"Hare Krishna Hare Krishna."* . . . This is what Lord Caitanya must have meant when he said, "So on the order of my spiritual master I chant the holy name of Kṛṣṇa, and I am now mad after his holy name. Whenever I utter it, I forget Myself completely; sometimes I laugh, sometimes I cry, and sometimes I dance like a madman." Some of the devotees go even further and collapse on the white floor in sheer ecstasy. To them they are momentarily one with Krishna.

Who are these people who get so wrapped up in their devotion? What are they like? Most are young, few being older than thirty. Yet, according to Swami, some parents and grandparents of the disciples have seen such remarkable changes in the younger people that they too have become ISKCON enthusiasts. Anyone can be an enthusiast since you needn't be a full-time member. This way you don't have to observe all the requirements of full renunciation. But the real devotees are full-time.

Full-time members in America and Canada number between 4,000 and 5,000. They break down into four categories. There are *brahmacaris,* the unmarried students, both male and female, who have taken several vows of renunciation, including celibacy. These people devote their entire waking consciousness to God. They live, several to a sparse room, in the temples. Their sleeping bags on the floor are their greatest possession. Theirs is a life of austerity.

The second class of full-time membership is householder, married people who live together solely to procreate. They live outside the temples and don't participate as fully as the single people since they must take full responsibility for their families.

The third order of ISKCON is for *vanaprasthas,* the retired householders. The life of vanaprasthas is one of pilgrimage and seeking enlightenment, and is pursued right after the householders' children are of age to leave the nest. These couples travel together all over the world gaining wisdom and spreading the word of the Lord.

The final stage is *sannyasi,* the life of full renunciation. Here, if you went through the married route, you give up even your spouse. All your thought should now be devoted to God. You take extra vows, then spend the rest of your life teaching. This is the only stage when you are eligible to become a swami. Since 1966 several advanced teachers have been initiated as swamis.

All ISKCON members constantly remind the world and themselves of Krishna by their attire. Both men and women paint parts of their bodies with white clay as symbols of God. The most pronounced of these marks, or *tilaks,* is a V symbol on the forehead. Full-time men also shave their heads as a sacrifice to Krishna because he asked for this in the Gita. Little pigtails are left on at the back to signify that Krishna is a transcendental being. Single men wear saffron robes because the color is believed to induce higher thought processes. Householder men wear white to signify their special status. The women pierce their noses and wear bright saris in all colors and patterns. Yet ISKCON ladies are the epitome of feminine decorum. This prompted one visiting Roman Catholic to remark how pleasant it was to see such chaste women. He complained that in his own church he was constantly distracted from the services by all the short skirts.

The life of an ISKCON devotee is simple and free of most material problems. But it's highly regulated. Every morning at 4:30 the Lord is greeted by the devotees in the temple with a communal samkirtan. The same happens five more times during the day. In between is eating, Bhakti yoga, study of Vedic literature and, of course, the 1,728 repetitions of the Hare Krishna mantra. The diet is vegetarian because Krishna asked for that. Alcohol, tobacco and drugs are out, as is gambling. And sports are considered useless.

Yet, in this materialistic world ISKCON has to exist. So ISKCON combines business with evangelism. Swami Prabhupāda is constantly writing spiritual books via dictaphone. ISKCON Press publishes them. And the Society's New Dvaraka book warehouse distributes them for sale, handling up to 500 tons of books at a time. The Swami's weekly lectures are available on tape from Golden Avatar Productions which, so far, has sold over 25,000 cassettes. It also puts on a weekly radio program about the Hare Krishna Movement. Spiritual Sky Scented Products Company makes soap, shampoo, oils, incense and other aromatic products and is the largest incense company in the world. In 1974 it made over $1 million profit. Like all the other ISKCON businesses, it is staffed solely from the membership.

And since each temple must be self-supporting, each is in business too. The members fan out daily onto the streets to sell ISKCON publications. Each temple has a colorful store displaying the Swami's books along with magazines, an excellent vegetarian cookbook, the society's incense, records and beautiful poster reproductions of oil paintings in the temples. Yet during all their work, the main thought on each devotee's mind is Krishna. That even goes for the computer at Spiritual Sky Scented Products. When it isn't taking inventory or figuring profits, you will always see the Hare Krishna mantra on its read-out screen.

Perhaps the most important of ISKCON's enterprises is reserved for the children. Since the Lord Krishna is considered the real seed-giving parent, earthly parents think of themselves only as carriers, as temporary custodians of their children. So at about age five each child is given over to Krishna and sent away to school to be educated according to the Gita. The Gurukula School in Dallas has fifty specially trained devotees who live with the children and teach them the simple pure life of Krishna Consciousness. The children dress like the adults and learn the same temple practices, though of course, the 150 boys and girls pick up worldly education as required by law. When the children reach the age of ten they move to a 1,000 acre farm in West Virginia where they learn about nature. They may, if they wish, visit their parents once a year, but it is expected that when ISKCON children have completed the whole educational program their devotion will be solely to Krishna.

Over and above sustaining itself and teaching its own children, ISKCON is dedicated to awakening all mankind to Krishna Consciousness. Swami says: "Just as there are many mental hospitals like Bellevue, established for the purpose of bringing a crazy man back to his original consciousness, similarly the purpose of this Kṛṣṇa consciousness movement is to bring all crazy men back to their original consciousness."

So ISKCON's meditations, lectures, feasts and festivals are open to the public. You are welcome at any temple every day between 4 a.m. and 9 p.m. Each temple hold classes six nights a week on Vedic philosophy as it appears in scripture, in literature, in drama and in art. All free of charge. Devotees also teach some academically accredited college courses on the science of the Gita. In order to entice people to hear their lectures and chants, ISKCON often distributes free food on the streets or at fair grounds. Two groups of brahmacharis, each headed by an American born swami, travel all over the country in buses converted to mobile temples. They spread the word through ceremonies, from literature, by lectures and with their famous mantra.

But not all is work. Krishna said that spiritual life should be colorful and fun. So every Sunday at 4 p.m. you are invited to take *Purshadam.* There is chanting in the temple, then dancing or a drama to depict some aspect of Krishna's history. Perhaps that's followed by a lecture or group singing to glorify God. The finale is a lavish meal of Indian vegetarian food.

However, the real fun comes once a year at the Jagganath Rathayatra festival. It is dedicated to three of the Deities found in all temples, and its highlight is a large noisy parade that features three enormous chariots. These huge vehicles carry templelike structures, some up to 45 feet high, made of exquisite fabrics, flowers, ornaments and festooned with bells and flying banners. They are drawn by laughing, dancing, chanting devotees and any spectators who may have joined the parade. The whole show culminates at the nearest temple where the assembled throng joyously chants before gorging itself on a six-course vegetarian feast. The 1974 festival that paraded through San Francisco's Golden Gate Park drew over 10,000 spectators and potential converts.

Tulasi Das summed up the festival this way: "You meet all kinds of people at these. And they find out that, although we are singing Hare Krishna and looking sentimental, there's some intelligence behind it. There's a great philosophy here, a great logic."

Then he added, "I'm enjoying that I'm advancing in spiritual life. I'm enjoying that I'm becoming free from looking at my fellows in the mood of exploitation. I'm enjoying becoming a useful asset. I'm enjoying hearing about Krishna and serving Krishna. I'm enjoying becoming purified. In so many ways I'm enjoying. I'm enjoying nice spiritual food and the simple life. I'm enjoying such nice friendships here. It's unbelievable. In so many things and so many ways I am appreciating Krishna consciousness. I started out with awe toward God and ended up as a lover."

That seems to sum up why in every major city you can hear more and more of Tulasi Das's fellow lovers chanting *"Hare Krishna Hare Krishna Krishna Krishna Hare Hare Hare Rama Hare Rama Rama Rama Hare Hare. . . ."*

Chapter 10

WHICH WAY FOR YOU?

So there you have it. What you read in the previous chapters represents most of the spectrum of mental practices. It spans numerous philosophies and lets you know a little about the variety of teachers available. It gives samples of the many ways of psycho-spiritual growth that in recent years have become accessible to the people of North America. And as the North American movement grows, these ways and more should spread to more people throughout the world. Oscar Ichazo, creator of Arica Training, put this a little more poetically when he said, "We are living in the time of the transformation. All history up to this point has been winter. Now spring is coming for sure."

He's speaking, of course, not only of the diversity, but of the mushrooming growth of the self-realization movement. He includes the emerging new practices, the revived old ones and the eclectic systems like his own. That means everything from analytical psychology through the humanistic and transpersonal disciplines to the most esoteric concepts of mysticism. And why does he see them all as beneficial? Because he knows that all the diverse schools, no matter how different they appear outwardly, have essentially the same purpose. Each in its own way and within its own limits reveals to you the nature of your psyche; and many hint at your relation to the universe. All of them, no matter how different they appear, provide you with some realization of an essentially single truth. As the Vedas proclaim, "The Truth is one, only the sages call it by different names."

But it's all those different names that cause confusion; and the seemingly different practices too. Because if not in the long run, at least in the short run, their differences produce different results. With so many books, hypnotists, psychologists, encounter leaders, yogis, mind-training organizations and mystery schools abounding, there's no problem finding something or someone to help you plumb the depths of your psyche or to guide you to the greatest spiritual heights. The real problem is to find the best ones specifically suited to you.

Abraham Maslow, that early giant of humanistic psychology, once said that the majority of people, those whom he considered "normal," weren't even interested in self-realization. But he did single out some people as being spiritual seekers whom he considered more highly developed than "normals." Similarly, the ancient mystery schools spoke of different degrees of spiritual evolution. To some extent they, like Freud, attributed the differences in people to experiences they have during their present lifetimes. But most of what you are, according to mystic tradition, was accumulated over hundreds of previous lives. It is said that your complexes, your drives, everything that makes up your personality is founded in what you experienced in this and past incarnations. That, of course, is what Hindus call karma. The Judeo-Christian concept of original sin as being an inherent human characteristic is another way of looking at karma. It might be likened more to Carl Jung's archetypes. But whichever of these concepts best expresses reality, they all imply one thing. You have something hidden in you that makes you what you are right now. For you to evolve spiritually, that something must change. It has to be worked through. So whether that something is Freudian complexes, past incarnations, original sin or archetypes, "karma" seems like a good word to express it. And self-analysis, good deeds, repentance, surrender—all of these are ways of purging your karma.

There is also something in karma that urges certain people more than others to seek self-realization. There is something in karma that determines your degree of spiritual evolution, just as the degree you have evolved spiritually influences how you receive any specific type of psychic or spiritual training. So there can be no guarantee that any form of training will automatically put you into any specific psychic state.

In fact, there isn't even agreement on what the definition of any specific state is. No one agrees on the relativity of terms like Self-Realization, Self-Actualization, Self-Remembering, Peak Experience, Permanent 24, Clear, Cosmic Consciousness, Samadhi and all the other terms for advanced states of consciousness. These are all subjective terms and can't be compared. Still, it is possible to gauge levels of spiritual awareness to some degree. Oscar Ichazo identified fourteen different levels of consciousness. The Buddhist text *Vissuddhimagga* details nine of them. But these are states of consciousness, not indicators of where you stand on the ladder of spiritual need. Yet even the rungs of that ladder can be crudely categorized. So for this discussion, let's say that beyond what Maslow calls "normal" there are three evolutionary steps, and that each is characterized by different goals.

One level of evolution might be called "Premystic." People in this category recognize the power of their subconscious and want to control it primarily so they can perform better in the material world. They get deep into encounter, Gestalt and other purgative approaches which relieve anxieties and annoying hang-ups. Or they learn self-hypnosis and other forms of mental control in order to improve their concentration and regulate their emotions. They are satisfied with the workaday world as most people define it, but realize that control over their emotions and other subconscious functions will help them operate better in the workaday world.

Then there is the level of the "Worldly Mystics." These people also accept the material world. But they don't look upon it with a workaday attitude. They see it as a place for experience, a place to enjoy to the fullest. They recognize the spiritual and mystical nature of the universe, and possibly accept that the world is no more than cosmic imagination. But they enjoy that imagination and revel in the excitement of it, savoring every moment as a divine gift. Many modern mystical schools stress this level of spiritual achievement.

The last category might be called that of the "Cosmic Mystic." These people see the *Mind* that created the world as the most important thing. To many of them the world is a dream-like illusion from which they wish to awaken. To them merging with the divine consciousness is the goal. To them the only pleasures are seeking and serving their god until the merger occurs. A few, the bodhisattvas, put off their personal fusion, but only so long as they can help all mankind merge. Most of the ancient mystical schools fall into this philosophical category.

Where do you stand on the ladder of spiritual evolution? More than likely, since you were interested enough to read this book, you are one of those few spiritual seekers Maslow spoke about. Still, you and other readers of this book all have different capacities, different motivations and consequently, different goals. Perhaps you already know exactly what you want. That's good. Or maybe you are playing it as you go, being guided by your inner spirit. That's good too. But in both cases, it helps to know how far up the spiritual ladder you can comfortably climb.

Generally, most people discover their real human nature before they are ready to tackle their higher selves. True, you can have peak experiences while purging yourself, and a few rare people can bypass the purgative process through fervent worship, through Bhakti yoga. But for most it is a step by step process of cleaning out the personal garbage to clear a path to Cosmic Consciousness. And all of this requires effort. How much of yourself are you willing to give to do it? How much will you sacrifice in money, time, repetitious practice and subordination to a guru— even all your worldly possessions to enter monastic life? Is your act of giving up going to be unduly unpleasant? Does it seem like too great a sacrifice? If so, maybe you are shooting too high.

On the other hand don't aim too low. That happens to so many people, mainly because of lack of exposure. Perhaps you have an inner karmic urge for spiritual growth that is alive and strong, but is lying dormant. Maybe it needs exposure to spiritual ideals, to people with high motivations and to inspiring philosophies. Perhaps it needs but one spark to ignite it into flames of activity. Remember what the Buddha said about right living and associating with people of a spiritual nature. This book may have helped to a small extent in rousing your curiosity, if not your urge for greater growth. But exposure to the real thing is the only way to evolve.

Vedantists are emphatic on this. They say never blindly accept what someone else tells you. You have to experience in order to really understand. The Sufis sum up the same thing with the simple statement "He who tastes knows."

No one method is better than another. Each has its function for specific situations and for specific people. If you want a dramatic exposure to your subconscious, self-hypnosis is a good starter. It's a striking demonstration of the power of your hidden psyche. It can enhance your life in the workaday world too, by improving your memory, your concentration or your self-discipline. And it can help in spiritual pursuits by allowing you to shift more easily from "normal" to altered states of consciousness, something that usually comes through conditioning built up over years of practice.

For people with emotional problems who want to deal with them intellectually, yet don't mind anguishing while doing it, encounter and similar group methods are ways to ease into the psycho-spiritual game. Those who benefit most from these are people with a strong urge for self-awareness and better personal relationships, yet who are not so defensive and sensitive that they suffer unduly if the encounter is unpleasant. If you have difficulty in a stress situation, encounter isn't the game for you. The same holds for people who aren't prepared to bare their innermost secrets to a group. These people usually prefer the intimacy of sessions with a single therapist whom they trust. Such disciplines as Gestalt, bioenergetics and Rolfing may be best for them. Scientology also involves intimacy, often with several different auditors. Subud and *est* take you deep into your psyche too, where you discover your innermost thoughts. And with these latter you are the only one privy to your awesome secrets.

Methods like Transcendental Meditation, Arica and Psychosynthesis get into your psyche in a different way. What they dredge up doesn't seem so painful. In fact lots of it is delightful. These methods place more emphasis on the mystical, and people drawn to them are not so much after their hang-ups as they are the ethereal aspects of their being. Sufi, Tibetan and many Hindu movements appeal to these same people. And for those who aren't concerned with complexes at all, but are motivated solely toward God, there are the religious schools like the Jesus Movement or Krishna Consciousness. These are the schools of complete surrender, and attract people who are willing to devote their whole lives to spiritual evolution. However, many spiritually oriented people find it easier to surrender their egos to a guru rather than to an ineffable Divine Consciousness. Thus, some groups emphasize adoration of

God and an enlightened master, often one from far-off India wearing strange exotic attire. And for worshippers inclined that way, this spiritual approach usually works.

So of the numerous growth and mystical schools, there are nearly infinite combinations of techniques and philosophies to suit almost any personality and any degree of spiritual development you may have attained. More than likely, there is some teacher or group or school just right for you.

So usually it isn't wise to rush in and join the first organization you run across. At least that's the consensus of most growth and spiritual leaders interviewed during the writing of this book. In fact, that and lots of other advice in this chapter comes directly from their lips. Don't be hasty. That's the first warning those who know the business will give you. It's so easy to get excited about something that seems exotic or esoteric, especially if you investigate only superficially. Then if you make the wrong choice, you could waste a lot of time. Worse, you could become so turned off by your misadventure that you might drop out of the growth game altogether.

So leaders and teachers advise that you learn as much about an organization or method as you reasonably can. Investigate more than one organization if you like. Read material about their philosophies and the memberships. Don't be satisfied with generalities like, "We believe in God" or "Love is our creed." Most growth centers, churches and other groups will tell you a lot more. The sincere ones give free lectures, seminars and demonstrations of their techniques and philosophies. They often give introductory courses free or for a modest fee so you can get your feet wet without full commitment. Talk with former students. Talk with teachers. Do you trust them? What are their credentials? Do their theories square with your understanding of psycho-spiritual development? Look at the product of their training. What is the attitude of their pupils? Observe members of the group on their own premises. Are they open, happy and enthusiastic about their work? Are they tolerant? Or are they dogmatic, pretentious and on ego trips, claiming theirs is the only way? If so, you will be expected to embrace the teachings unquestioningly. That's not to say that's wrong if you can do it. But a lot of people can't.

Many organizations or forms of instruction have names or make claims that don't exactly define what they really teach.

Sometimes it's hard to know what you will get before you put up your money or time. So make sure you know what you are getting into before investing large sums of money, and more important, too much time. Since you are interested in controlling your mind, determine whether the instructor really understands mental functioning, or is just parroting the organization's line.

If you're considering encounter, you are probably most interested in better understanding yourself and the rest of the world. Make sure the type of group and training matches your personality. Beware of joining groups with friends or business associates. Since you spill your innermost secrets there, it's a lot easier to trust strangers. Also be wary of encounter leaders who set up conditions —sanctions, punishment and even ostracism—to force behavioral changes like being more open, honest and loving. Often your defenses are stripped apart with no guarantee they will be put back together. Barry Certner of NTL Institute warns: "The danger is that in many cases people who lead change-focused encounter groups are really masquerading as therapists without a comprehensive knowledge of the change process, personality theory, psychopathology, and other of the ingredients which comprise competent practice." In fact, many group leaders aren't much more advanced in the encounter game than you are—just enough sometimes to boost their own egos at your expense.

You will find teachers in all types of growth systems who like to be center stage, especially the self-proclaimed gurus who will start pontificating the moment they enter a room. Many prefer to shock their audiences more than instruct them. One sheet-clad Hindu demonstrated this tendency in a dramatic fashion. While describing the virtues of breathing and breath control, he lit a cigarette and wisecracked that even a guru on occasion should maintain his strength by wrestling the devil. The devil must have been the stronger this time because within minutes the master of breath control had to leave the room in a fit of coughing.

It's important to respect and trust your teacher. The Upanishads tell us, "The teacher must be wonderful and the disciple must be wonderful; where this combination is found there grows the beautiful tree with flowers and fruit." So you may have to look at several different schools before your spiritual tree comes into blossom. Brother Bhavananda of the Self-Realization Fellowship believes you don't actually find a real guru. He finds you. You are drawn to him—and then only when you are spiritually advanced enough to get the most from his teaching. But when you and your real guru do meet, you will know it. That's when your true teacher-disciple relationship begins.

There's one thing all the teachers caution: beware of the fly-by-nighters. That doesn't necessarily mean they are charlatans. Many well-intentioned and often qualified people start a growth or spiritual group only to suffer a scarcity of disciples, and thus soon go out of business. Others are notoriously nomadic and have an itch to move all over the continent. So if you are interested in pursuing a specific training for any period of time, the established organizations are more likely to be around long enough for you to complete your work. It may not be axiomatic, but it is reasonable to assume that if an organization has been in business a long time and if lots of people have been processed by it, there is a good chance its practices are not only effective, but are likely to be available when you need them. That's one reason larger and more extensive schools have been emphasized in this book.

But large organizations have their pitfalls. More than likely the founder won't be your teacher, so you will have to settle for someone who may not measure up to the high standards the leader set. Bad apples can slip by anywhere. In organizations with numerous teaching houses or ashrams, the house leaders are appointed and may not be fully evolved spiritually. Some develop messiah complexes and dictate in a harsh and unreasonable fashion. Also, worldwide societies tend to standardize their practices, and when the founders depart this material world, there is a tendency to canonize them and sanctify their pronouncements. This can result in stifling inflexibility, especially if the organization claims to be the *only way,* to have a corner on the world. That could be, but test the philosophy. It should be practical and have value for you in the here-and-now. It should be demonstrable rather than just having a holy or occult aura. And if there are rituals, they should make sense. But that way they aren't really rituals. As Gurucharn Singh of 3HO said, "A technique which has lost its meaning or is out of context is a ritual; a living ritual which is fully understood is a technique."

Don't be put off by *minor* details of a teaching that may not square with your logic, especially if the scheme as a whole looks good. Most people have difficulty distinguishing between the methods of an organization and its philosophy. So if they can't buy the philosophy, they automatically reject the techniques. Yet most philosophies, especially those pertaining to gods, the cosmos, and creation, are often based on centuries-old lore no longer compatible with modern thought. Techniques, on the other hand, are observable and measurable. They are material-world reality. So let them be your guide. No one really knows what electricity is, but who buys batteries based on the manufacturer's theory of electrostatics? Besides, if you listen or read extensively enough you will find that many diverse philosophies are really just different ways of saying the same thing . . . that guidance by guardian angels may be the same as unconscious revelations. Who cares so long as the techniques to bring about the phenomena work?

How fast should you proceed in your quest for enlightenment? John Miranda of Arica likes efficiency. So he says, "I've looked around all the different groups and seen their goal is the state of unity, the state of void, the state of satori, of samadhi. From my personal opinion, it simply makes sense to get to that state as quickly as possible. To eliminate as much suffering as fast as possible." For lots of people in the right training that works well. But other teachers believe you should proceed at the rate best suited to you. They don't consider speed nearly as important as how comfortable you feel with teachers or groups. Do they speak your language? Are you compatible with them? Is your age much different from the average of your spiritual companions? Does your socioeconomic situation allow you to be comfortable with them? And remember, always reserve the right to test all practices for their naturalness for you.

Do severe abstentions turn you off? Then go slow in giving up things. If the rewards you expect from sacrifice don't meet your expectations, you may become disenchanted with self-improvement in general. Some masters say abstentions in the early stages of your development aren't really necessary, that as you grow spiritually many of your undesirable wants will automatically vanish anyway. But you have to help them a little. So if your life-style violates the major principles you learn during your development, eliminate conflicts by modifying your ways slightly.

But the most important thing to do on the path to self-realization is to take the first step. If you aren't sure how far to go or which path you want to take, try several programs. Werner Erhard of *est* advises that you become familiar with different approaches. Attend seminars or weekend workshops. Take a few lessons. Use your senses, Erhard says. See what the different approaches are like. Get a *feel* for them. He means that literally. Don't select solely on logic. Let your inner senses guide you. It's not really difficult to select what is right for you if you let your feelings in on the decision. You will be drawn to what's right.

Once you have selected a path that can take you to a goal that appeals to you, *stick* with it. At least stick with it long enough to give it a chance. If your needs are answered, fine; that's where you belong. If not, in six months or more you may want to change. But a word of caution. In most trainings some students reach a plateau, a stage where progress seems to stop, where they become totally discouraged, where they hate the work. They don't like the people in the movement. Many feel above the teachings. But if they don't drop out too soon, most discover they have unknowingly slipped into a higher state of consciousness. It's as if all the negativity is a product of their metamorphosis, only to vanish when the transformation is complete. Then their new state is one where personal consciousness has met cosmic consciousness. They cannot turn back. Try as they may to regain it, their material world is never again the same. They have discovered a basic truth. They know now that reality is different. Werner Erhard describes it this way: "You're God in your universe—you caused it—you pretended not to cause it so you could play in it—and you can remember you caused it—any time you want to."

That basic truth exists no matter where you live. But where you live may determine how soon you learn that basic truth, or any truth. Your home may not be near the right teacher or program for you. Self-realization is a relatively new practice in many parts of the United States and Canada. Your town may not have exactly what is best for you. If it does, great! If not, don't despair. Everyone's mailbox is a direct link to all kinds of religious and esoteric correspondence courses (see Appendix B).

However, at least three-quarters of the American population (less in Canada) live within an hour's drive of a metropolitan area where one or more growth centers, spiritual churches, mystical schools or adult education encounter groups provide workshops, services or yoga courses. These people can commute easily on a regular basis.

If you are lucky enough to live in or near Boston, Chicago, New York, or Montreal, you shouldn't have much difficulty finding what you need. These cities are spiritual Meccas and very likely you will find exactly what you like there. Residents in the vicinity of Los Angeles or San Francisco have a hard time keeping from becoming enlightened. They are literally surrounded by the greatest variety and number of growth and spiritual centers in the entire world. The Golden State has over 1,100 growth and spiritual organizations—that's one-third of all the groups in the country.

So wherever you live in the United States or Canada, the psycho-spiritual movement is growing . . . and growing fast. Many old schools of self-realization are expanding, and new ones are constantly springing up. Superficially they may seem quite different, but they really aren't. As the Hindus say: "Cattle are of different colors, but all milk is alike; systems of faith are different, but God is one."

That describes the self-realization movement succinctly. Another way would be to liken it to a huge mountain, a mountain with tremendous diversities in landscape. On the plain around its base are scattered many camps full of all types of people. From each camp the mountain looks different, and in these camps are guides who know at least one path up the mountain. But all the paths seem different, and some go higher than others. A few routes follow canyons and rocky streams. Others cross broad grasslands or meander through rich forests. Some are said to be fast approaches to the top, but they scale steep escarpments. Some trails are easier and traverse many types of countryside, with lots of stopping places on the way. Many trails interconnect. As the trails near the summit they get closer together and their landscapes become more similar. The vegetation looks more alike and the high altitude makes you equally giddy on all of them. A few of the paths go all the way to the summit where they meet and become one—as do the climbers. The summit is where the snowy peak merges with swirling white clouds; where earth and heaven join; where man finally awakens and meets his Being; where there is nothing but oneness in the universe. This is the limit of the world of illusion—the end of individuality. It is where the cosmos begins.

And all of us can climb at least one path up that mountain. All we have to do is start.

PARTIAL LIST OF PSYCHO-SPIRITUAL SCHOOLS

Most of the following organizations, though not specifically researched and interviewed, seem of sufficient merit to be included in this appendix as alternatives to those described in the text. The latter are also included in this appendix for comparative purposes and to provide their mailing addresses in a convenient format. The descriptive material, for the most part, was supplied by the organizations themselves.

An asterisk (*) indicates instruction is available by mail. See Appendix B for a comprehensive list of correspondence instruction.

AGNI YOGA SOCIETY
319 West 107th Street, New York, NY 10025

Publishes and disseminates literature about Agni Yoga, a synthesis of all yogas. Participants must complete three years of study before acceptance as members into the Esoteric Group.

Books published by the Society are available by mail.

Study groups throughout the U.S. Write for names and addresses.

ALTORA SOUL SCIENCE ACADEMY
625 Polk Street, Apt. 405 San Francisco, CA 94102

Nonprofit School of Spiritual Unfoldment. Public lectures and private instruction, preparing for advanced arcane training. Emphasis on ethical Soul-Culture, magnetic healing, regeneration and occult sciences.

* Guidance letters. Books on Atlantis, Alchemy, Rose Cross, Initiation, Occult Science, Seership, Prenatalism.

Affiliated with Beverly Hall Corporation
Philosophical Publishing Company
P.O. Box 220
Quakertown, PA. 18951

AMERICAN CENTER FOR THE ALEXANDER TECHNIQUE
142 West End Avenue, New York, N.Y. 10023

Expansiveness, lightness, ease of movement and ease of attitude are the common results of kinesthetic awareness-movement re-education process. Individual and group classes, lecture-demonstrations.

List of U.S. teachers and free brochure upon request

931 Elizabeth Street, San Francisco, CA 94114

Affiliated teachers: Berkeley, Los Angeles, San Francisco, Santa Cruz, Santa Monica, CA; Glencoe, IL; Cambridge, MA; Lincoln, NE; New York, Rockland County, NY.

AMERICAN FOUNDATION FOR THE SCIENCE OF CREATIVE INTELLIGENCE (AFSCI)
See World Plan Executive Council

AMERICAN HUMANIST ASSOCIATION
See Humanism

A.M.O.R.C.
See Rosicrucians

ANA FOUNDATION
20204 Catalina Drive, Castro Valley, CA. 94546

Metaphysical teachings mainly through trance lessons, healing groups, development classes, lectures, hypnosis and individual guidance.

The teachings of Ana available in book form or on tape.

ANANDA MARGA (the "Path of Bliss")
854 Pearl Street, Denver, CO 80203

Spiritually oriented, socially active. Teaches meditation, yoga postures, and other practices related to attainment of a balanced personality. Emphasis on establishing a progressive society through various social service activities. Public talks, individual instruction, multimedia presentations, and classes given free of charge.

Books on social and spiritual philosophy available from Ananda Marga Publications, 854 Pearl Street, Denver, CO 80203

North American headquarters: Los Altos Hills, CA; Colorado Springs, CO; Atlanta, GA; Chicago, IL; Cambridge, MA; Philadelphia, PA; Austin, TX; Vancouver, B.C.; Ottowa, ONT.

Centers: Birmingham, AL; Anchorage, Fairbanks, AK; Phoenix, Tucson, AZ; Los Altos Hills, Los Angeles, Oakland, Sacramento, Santa Cruz, CA; Boulder, Denver, Littleton, CO; Milford, New Haven, CT; Gainsville, FL; Athens, Atlanta, GA; Hilo, Honolulu, HI; Moscow, ID; Carbondale, Chicago, Peoria, IL; Bloomington, IN; Des Moines, IA; Emporia, Wichita, KS; Louisville, KY; New Orleans, LA; Baltimore, Silver Springs (Washington, DC), MD; Amherst, Cambridge, MA; Allendale, MI; Kansas City, MO; Duluth, Minneapolis, MN; Bozeman, Missoula, MT; Reno, NV; Hanover, NH; Jersey City, NJ; Albuquerque, Santa Fe, NM; Bellmore, Ithaca, Kings Park, New Platz, New York, Rochester, Ronkonkoma, NY; Raleigh, NC; Cleveland, OH; Oklahoma City, Tulsa, OK; Eugene, Portland, OR; Greensburgh, Philadelphia, Pittsburgh, Scranton, PA; Columbia, Isle of Palms (Charleston), SC; Sioux Falls, SD; Memphis, Nashville, TN; Austin, Denton, Franklin, Waco, TX; Salt Lake City, UT; Perkinsville, Warren, VT; Blacksburg, VA; Bellingham,

Seattle, Spokane, WA; Madison, WI; Burnaby, Grand Forks, Vancouver, Vernon, B.C.; Winnipeg, MAN; Campbellville, Kitchner, London, Ottawa, ONT; Montreal, QE.

ANTHROPOSOPHICAL SOCIETY IN CANADA

151 Carisbrooke Crescent, North Vancouver, B.C. Canada

Study groups on Rudolf Steiner's Spiritual Science. Public lectures. Books for sale and lending library. Waldorf School, Bio-Dynamic farming, Eurythmy.

Books available from Steiner Book Centre, 151 Carisbrooke Crescent, North Vancouver, B.C.

Vancouver, B.C.; Edmonton, ALTA.; Toronto, ONT.; Longueuil, QUE.

AQUARIAN FELLOWSHIP CHURCH

1101 Park Avenue, San Jose, CA 95126

Teaches psychic development with emphasis upon its morals and ethics; mediumship. Church services, children's lyceum, psychic demonstrations, billet reading, aura analyses, etc., at weekly services.

Books and magazine quarterly available by mail.

San Jose, CA; Dayton, OH.

AQUARIAN RESEARCH FOUNDATION

5620 Morton Street, Philadelphia, PA 19144

Dedicated to bringing in a whole new age peacefully, joyfully, and quickly by reducing society's resistance to change. A mailing list of over 350 and constantly growing.

Staff lives at this address sharing common household.

Unpopular Science (which contains first 4½ years' newsletters)
The Natural Birth Control Book
Newsletters of the A R F.

ARCANA WORKSHOPS

407 North Maple Drive Apt. #214, Beverly Hills, CA 90210

Group meditation training is designed to connect the contemporary meditator to his environment by linking him and his creative potential to the soul. Service is an inherent soul urge, a soul attitude. Therefore, contemporary meditation becomes training for service.

* Meditation training is offered in workshops and through correspondence. Books, publications, and tapes.

ARICA INSTITUTE, INC.

24 West 57th Street, New York, NY 10019 (national headquarters)

Offers training from one hour to 40 days for integration of body, mind, emotion, and spirit. Scholarships available. Other participation could be as a volunteer worker, an associate (graduate of 40-day training), or further training and participation as a member of a teaching house.

* Arica Audition, 2-record set, exercises and mantram. Arica Heaven, 1 record, music for listening. Books and correspondence courses in preparation. Write for the nearest Teaching House to you.

ARUNACHALA ASHRAM—BHAGAVAN SRI RAMANI MAHARSHI CENTER, INC.

342 East 6th Street, New York, NY 10003

Path of practice of self-enquiry, of *Who Am I?* Every evening at 7:00 p.m.— recitation, chanting and short reading.

Books and photographs available.

Glendale, CA; Brooksville, FL; New York, NY—Bridgetown, Novia Scotia, Canada.

ASSOCIATION FOR HUMANISTIC PSYCHOLOGY

325 Ninth Street, San Francisco, CA 94103

List of growth centers throughout the United States and Canada available on request for $2.00.

ASSOCIATION FOR RESEARCH AND ENLIGHTENMENT

P.O. Box 595, Virginia Beach, VA 23451

Dedicated to the study and dissemination of the psychic readings of Edgar Cayce. Year-round programs of lectures and conferences along with extensive library of Cayce's readings at Virginia Beach.

Numerous study groups in U.S. and Canada that meet weekly for discussions, growth and fun.

ASTARA

261 S. Mariposa Avenue, Los Angeles, CA 90004

Secret mystical society with an organized plan for enlightenment and soul progression. Teaches developing inner facilities, esoteric nature of the Cosmos and psychic healing.

* Principal instruction through correspondence lessons. Books and recordings also available.

ASTRO CONSCIOUSNESS INSTITUTE FOR SELF ENLIGHTENMENT AND PEACE

1627 South Emerson Street, Denver, CO 80210

A personalized program of self enlightenment based on "The Life and Teachings of the Masters of The Far East." This is accomplished through the inner control of personal energy outflow. A New Age educational concept for the training of the "Citizen of the Universe." The emphasis is on "how" rather than theory.

AUM ESOTERIC STUDY CENTER

2405 Ruscombe Lane, Baltimore, MD 21209

A nonprofit, tax-exempt, state-approved esoteric study center. Located at Savitria (founded in 1969), a spiritual community based on the Ageless Wisdom Teachings. Being state-approved, AUM is able to grant three certificates in the areas of Mystic Arts, Occult Sciences and Religious Metaphysics.

A gift catalog is available by mail, specializing in Esoteric Americana and Great Seal Medallions, etc. Working on correspondence courses and tapes of courses and guest lectures.

THE BARKSDALE FOUNDATION FOR FURTHERANCE OF HUMAN UNDERSTANDING

P.O. Box 187, Idyllwild, CA 92349

Seminars, workshops and self-led Study Groups in building self-esteem.

* *Building Self-esteem, Study Guide for Building Self-esteem* Follow-up Workbook, various leaflets and tape cassettes on self-esteem.

Workshops available in many cities in the United States. Inquire at above address.

BAY AREA YOGA TEACHERS ASSOCIATION

947 Larkspur Road, Oakland, CA 94610

Association of Yoga teachers in the San Francisco area to increase teaching skills through weekly and monthly seminars. Also referral service to potential students.

DAVE BENT—Coordinator Aquarian Activities
P.O. Box 766, Fort Lauderdale, FL 33302

Acts as information center and advisor to New Age individuals and groups.

BUDDHIST ASSOCIATION OF THE UNITED STATES
3070 Albany Crescent, The Bronx, New York, NY 10463

Teaches Buddhist theory and meditation with heavy emphasis on Sutra reading and discussion. Occasionally, lectures are given in Chinese and/or English on various aspects of Buddhism. Some publications of the Association are available on request.

BUILDERS OF THE ADYTUM
5105 N. Figueroa St., Los Angeles, CA 90042

Teaches practical mysticism, based on the Kabbala. Includes the occult or hidden psychology, Tarot transmutation, climbing the 32 Paths of Wisdom to spiritual attainment, Chanting, group ritual and ceremonial, Mystical Alchemy, Esoteric Astrology, etc. Public classes, Sunday healing services, and esoteric instruction to qualified members.

* Correspondence courses in all of the above.

Sacramento, San Francisco, CA; Boston, MA; Tulsa, OK; New York, NY.

CALIFORNIA INSTITUTE OF ASIAN STUDIES
3494 21st Street, San Francisco, CA 94110

Evening graduate school offering M.A. and Ph.D. degrees and diplomas in Asian languages, comparative religion, philosophy, psychology, eastern self-disciplines (yoga, Tai Chi Chuan), art and music therapy; Sunday lectures; Sunday school; Guest speakers. Also Counseling Psychology center for those desiring growth and guidance. Auditors welcome.

Philosophical, religious, psychological, Asian language, Individual Lecture Tapes and art books for sale.

CAMPUS CRUSADE FOR CHRIST INTERNATIONAL
Arrowhead Springs, San Bernardino, CA 92404

College level Christian societies. Provide instruction, inspiration and fellowship in a Christian environment. Available on many university and college campuses.

CANADIAN ACADEMY OF YOGA
71 Boulton Drive, Toronto, 190 ONT.

Teaches integral yoga for certification of yogins. Affiliate Canadian Yoga Teachers Association fosters standards for teachers of yoga. Affiliate House of Yoga is an ashram for practical application of yogic techniques.

Vancouver, B.C.; Winnipeg, MAN; Halifax, Nova Scotia; Toronto, ONT.

CENTER FOR SPIRITUAL AWARENESS
Box 7, Lakemont, GA 30552

Teaches meditation, yoga, and awareness procedures. Seminars are given in the summer months; occasional classes at other times. Tours are made to about 60 cities a year to offer classes.

* Correspondence course in meditation

and occult sciences. Also, self-help and meditation books.

Headquarters is at Lakemont, Ga. About 30 study groups in the U.S., Canada and West Africa.

CENTER FOR SPIRITUAL STUDIES
1561 N. Benson Rd., Fairfield, CT 06430

Diverse teachings and philosophies. Program includes lectures, yogic postures and meditation. Emphasis is on love in action.

CHAKPORI-LING FOUNDATION SANGHA, INC.
P.O. Box 73475, Metairie, LA 70033

Mahayana-Tantra (Tibetan) Buddhism; Kung-Fu, a Shao-lin Buddhist art that includes Sino-Tibetan yoga; Oriental cookery based on yin-yang, Trapa training; monk and nun training, etc. (Future plans include acupuncture with a Ph.D. award)
* Future correspondence course in acupuncture.

Metairie, LA; Houston, TX.

CHABAD-LUBAVITCH (Hasidism)
770 Eastern Parkway, Brooklyn, NY 11213

Revitalized Jewish movement emphasizing feeling and emotion along with orthodox scholarship. Teaches a mystical view of God and creation in terms that everyone can understand. Advocates marrying both the spiritual and worldly pursuits into a single harmonious life-style.

Phoenix, Tuscon, AZ; Little Rock, AR; Berkeley, Encino, Long Beach, Los Angeles, San Diego, Santa Monica, Westwood, CA; Denver, CO; Bridgeport, New Haven, Orange, CT; Washington, DC; Miami Beach, FL; Atlanta, GA; Chicago, IL; Baltimore, Silver Springs, MD; Boston, Brookline, Mattapan, Springfield, Worcester, MA; Ann Arbor, Detroit, Farmington, Oak Park, MI; Minneapolis, St. Paul, MN; Kansas City, St. Louis, MO; Maplewood, Morristown, Newark, Passaic, Paterson, NJ; Albany, Buffalo, Crown Heights, Greenfield Park, New York, Rochester, NY; Cincinnati, Cleveland, OH; Portland, OR; Philadelphia, Pittsburgh, Scranton, PA; Providence, RI; Memphis, Nashville, TN; Dallas, Houston, TX; Richmond, VA; Seattle, WA; Madison, Milwaukee, WI; London, Toronto, Windsor, ONT; Lacdesert, Montreal, QUE; Winnipeg, SAS.

THE CHILDREN OF GOD
GPO 3141, San Juan, PR 00936

Full-time communal living according to Book of Acts in the Bible; also have associate colonies, widow colonies, catacomb colonies.

Phoenix, AZ; Los Angeles, San Francisco, CA; Denver, CO; Washington, DC; Miami, FL; Atlanta, GA; Honolulu, HI; Chicago, IL; New Orleans, LA; Baltimore, MD; Boston, MA; Minneapolis, MN; St. Louis, MO; New York, NY; Cincinnati, Cleveland, OH; Portland, OR; Philadelphia, Pittsburgh, PA; San Juan, PR; Dallas, Houston, TX; Seattle, WA; Vancouver, B.C.; Toronto, ONT.

CHRISTIAN SCIENCE See Church of Christ, Scientist

CHRISTIAN WORLD LIBERATION FRONT
P.O. Box 4307, Berkeley, CA 94704

Christian family with rural farm for retreats and rehabilitation.

Publish monthly paper, *Right On*, P.O. Box 4309, Berkeley, CA 94704

CHURCH OF CHRIST, SCIENTIST

Christian Science Center, Boston, MA 02115

A biblically based Christian teaching, emphasizing healing through the prayer of spiritual understanding. Sunday and Wednesday church services, public lectures, practitioners. Class instruction for church members only.

Books, pamphlets and periodicals of the Christian Science Publishing Society, Boston. Available at all Christian Science Reading Rooms.

2,316 Churches of Christ, Scientist, and Christian Science Societies throughout the United States and Canada. (See your local phone book.)

CHURCH OF SCIENTOLOGY

5930 Franklin Avenue, Los Angeles, CA 90028

A pan-denominational applied religious philosophy dealing with the study of knowledge which, through the application of its technology can bring about desirable changes in the conditions of life, and increase the abilities of the individual. It provides spiritual counseling and courses in communication. Also provides community services.

All Scientology books and records are available to the public at all centers.

Centers: La Jolla, Los Angeles (4), San Francisco, CA; Washington, DC; Miami, FL; Honolulu, HI; Boston, MA; Detroit, MI; Minneapolis, MN; Las Vegas, NV; Buffalo, New York, NY; Portland, OR; Austin, TX; Seattle, WA;—Toronto, ONT.

Also 75 missions throughout the United States and Canada

CHURCH OF THE TRUTH & NEW AGE BOOKS AND ARTS

919A–17th Avenue S.W., Calgary, Alberta, T2T OA4

Teaches Positive Living, New Thought, Meditation. Public Lectures, Free Courses, Children's Positive Living program, Leadership Training program, counseling. Courses in Positive Motivation for Business and Sales groups.

Bookstore with over 600 titles on metaphysics and self-help. Mail Order on books and tapes. Fine arts, tiles, batik.

CIMARRON ZEN CENTER OF RINZAI-JI See Zen

CULTURAL INTEGRATION FELLOWSHIP, INC.

3494 21st Street, San Francisco, CA 94110.

Universal and humanistic religious services with a focus on balanced personality growth and creative freedom. Teaches various spiritual disciplines including integral yoga, dialectical meditation, Zen, tantra, Tibetan mysticism, Sufism, Christian and Jewish mysticism. Interreligious, international marriages performed.

The Ashram Bookstore sells books and tape recordings on Asian wisdom, meditation techniques, spiritual disciplines, yoga therapy, comparative psychotherapy, etc.

DIAMOND SANGHA See Zen

DIVINE LIGHT MISSION

P.O. Box 6495 Denver, CO 80206

Informs public about "Knowledge," the meditation revealed by Guru Maharaj Ji, which puts one in touch with the energy animating all creation.

Regular discourses are given at Divine Light Centers where devotees may live together if they choose.

Magazine: *And It Is Divine*, and newspaper, *Divine Times*, available by subscription. Cassette tapes of discourses on knowledge by Guru Maharaj Ji.

Phoenix, Tuscon, AZ; Kingston, Lincoln, AR; Chico, Los Angeles, Menlo Park, Sacramento, San Francisco, San Jose, Santa Barbara, Santa Cruz, CA; Aspen, Denver, CO; Lakeville, New Haven, CT; Wilmington, DE; Washington, DC; Fort Walton Beach, Gainsville, Miami, Ocala, Pinellas Park, Tallahassee, Tampa, FL; Atlanta, GA; Honolulu, HI; Carbondale, Chicago, IL; Indianapolis, South Bend, IN; Davenport, IA; Lawrence, KS; New Orleans, LA; Portland, ME; Boston, Boxford, Northampton, MA; Ann Arbor, Detroit, Kalamazoo, Lansing, MI; Minneapolis, MN; Jackson, Gulfport, MS; Kansas City, St. Louis, MO; Omaha, NE; Reno, NV; Contoocook, NH; East Brunswick, West Orange, NJ; Alburquerque, NM; Albany, Buffalo, Ithaca, New York, Rochester, NY; Asheville, Hurdle Mills, NC; Cincinnati, Columbus, OH; Portland, OR; Erie, Philadelphia, Pittsburgh, PA; Newport, Providence, RI; Columbia, SC; Sioux Falls, SD; Houston, Lubbock, TX; Salt Lake City, UT; Richmond, VA; Seattle, Spokane, WA; Milwaukee, WI.

ECKANKAR
P.O. Box 5325, Las Vegas, Nevada 89102

The Path of Total Awareness, achieved through the science of Soul Travel

* Membership Discourses, books, records, tapes, jewelry, sheet music, brochures, prints, charts, parchments available by mail.

Representatives available in all major cities.

ELYSIUM INSTITUTE
5436 Fernwood Avenue, Los Angeles, CA 90027

Provides a clothing-optional supportive environment on a country estate for individuals and families to experience the essential wholesomeness of the human body. Also offers professionally led workshops and seminars in a wide variety of disciplines. Some seminars are held at the In-Town Center in metropolitan Los Angeles.

Elysium Journal of the Senses (quarterly) available, as well as curriculum material for courses on Human Sexuality.

ESALEN INSTITUTE
1793 Union Street, San Francisco, CA 94123

World's largest growth center. Offers a potpourri of workshops in personal growth, interpersonal relations, body consciousness, sports, parapsychology, altered states of consciousness and psychosynthesis.

Free catalogue on request.

Big Sur, San Francisco, CA

EST (ERHARD SEMINARS TRAINING)
1750 Union Street, San Francisco, CA 94123

A 60-hour experience over two consecutive weekends to transform your living so that the situations you have been trying to change or have been putting up with clear up just in the process of life itself. Available after the Training: an ongoing Seminar Program and Educator Workshops. Communication Workshops exist for individuals, professionals, and business groups.

Informational material available by calling or writing any est office.

San Francisco, San Jose, Santa Monica, CA; Aspen, CO; Honolulu, HI; New York, NY.

ESP LABORATORY
7559 Santa Monica Blvd. Los Angeles, CA 90046

Teaches unfolding of psychic faculties, mysticism and magic for enhancement of daily living. International membership participates by mail. Local classes and research.

* Correspondence courses in occultism, mysticism, Tarot, I Ching, magic. Occult supplies and books.

Small groups meet in members' homes throughout the country.

FAMILY UNITY FOUNDATION
P.O. Box 907, San Juan Capistrano, CA 92675

Teaches Religio-therapy, a true synthesis of science and religion. A scriptural truth is thought to be a psychological truth. World Center at Elsinore, CA sponsors free seminars, workshops, lectures, teaching and school.

Books, cassette lectures and *Journal of Vision* for sale.

Elsinore, San Diego, CA.

THE FARM
Summertown, TN

A family monastery of students of Stephen, considered to be a living prophet. He teaches principles of the spiritual life. Day to day living on The Farm is an expression of these principles.

Books and records for sale.

Rural locations in Arizona, Tennessee, West Virginia, Wisconsin.

FRANSISTERS
2168 S. Lafayette Street, Denver, CO 80210 (Mail only)

Interreligious, philosophical; emphasis on importance of women as "form-givers" to ideals in all society—"giving birth to the best" in others as themselves. Conduct Silent Retreats for churches, groups and form retreat places close to nature. Weekly meetings. Occasional guests.

Gentle Living Publications—numerous books to help and inspire. Especially *Toning, the Creative Power of the Voice.*

Centers: Deer Creek, Denver, CO. Teaching only: Arcadia, Lincoln, CA

GANDALF INSTITUTE FOR INNER RESEARCH
#1 Lighthouse Road, Horton Point, Southold, Long Island, NY 11971

A center for retreat, meditation, study, research and spiritual guidance. All disciplines studied. Residency permitted only after a series of interviews. Publications and *GANDALF Gazettes* available in:

Los Angeles, San Francisco, CA; New York, NY; Toronto, ONT.

GAYATRI CENTRE AUM
602 N. 4th Avenue, Tucson, AZ 85705

Classes in astrology, yoga, poetry.

Books and records available by mail. Write for catalog/newsletter (semi-annual).

GESTALT INSTITUTE OF CANADA
P.O. Box 39, Lake Cowichan, B.C.

Founded by Fritz Perls and provides Gestalt therapy as well as training for Gestalt therapists.

GLOBAL YOUTH EVANGELISM
23946 Summit Road, Los Gatos, CA 95030

Training center for Christian ministers. Services open to the public.
* Correspondence course in the Bible. Grass Valley, Los Gatos, CA

GUILD FOR STRUCTURAL INTEGRATION
1776 Union Street, San Francisco, CA 94123

Write for qualified Rolfers near you.

GUNZULUS UNIVERSITY OF SPIRITUALISM
515 Blake Street, Indianapolis, IN 46202

Teaches Bible, occult sciences, Theosophy, astrology, metaphysics, spiritualism, Tarot, numerology, yoga, angelology, theo-therapy and parapsychology. Some free classes open to general public.

Affiliated with American Research University of Astrology and Theosophy, Universal Christian Spiritualist Association and Christian Spiritualist Church—all located at above address.

HARE KRISHNA MOVEMENT
See International Society for Krishna Consciousness

HAROLD INSTITUTE
P.O. Box 11024, Winston-Salem, NC 27106

Promotes the work of Preston Harold, author of *The Shining Stranger* and *The Single Reality*, which brings into harmonious relationship all religions, science, and psychology. Presents a new interpretation of Jesus and other great religious figures that offers a dynamic depth psychology and a new concept of humankind.

Offers Harold's books for sale, cassette tapes and transcripts for group study.

Presents seminars at Centers of other organizations throughout the United States.

HASIDISM See Chabad-Lubavitch

HEALTHY HAPPY HOLY ORGANIZATION—3HO Foundation
1620 Preuss Road, Los Angeles, CA 90035

Classes in Kundalini yoga (Breathing, postures, meditation, chanting) as taught by Yogi Bhajan.

Quarterly magazine—*Beads of Truth*—books and music on tapes and records.

Ashrams: Anaheim, Berkeley, Fairfax, Kings Beach, Long Beach, Los Angeles (6), Palo Alto, Pomona, Redlands, San Francisco, San Rafael, Santa Cruz, Santa Rosa, CA; Boulder, Colorado Springs, Denver, CO; Hartford, CT; Newark, DE; Washington (2), DC; Jacksonville, Miami, Orlando, FL; Atlanta, GA; Honolulu, HI; Boise, ID; Chicago, IL; Ames, IA; New Orleans, LA; Canaan, Milo, ME; Dorchester, Millers Falls, Montague, Worcester, MA; Ann Arbor, Detroit, MI; Minneapolis, MN; Kansas City, St. Louis, MO; Dover, NH; Princeton, NJ; Espanola, NM; Brooklyn, Buffalo, Ithaca, Lyons, New York, Rochester, Syracuse, NY; Durham, NC; Cleveland Heights, Columbus, OH; Oklahoma City, OK; Bend, Corvallis, Eugene, Portland, Salem, OR; Philadelphia, PA; San Juan, PR; Austin, Dallas, Houston, San Antonio,

TX; Salt Lake City, UT; Richmond, VA; Seattle, WA; Madison, WI;— Whonnock, B.C.; Ottawa, Toronto, ONT.

Teaching centers in other communities.

HOLY ORDER OF MANS

International Headquarters, 20 Steiner Street, San Francisco, CA 94117

A service and teaching Order based on the teachings of Jesus Christ and the Ancient Wisdoms. Provides spiritual leadership and Sacraments through a program of Christian Communities, as well as a Lay Order of Discipleship, in addition to training Brothers, Sisters, and Priests within the Order itself.

* Correspondence course in Lay Discipleship and Tarot. Books through The Rainbow Bridge, P.O. Box 40208, San Francisco, CA 94140

San Francisco, CA; Wichita, KS; Cheyenne, WY.

HUMANISM

Nonreligious philosophy that affirms the true, the good and the beautiful in human life. Works to discover the truth and to promote the welfare of individuals. Involved with programs of social welfare as well as those devoted to personal growth and self-understanding.

AMERICAN HUMANIST ASSOCIATION

602 Third Street, San Francisco, CA 94107

Affiliated Chapters: Phoenix, Tucson, AZ; Berkeley, Monterey, Los Angeles, San Diego, San Francisco, San Jose, San Luis Obispo, CA; Fairfield County, CT; Washington, DC: Coral Gables, Jacksonville, Miami, No.

Dade County, Orlando, FL; Atlanta, GA; Chicago, IL; Williamstown, MA; Camden, ME; St Paul, MN; St. Louis, MO; Middletown, New York, NY; Cleveland, Toledo, OH; Tulsa, OK; Philadelphia, Pittsburgh, PA; Providence, RI.

HUMANIST ASSOCIATION OF CANADA

521 Fraser Avenue, Ottawa, 13, ONT.

Affiliated chapters: Calgary, Edmonton, ALTA.; Vancouver, B.C.; Winnipeg, MAN.; Belleville, Hamilton, London, Ottawa, Toronto, ONT.; Montreal, QUE.; Saskatoon, SASK.

IDA P. ROLF FOUNDATION

P.O. Box 1868, Boulder, CO 80302

Training for those wishing to become Rolfing therapists.

INNER LIGHT FOUNDATION

P.O. Box 761, Novato, CA 94947

Teaches simple form of meditation for spiritual growth, inner peace and awareness. Free meditation groups open to all. Foundation is nonprofit, nondenominational, sponsors lectures, publications, radio-TV appearances by head of Foundation, Betty Bethards, mystic and meditation teacher. Also involved in spiritual healing.

Meditation booklet "Way to Awareness" available through Foundation— teaches meditation. Publication list available free by mail.

Free meditation group meetings in private homes at Berkeley, Carmel, Los Angeles, Marin County, Napa, Oakland, Palo Alto, Placerville, Salinas, San Diego, San Francisco, San Jose, Santa Rosa, Solano, Sonoma, Stockton, CA.

INNER NATURE FOUNDATION AND INSTITUTE

1307 Seabright Avenue, Santa Cruz, CA. 95062

P.O. Box 1376 Santa Cruz, CA. 95061

Uniting various groups—Eastern and Western cultures; sharing learning and knowledge with mankind through the media of classes, lectures, seminars, services, etc. Meditation loft and library, Chapel of Inner Man, book store and gift shop. Nondenominational—metaphysical—spiritual—parapsychology.

Publications and tapes.

Associated with Universal Mind Science centers in Hollywood, Long Beach, Mountain View, Redwood City, Santa Barbara, CA.

INNER PEACE MOVEMENT

5103 Connecticut Avenue N.W., Washington, DC 20008

Self-understanding through local group meetings and Camp Programs of the American Leadership College in various locations.

INSTITUTE OF ABILITY

P.O. Box 798, Lucerne Valley, CA 92356

Basic teachings deal with how to relate with other people by discovering your true nature. Specializes in the Enlightenment Intensive, a 3-day marathon where students answer the question, "Who are you?" over and over until they have an inner awakening. Affiliated with Santana Dharma Foundation.

* 30-lesson correspondence course for beginners.

Also books available by mail.

Field instructors: Los Angeles, San Diego, San Francisco, CA; New York, NY.

INSTITUTE OF HUMAN ENGINEERING

3680 E. Fall Ck. Pky, Indianapolis, IN 46205

Integrates the findings of philosophy, science, and religion and combines them with psychology, economics, physics and metaphysics for correlation of the social, political, economic and religious aspects of life.

* Home Study *Science of Man*—48 lessons.

Fundamentals of Human Engineering—Textbook.

INSTITUTE OF MENTALPHYSICS

213 South Hobart Blvd., Los Angeles, CA 90004

Teachings based on the experiences of the founder, Edwin J. Dingle, in China and Tibet. Oriental mysticism based on positive mental attitude, meditation and prana breathing. Classes and correspondence instruction. Sunday services open to the public.

* Principal instruction is through correspondence courses. Books also available.

Los Angeles, Yucca Valley, CA

INSTITUTE OF PSYCHIC SCIENCE, INC.

2015 South Broadway, Little Rock, AR 72206

Classes and workshops in ESP, self-hypnosis, advanced metaphysics, yoga, psychic art, astrology, natural foods, and similar topics. Annual conference of psychic researchers, and monthly seminars of guest speakers. Esoteric Bookstore, magazine *Breakthrough!*

Esoteric and metaphysical books by mail. Catalog—$1.00 refundable with first order. Over 1000 titles.

INTEGRAL YOGA INSTITUTE
P.O. Box 108, Pomfret Center, CT 06259

Teaches theory and practice of meditation, yoga postures, chanting, breath control, deep relaxation, selfless-meditative work. Yoga retreats and public lectures available. Communal spiritual living and teaching centers. Instruction for beginners and advanced students. Yoga instruction in schools and prisons, teacher training programs, community services and drug rehabilitation program.

Record album, cassette tapes of lectures and biography of Sri Swami Satchidananda. Also *Integral Hatha Yoga*, spiritual books and other publications available. Write above address for details.

Integral Yoga Institutes: Los Angeles, San Diego, San Francisco, Santa Cruz, CA; Denver, CO; Washington, DC; Danbury, New Britain, CT; Davenport, IA; Cambridge, MA; Detroit, MI; Columbia, St. Louis, MO; Garfield, NJ; New York (2), NY; Dallas, San Antonio, TX;—Outremont (Montreal), QUE.

INTERNATIONAL CENTER FOR SELF ANALYSIS
102 David Drive, North Syracuse, NY 13212

Yoga centers and ashrams founded by Dr. Rammurti S. Mishra, M.D. Teaches spontaneous psychoanalysis and psychosynthesis, along with meditation. Instruction varies with each ashram, but is based on Vedanta.

Books by Dr. Mishra for sale.

Benson, AZ; San Francisco, CA; Clearwater, Lake Wales, N. Miami Beach, FL; Atlanta, GA; Jamesville, Monroe, North Syracuse, Pulasky, Rochester, Watertown, NY; Columbus, OH; Bothel, WA;—Montreal, QUE.

INTERNATIONAL COOPERATION COUNCIL
17819 Roscoe Blvd., Northridge, CA 91324

A council of almost 150 organizations which "foster the emergence of a new universal man and civilization based upon unity in diversity among all peoples." Includes displays, interest groups, lectures at annual festival, experiential services, workshops, projects throughout the year.

Magazine *The Cooperator*, annual Directory, and monthly newsletter *Spectrum* available by mail.

Los Angeles, San Diego, San Francisco, Santa Barbara, CA; Colorado; Washington, DC: Southern Florida; Chicago, IL; Boston, MA; Kansas City, MO; Las Vegas, NV; New York, NY.

INTERNATIONAL FOUNDATION FOR PSYCHOSYNTHESIS
Linde Medical Plaza, 10921 Wilshire Blvd., Suite 901, Los Angeles, CA 90024

INTERNATIONAL MEDITATION SOCIETY (IMS) See World Plan Executive Council

INTERNATIONAL SOCIETY FOR KRISHNA CONSCIOUSNESS
3764 Watseka Avenue, Los Angeles, CA 90034

Life devoted to worship of Krishna. May live-in full time or practice principles on your own. Nonsectarian, with many different levels of understanding and practice. Instruction to the public.

Birmingham, AL; Laguna Beach, Los Angeles, San Diego, San Francisco, CA; Denver, CO; Washington, DC; Gainseville, Miami, FL; Honolulu, HI; Chicago, IL; New Orleans, LA; Boston, MA; Detroit, MI; St. Louis, MO; Buffalo, New York, NY; Cleveland, OH; Portland, Or; Philadelphia, Pittsburgh, PA; Rio Piedras, PR; Austin, Dallas, Houston, TX; Seattle, WA; New Vrindavan, WV; Vancouver, B.C.; Ottawa, Toronto, ONT.; Montreal, QUE.; Regina, SASK.

KOINONIA FOUNDATION
P.O. Box 5744, Baltimore, MD 21208

An ecumenical spiritual and educational center. Resident terms of 1, 2 and 3 months, including classes, community life and work; weekend conferences in many subject areas; lectures and films; conference and retreat facilities; full-time resident staff community.

LAMA FOUNDATION
P.O. Box 444, San Cristobal, NM 87564

Full-time communal living, limited population. Farming, daily meditation practice, guidance of free school in Taos. A variety of visiting teachers throughout the year, none in residence. Please write for information.

Bountiful Lord's Delivery Service, a series of published teachings given at Lama, Series I or II available by mail.

LIGHT OF YOGA SOCIETY
2404 Kenilworth Road, Cleveland Heights, OH 44106

Classes in yogic philosophy and meditation. Also instruction in vegetarian nutrition. Lectures; Light of Yoga Society Good Food Store; vegetarian restaurant; bookstore.

* Available by mail: *Light of Yoga Society Beginners Manual*; Yoga exercise and meditation record; Alice Christensen and Swami Rama records.

LIVING LOVE CENTER
1730 La Loma Avenue, Berkeley, CA 94709

Teaches the Living Love Way, which is a modern, rapid method of growth towards higher consciousness. Offers weekend trainings which include the Keyes Seminar, the Consciousness Growth Intensive and the Concentrated Growth Experience. All interested are invited to Sunday evening open house at the Center.

Handbook to Higher Consciousness, and *How to Make Your Life Work or Why Aren't You Happy* by Ken Keyes and Tolly Burkan for sale.

THE LOUIS FOUNDATION
P.O. Box 210, Eastbound, WA 98245

Nonprofit spiritual organization whose basic tenet is "service to mankind," for in sharing with others one's spiritual destiny is realized. Many-faceted program: Conferences at Foundation and other locations; chapel services; meditation; instructional program; school for bright students. Opportunity to participate part- or full-time at Foundation Headquarters. Four-year study course for groups of 3 to 12 serious students.

Outlook Press publishes books privately.

THE LOVE PROJECT
4470 Orchard Avenue, San Diego, CA 92107

A way of life based on six basic principles which facilitate putting love into action in daily life. Practice sessions in channeling love energies, open dialogue sharings and group travel experiences offer Seekers the opportunity to seek alternatives which work to counter passive, apathetic, negative, hostile and violent living.

Publishes *The Seeker Newsletter* quarterly. *The Love Project* and other books and pamphlets for sale.

Made up of individuals across the land who are making their own lives viable alternatives of love and peace.

LUCIS TRUST
866 United Nations Plaza, Suite 566-7, New York, NY 10017.

The Lucis Trust is responsible for the Arcane School, Triangles, World Goodwill and the Lucis Publishing Company. Activities dedicated to the establishment of right human relations, promoting the education and the expansion of the human mind toward practice of spiritual principles and values.

* Correspondence course on esoteric training provided by the Arcane School. Books available from the Lucis Publishing Co.

MAHARISHI INTERNATIONAL UNIVERSITY See World Plan Executive Council

MAITRI
Old Forge Road, Wingdale, NY 12594

Residential community applying insights of Buddhist psychology to psychologically disturbed individuals. Training sessions for therapists and students of psychology are offered in conjunction with Naropa Institute, Boulder, CO.

MARK-AGE METACENTER, INC.
327 N.E. 20 Terrace, Miami, FL 33137

Teaches and demonstrates spiritual understanding, development, and mastership of life. Information and education for Second Coming. Weekly taped meditation programs for individuals and groups. University of Life self-study courses for spiritual growth. Healing Haven health department. Complete program for lifting man into his spiritual nature, heritage, powers for new cycle of evolution in Aquarius.

* University of Life courses; meditation and other tape recordings; Mark-Age books, periodicals, magazine by mail and bookdealers.

Santa Monica, CA; Minneapolis, MN; Syracuse, NY; Austin, TX.

MATAGIRI
Mount Tremper, N.Y. 12457

Small community devoted to the Integral Yoga of Sri Aurobindo. No formal classes. Visitors welcome. Serves also as center for information on Sri Aurobindo's teaching, Ashram and new city of Auroville.

Works of Sri Aurobindo, the Mother, their disciples and others sold. Incense and other ashram products sold.

Affiliates: Scottsdale, Sedona, AZ; Aptos, Los Angeles, San Francisco, CA; Boston, MA; Minneapolis, MN; New York, NY; Montreal, QUE.

MEHER BABA CENTERS
P.O. Box 487, Myrtle Beach, SC 29577

Based on the concept that Meher Baba is the God Incarnate of the present age. Members consider the most direct path to salvation is complete love and surrender to Meher Baba. Meetings consist of introduction to Baba and his works. In addition are meditations and prayers.

Books by Baba for sale.

Berkeley, CA; Boulder, CO; Fairfield, CT; Miami Beach, FL; Chicago, IL; Detroit, MI; New York, Schenectady, NY; Portland, OR; Myrtle Bach, SC.

MORENO INSTITUTE, INC.
259 Wolcott Avenue, Beacon, NY 12508

Sociometry, group psychotherapy, psychodrama, encounter groups, sensitivity training, group dynamics and creativity training. In-residence training program in Beacon only.

Affiliates: Phoenix, AZ; Berkeley, Long Beach, Los Angeles, CA; Denver, CO; Beacon, New York, NY;— Montreal, QUE.

NAROPA INSTITUTE See Vajradhatu

NICHIREN SHOSHU OF AMERICA
1351 Ocean Front Blvd., Santa Monica, CA 90401

A buddhist laymen's organization dedicated to achieving world peace through the happiness of each individual. Emphasizes chanting of a mantra and mass get-togethers. Discussion meetings are held in private homes.

Activity centers: Culver City, Montebello, San Diego, San Pablo, Santa Monica, CA; Denver, CO; Washington, DC: Atlanta, GA; Honolulu, HI; Chicago, IL; Boston, MA; Mt. Rainier, MD; New York, NY; Philadelphia, PA; Dallas, TX; Seattle, WA. Also Student Associations are active on most U.S. campuses.

NORTHERN CALIFORNIA ENLIGHTENMENT COOPERATIVE
2748 Grande Vista Avenue, Oakland, CA 94601

Offer Enlightenment Intensives similar to Abilitism. Also other forms of emotional release are taught.

NTL INSTITUTE
P.O. Box 9155, Rosslyn Station, VA 22209

The first organization to employ Sensitivity Training.

Laboratories in Professional Development, Management Development, Organization Development and Personal Interaction.

Laboratory centers: Santa Cruz, CA; Bethel, ME.

Most programs are conducted during the summer throughout the country.

NYINGMA INSTITUTE See Tibetan Nyingma Meditation Center

OASIS, MIDWEST CENTER FOR HUMAN POTENTIAL
6 W. Ontario, Chicago, IL 60610

Offers variety of lectures, films, classes, weekend seminars including astrology, meditation, massage, Tai Chi, Yoga, psychic training.

PSYCHIC WORLD NEWS
P.O. Box 5504, Fort Lauderdale, FL 33310

The purpose of this newspaper is to publish, as a service, correlative, authenticated sources of information derived from various research studies in the field of psychic sciences, including natural health; to act as a means of communication to the public; to pool scientific data for the further advancement and education of this knowledge.

Subscription to *Psychic World News* and international research participation memberships available. Free information upon request and advertising rates.

Ft. Lauderdale, Miami, FL.

PSYCHOSYNTHESIS

Synthesis of individual physical, mental and spiritual aspects into a harmonious operating whole. Professional training programs, workshops, individual consultation, and educational services. Most independent centers provide all the above services. Many also can provide books, articles and other materials on psychosynthesis and related subjects. Write for information to any of the following.

Independent Centers:

INSTITUTE CANADIEN DE PSYCHOSYNTHESE

3496 Avenue Marlowe, Montreal 260, QUE.

PSYCHOSYNTHESIS INSTITUTE

576 Everett, Palo Alto, CA 94301

PSYCHOSYNTHESIS RESEARCH FOUNDATION

40 East 49th Street, Room 1902, New York, NY 10017

RAINBOW ZEN

#22A Smith River, Drain, OR. 97435

Pantheistic communal anarchy. Gardening and simple crafts. No gas or electricity. Also, no unannounced guests, please.

Drain, Garrick Beck, OR.

RAJNEESH MEDITATION CENTERS (Neo-Sannyas International)

P.O. Box 143, East Islip, NY 11730; or P.O. Box 22174, San Francisco, CA 94122

Teaches Tantric, Sufi and nontraditional psychologically oriented techniques (including chaotic meditation) devised by Bhagwan Rajneesh. Lectures and evening, all-day, or weekend workshops at centers and throughout the USA and Canada on invitation. Books, magazines, reprints and tapes by Rajneesh for sale.

Los Angeles, San Francisco, CA; Washington, DC; Miami Beach, FL; Chicago, Urbana, IL; Boston, Cambridge, MA; Brooklyn, E. Islip, Larchmont, New York, NY; Portland, OR; Philadelphia, PA; Seattle, WA;—Toronto, ONT; Montreal, QUE.

RELIGIOUS SCIENCE INTERNATIONAL

P.O. Box 486, Fillmore, CA 93015

Two basic courses conducted by ministers locally. Advanced courses for those becoming practitioners or becoming ministers.

Mesa, Scottsdale, Tucson, AZ: Alamo, Altadena, Anaheim, Barstow, Canoga Park, Cathedral City, Costa Mesa, El Cajon, Escondido, Fillmore, Fresno, Glendale, Granada Hills, Hayward, Hollywood, Huntington Park, Inglewood, Long Beach, Los Angeles, Los Gatos, Monte Bello, Monterey, Palo Alto, Paradise, Redondo Beach, San Clemente, San Diego, Seaside, Simi, Thousand Oaks, Van Nuys, Visalia, CA; Cape Coral, Clearwater, Ft. Lauderdale, Lakeworth, St. Petersburg, Winter Park, FL; Kailua Kona, HI; Chicago, Peoria, IL; Ft. Wayne, IN; Closter, Morristown, Plainfield, NJ; Albany, New York, White Plains, NY; Cincinnati, Dayton, OH; Eugene, Medford, Roseburg, Salem, OR; Spokane, WA;—Calgary, ALTA.

RELIGIOUS SCIENCE, UNITED CHURCH OF, See United Church of Religious Science

ROLFING See Ida P. Rolf Foundation and various growth centers

THE ROSICRUCIAN FELLOW-SHIP

P.O. Box 713, Oceanside, CA 92054

Teaches esoteric Christianity; explains mystery of life and being; correlates science and religion; teaches spiritual astrology; offers spiritual healing.

* Correspondence courses in Philosophy, spiritual astrology and Bible for a free will offering. Books for sale.

Study Groups: Los Angeles, CA; Newark, NJ; Rochester, NY; Seattle, WA.

ROSICRUCIAN FRATERNITY

Beverly Hall Corporation—Philosophical Publishing Co.

P.O. Box 220, Quakertown, PA 18951

World headquarters of the organization known as the Fraternity of Initiates, which emphasizes the esoteric, the arcane and the occult; used as a place for ceremonials, rites and initiations and for study by selected students.

Also see Altora Soul Science Academy

ROSICRUCIAN ORDER— A.M.O.R.C.

Rosicrucian Park, San Jose, CA 95191

A nonsectarian body of men and women devoted to the investigation, study and practical application of natural and spiritual laws. The purpose of A.M.O.R.C. is to enable everyone to live in harmony with the creative, constructive cosmic forces for the attainment of health, happiness and peace.

* Principal instruction is by correspondence, which is a part of the membership privileges along with books, records and other paraphernalia.

Lodges: Long Beach, Los Angeles, Oakland, San Francisco, Sepulveda, CA; Miami, FL; Chicago, IL; Boston, MA; Detroit, MI; St. Louis, MO; New York, NY; Oklahoma City, OK; Portland, OR; Philadelphia, Pittsburgh, PA; San Juan, PR; Dallas, TX; Seattle, WA.—Vancouver, B.C.; Toronto, ONT.; Montreal, QUE.

Also Chapters and Pronaoi in many other cities throughout the United States and Canada.

RUHANI SATSANG— DIVINE SCIENCE OF THE SOUL

221 West Broadway, Anaheim, CA 92803

Class and personal instruction in morality, religious union and Surat Shabel (sound current) yoga. Initiation is by guru's grace, a subjective experience projected from Master Kirpal Singh. 2 Satsangs: Sunday—10:30 a.m. meditation, 11:00 a.m. Satsang Wednesday—7:30 p.m. meditation, 8:00 p.m. Satsang.

Books by Kirpal Singh available.

Anaheim, Arcata, Beaumont, Fresno, Glendale, Hollywood, Los Angeles, Monterey Peninsula, Oakland, Orangevale, Piru, San Diego, San Francisco, San Jose, San Juan, Capistrano, Santa Barbara, Santa Rosa, Silverado, CA; Colorado Springs, Denver, Fort Collins, CO; New Haven, CT; Washington, DC; Fort Lauderdale, Gainesville, Lake Worth, Miami, New Port Richey, Orlando, Pensacola, St. Petersburg, Tallassee, Tampa, Venice, FL; Atlanta, GA; Chicago, Evanston, Gilson, Urbana, IL; Louisville, KY; Clinton, ME; Amherst, Boston, Rockport, Vineyard Haven, MA; Detroit, Grand Rapids, Lansing, Mt. Clemens, MI; Minneapolis, St. Paul, MN; Hanover, Sanbornton, NH; Princeton, NJ; Santa Fe, NM; Buffalo, Croton-on-Hudson, Ithaca, Long

Island, New York, Rochester, Rockland, Syracuse, NY; Charlotte, NC; Cincinnati, Cleveland, Kent, Toledo, OH; Gold-Hill, Portland, OR; Philadelphia, State College, Wallingford, PA; Austin, Cookville, Dallas, Houston, TX; Salt Lake City, UT; Charlottesville, Richmond, Sumerduck, Vienna, VA; Seattle, WA; Greenfield, WI; Edmonton, ALTA.; Powell River, Vancouver, Victoria, B.C.; Toronto, ONT.; Montreal, QUE.

SANTANA DHARMA FOUNDATION
Crystal Valley Retreat, P.O. Box 798, Lucerne Valley, CA 92356

Retreats and ongoing residential programs in Sahaj Yog, the natural yoga, as revealed to Yogeshwar Muni (Charles Berner) by Swami Kripaliananda. It is a yoga of opening your mind to the indwelling Divine experience. Write for prerequisites.

Affiliated with the Institute of Ability (which see).

SAN FRANCISCO ZEN CENTER
See Zen

SATHYA SAI BABA CENTER AND BOOK STORE
7911 Willoughby Avenue, Los Angeles, CA 90046

Bookstore open weekdays—check for current hours.
Thursday evening—8 p.m., *Bhajans* (devotional songs) and meditation.
Friday evening—8 p.m., *Bhajans,* meditation, films and guest speakers.

Books, records, tapes, photos, films and slides available by mail.

Affiliates: San Diego, Santa Barbara, San Francisco, Grass Valley, Tustin, CA; Madison, WI; S. Glastonbury,

CT; Honolulu, HI; New York, NY; Chicago, IL.

SCIENCE OF MIND See Religious Science International and United Church of Religious Science

SCIENTOLOGY See Church of Scientology

SELF-REALIZATION FELLOWSHIP
3880 San Rafael Avenue, Los Angeles, CA 90065

Founded by Paramahansa Yogananda, author of *Autobiography of a Yogi.* Presents his Raja yoga teachings through printed studies, public lectures and classes, and counseling for members.
* Printed correspondence studies, books, a quarterly magazine, records and cassettes available.

Inquiries into the teachings and center locations for Self-Realization Fellowship should be directed to the above address.

SHORES OF LIGHT
P.O. Box 35933, Houston, TX 77035

Attempting to form a bridge between East and West. Explores various philosophies and paths such as Zen, Taoism and Buddhism. Offers courses through the University of Thought, a community university. Public lectures, group and individual instruction.

Carries on correspondence with interested people.

SILVA MIND CONTROL INTERNATIONAL, INC.
P.O. Box 1149, 1110 Cedar Avenue, Laredo, TX 78040

Mind Control Basic Course (40–48 hours)

taught all over U.S. and Canada. Instruction in controlled relaxation, general self-improvement, effective sensory projection and applied effective sensory projection. *Mind Control Graduate Course (30–35 hours)* taught in U.S. and Canada. In-depth study of history and theories of mind, examples of mind functioning in altered states of awareness and advanced techniques in self programing.

Some books for sale—tapes available to graduates.

Courses taught in over 100 cities and towns throughout the U.S. and Canada. Inquire at above address.

SIDDHARTHA FOUNDATION FOR THE STUDY OF HIGHER CONSCIOUSNESS
91 Dobbins Street, Waltham, MA 02154

Produces radio and TV programs dealing with higher consciousness and New Age awareness. Offers lectures, workshops and panels on these topics, especially on Positive Energy and Healing, to organizations, schools and foundations. Broadcast inquiries invited.

Offers books and over 90 half-hour interviews "On the Path to Higher Consciousness"—talks with New Age Leaders. List on request.

SIVANANDA YOGA ASHRAM
8th Avenue, Val Morin, QUE.

Permanent living facilities and camp for guests. Teaches all aspects of yoga. Strong emphasis on Hatha Yoga, meditation and Hindu philosophy. Also offers a yoga teachers training course.

Branch centers: Los Angeles, San Francisco, CA; Washington, DC; Fort Lauderdale, Orlando, Palm Beach, FL; Chicago, IL; New York, NY;— Hamilton, Toronto, ONT.; Montreal, Quebec, QUE.

THE SKY (SWAMI KUVALAYAN-ANDA YOGA) FOUNDATION
10 South Front Street, Philadelphia, PA 19106

Scientifically oriented yoga institute. Interested in research. Deals with physical, mental and spiritual aspects of yoga. Teaches yoga techniques and philosophy to a variety of people— young, old, normal, sick and addicts. Participation can be part- or full-time.

Books, journals, records and tapes available by mail.

Affiliates: Rutherford, NJ; Elkins Park, PA.

SOHAM YOGA CENTER
63 East Adams, Chicago, IL 60603

Offers classes in exercises, philosophy, positive mental techniques, asanas, breathing, meditation.

Books available at the center.

S.O.M.A. INSTITUTE
526 Green Street, Cambridge, MA 02139

Classes in Sufi dancing, meditation, healing herbology, music therapy, art therapy, Drums as Melody, Principles of Sound, African Dance, Roots of Religion.

Also available from above address are 90-minute cassette tapes of chants and songs of the Guru Blanket Band.

SRI CHINMOY CENTRE
P.O. Box 32433, Jamaica, NY 11431

Sri Chinmoy is a God-realized master who teaches the path of Love, Devotion and Surrender to God. He guides his disciples inwardly in meditation, bringing forth the individual soul of each disciple. Group meditations are held at each center and arrangements can be made to attend by contacting the respective center.

Books by mail from Aum Publications, 85-45 149th Street, Jamaica, NY 11435

Phoenix, AZ; Corona del Mar, Los Angeles, San Francisco, Santa Barbara, CA; Norwalk, CT; Washington, DC; Miami, FL; Honolulu, HI; Chicago, IL; Kansas City, St. Louis, MO; Jamaica, New York, NY; Toledo, OH; Eugene, OR; Ponce, San Juan, PR; Milwaukee, WI;—Vancouver, Victoria, B.C.; Halifax, N.S.; Ottawa, Toronto, ONT.; Montreal, QUE.

STRUCTURAL INTEGRATION
See Ida P. Rolf Foundation and various growth centers

STUDENTS INTERNATIONAL MEDITATION SOCIETY (SIMS)
See World Plan Executive Council

SUBUD, U.S.A.
P.O. Box 1166, San Rafael, CA 94902

Group practice of direct opening up to God, resulting in self-knowledge, revelation and enlightenment.

Numerous chapters throughout the country. See your local phone book or inquire at above address.

SUFI ORDER
408 Precita Avenue, San Francisco, CA 94110

A universal esoteric school which teaches meditation, spiritual dance and walk, music and other New Age methods to awaken the inner being of mankind. Public meetings are held and there is individual and group instruction for members.

* An instructional manual giving meditation techniques is available from Meditation Manual, 147 Humbolt Avenue, San Anselmo, CA 94960. Esoteric books available through Rainbow Bridge, 3548 22nd Street, San Francisco, CA 94114

Tucson, AZ; Corte Madera, Hollywood, Novato, San Anselmo, San Francisco, Santa Cruz, CA; Boulder, CO; Chicago, IL; Bloomington, IND; Boston, Cambridge, MA; New York (3), Unidilla, Woodstock, NY; Berea, Cleveland, OH; Portland, OR; Philadelphia, PA; San Antonio, TX;—Toronto, ONT.

SYNANON FOUNDATION, INC.
1215 Clay Street, Oakland, CA 94612

Synanon is an alternative lifestyle, 24 hours a day for ex-drug addicts, character-disordered persons, and normal individuals alike. There are approximately 1,300 men, women and children living in an environment free of drugs, tobacco and alcohol.

Literature upon request.

Badger, Marshall, Oakland, San Francisco, Santa Monica, CA; Detroit, MI; New York, NY.

TEACHING OF THE INNER CHRIST (TIC)
2333 Albatross Street, San Diego, CA 92101

Sunday meetings, 9:30 and 11:00 a.m., Wednesday Healing Meetings, 8:00 p.m., week night classes in Inner Christ contact, meditation, Inner Sensitivity, Prayer Therapy, Leadership, and ministerial training. No communal living facilities. Youth meetings Sunday, 7:00 p.m.

Books available by mail.

Berkeley, Chula Vista, Escondido,

Long Beach, San Diego, CA; Salt Lake City, UT.

THE ZEN CENTER See Zen

3HO See Healthy Happy Holy Organization

TIBETAN NYINGMA MEDITATION CENTER

2425 Hillside Avenue, Berkeley, CA 94704

Center for the study of the religious practices of Tibetan Buddhism, under the direction of the reincarnate lama, Rinpoche, Tarthang Tulku. There are about 70 students living and working on various projects for the preservation of Tibetan culture and philosophy, operation of Dharma Press and Dharma Publishing. Open to new students by application and interview.

Books and posters available from Dharma Publishing, 5856 Doyle Street, Emeryville, CA

Affiliates:
Myingma Institute of Phoenix—Phoenix, AZ
Nyingma Institute—Berkeley, CA

TOPANGA CENTER FOR HUMAN DEVELOPMENT

2247 North Topanga Canyon Blvd., Topanga, CA 90291

Weekend workshops, Friday and Saturday night drop-in group programs, on-going groups, training course in facilitating communication.

TRADITIONAL MARTINIST ORDER

Rosicrucian Park, San Jose, CA 95191

A system of Christian mysticism, much of which is based on the Kabbala. Teaches how to commune with the Divine consciousness within and how to apply such wisdom to the earthly realm.

Los Angeles, San Jose, CA; Chicago, IL; New York, NY

TRANSCENDENTAL MEDITATION (TM) See World Plan Executive Council

THE UNIFICATION CHURCH INTERNATIONAL

1365 Connecticut Avenue N.W., Washington, DC 20036

Based on an evolution of Judeo-Christian thought and incorporating aspects of Oriental philosophy, the Church teaches that mankind is entering a new spiritual age—the age when one world family will emerge and God and Man will become one. The Church was founded by the Rev. Sun Myung Moon of Korea.

Books containing the teachings of the Church and speeches by Rev. Moon are for sale.

Birmingham, AL; Anchorage, AK; Phoenix, AZ; Little Rock, AK; Alhambra, Berkeley, Fresno, Fullerton, Menlo Park, Oakland, Sacramento, San Diego, San Francisco, San Jose, Van Nuys, CA; Boulder, CO; New Haven, CT; Wilmington, DE; Washington, DC; Miami, Tampa, FL; Athens, Atlanta, Savannah, GA; Honolulu, HI; Boise, ID; Chicago, IL; Indianapolis, IN; Ames, Des Moines, Dubuque, Iowa City, IA; Wichita, KS; Louisville, KY; Baton Rouge, New Orleans, LA; Bangor, Portland, ME; Baltimore, MD; Amherst, Brookline, Worcester, MA; Detroit, MI; Duluth, Mankato, Minneapolis, MN; Jackson, MS; Kansas City, St. Louis, Springfield, MO; Bozeman, Helena, Missoula, MT; Lincoln, Omaha, NE;

Las Vegas, NV; Durham, Manchester, NH; Hightstown, Princeton, NJ; Albuquerque, NM; Albany, Flushing, Forest Hills, Hempstead, L.I., Ithaca, New Rochelle, Staten Island, White Plains, New York, NY; Raleigh, NC; Fargo, ND; Cincinnati, Columbus, OH; Philadelphia, Pittsburgh, State College, PA; Cranston, RI; Columbia, SC; Sioux Falls, SD; Nashville, TN; Austin, Dallas, Houston, TX; Salt Lake City, UT; Burlington, Montpelier, VT; Reston, Richmond, VA; Seattle, Spokane, QA; Charleston, Huntington, WV; Milwaukee, WI; Laramie, WY.

UNITED CHURCH OF RELIGIOUS SCIENCE

3251 West 6th Street, Los Angeles, CA 90020

Teaches that you create your own destiny. Provides three 8-month-long courses locally in how to do that, along with ministerial and doctoral training. Public is invited to all services.

* 48 lesson correspondence course in lieu of the 1st local course.

Authorized teaching chapters: Phoenix, Tucson, AZ; Alamo, Apple Valley, Bakersfield, Beverly Hills, Burbank, Claremont, Covina, Downey, El Centro, Fresno, Fullerton, Hemet, Huntington Beach, Huntington Park, La Crescenta, Laguna Beach, La Jolla, Lakewood, Lancaster, Long Beach, Los Angeles, Magnolia Park, Manhattan Beach, Modesto, Napa, Newport Beach, North Hollywood, Oakland, Palmdale, Palm Desert, Palm Springs, Paradise, Pasadena, Redlands, Reseda, Riverside, Sacramento, San Bernardino, San Diego, San Fernando, San Francisco, San Jose, San Mateo, San Pedro, Santa Ana, Santa Barbara, Santa Cruz, Santa Rosa, Seal Beach, Sun City, Vellejo, Ventura, Vista, Westchester, Whittier, CA; Colorado Springs, Denver, CO; Lakeland, Miami, Orlando, FL; Atlanta, GA; Honolulu, HI; Boise, ID; St. Louis, MO; Las Vegas, Reno, NV; Albuquerque, Santa Fe, NM; Cincinnati, Cleveland, OH; Oklahoma City, Tulsa, OK; Portland, OR; Arlington, Dallas, Ft. Worth, TX; Seattle, WA—Vancouver, B.C.

UNIVERSAL GREAT BROTHERHOOD, AQUARIAN UNIVERSAL MISSION

6002 Pershing, St. Louis, MO 63112

The U.G.B. promotes social services and centers for the study and practice of Aquarian Disciplines—yoga, meditation, cosmobiology, esoteric and exoteric study and service. These Centers serve as training grounds for the INIATIC SCHOOLS, which are the ancient schools of wisdom that the U.G.B. has been authorized to reopen publicly in the New Age.

Teachings of the Masters—translated and distributed by the U.G.B.—are available from the Initiatic Esoteric Service, 6002 Pershing, St. Louis, MO 63112

Montebello, National City, San Diego, CA; Carlinville, IL; Ann Arbor, Ypsilanti, MI; Arnold, Bridgeton, St. Louis, MO; Tulsa, OK; Oakland, OR.

UNIVERSITY OF THE TREES

P.O. Box 644, Boulder Creek, CA 95006

Students work daily on a three-year course either at Boulder Creek or by correspondence. Weekly meditation and discussion sessions on Fridays at 7 p.m. at 13185 Pine Street, Boulder Creek. Inquire first.

* Three-year correspondence course in Direct Enlightenment.

Affiliate: Center Nucleus and World Yoga Society, 131 West 75th Street, New York, NY 10023

URANTIA FOUNDATION
633 Diversy Parkway, Chicago, IL 60614

Teaches the nature of the Cosmos as revealed in its cosmological bible, supposedly found in its complete form by the Foundation.

* Urantia Book, a complete form of the found bible available by mail.

Urantia brotherhood centers throughout the country. Inquire at the above address.

VAJRADHATU
1111 Pearl Street, Boulder, CO 80302

Buddhist meditation under direction of Chogyam, Rinpoche, a Tibetan lama.

Vajradhatu Recordings and recordings of seminars and lectures available by mail.

Centers: Berkeley, CA; Boulder, Farista, Livermore, CO; Barnet, VT

Dharmadhatus: Berkeley, Los Angeles, San Francisco, CA; Washington, DC; Chicago, IL; Bloomington, IN; Boston, MA; Austin, Houston, San Antonio, TX;—Toronto, ONT.; Montreal, QUE.

Affiliates:
Naropa Institute—Boulder, CO
Maitri—Elizabethtown, NY

VEDANTA SOCIETIES

All teach Jnana, Bhakti, Karma and Raja yoga to suit your specific personality. Swamis provide lectures, classes and individual instruction to serious seekers. Weekly services open to the public. ·

Most Vedanta Societies have books and literature for sale on the premises. Inquire for mail order.

Independent Vedanta Societies:

VEDANTA SOCIETY OF NORTHERN CALIFORNIA
2323 Vallejo Street, San Francisco, CA 94123
Affiliates—Berkeley, Carmichael, CA

VEDANTA SOCIETY OF SOUTHERN CALIFORNIA
1946 Vedanta Place, Hollywood, CA 90028
Affiliates—Santa Barbara, Trabuco Canyon, CA

VIVEKANANDA VEDANTA SOCIETY
5423 South Hyde Park Blvd., Chicago, IL 60615

THE RAMAKRISHANA—VEDANTA SOCIETY OF MASSACHUSETTS
58 Deerfield Street, Boston, MA 02215

THE VEDANTA SOCIETY OF ST. LOUIS
205 South Skinner Blvd., St. Louis, MO 63105

RAMAKRISHNA-VIVEKANANDA CENTER
17 East 94th Street, New York, NY 10028

VEDANTA SOCIETY
34 West 71st Street, New York, NY 10023

VEDANTA SOCIETY OF PORTLAND
1157 South East 55th Avenue, Portland, OR 97215

THE VEDANTA SOCIETY OF PROVIDENCE
224 Angell Street, Providence, RI 02906

RAMAKRISHNA VEDANTA CENTER
2716 Broadway East, Seattle, WA 98102

VEDANTA SOCIETY
5 Hookwood Drive, Agincourt, ONT.

WAILUA UNIVERSITY OF CONTEMPLATIVE ARTS
Kapaa, On the Garden Island, HI 96746

Founded by Master Subramuniya. Teaches the Hindu tradition of Bhakti, Karma, Raja, and Jnana yoga with the stress on Siva worship. Advanced training requires a disciplined monastic life at one of the monasteries in Nevada, California or Hawaii. Courses and temple services are available to students only.

* *"The Master Course*—Part One" is a 12-week cassette course in meditation and Hindu mysticism. Books of Master's teachings are available through Comstock House in Virginia City, Nevada.

San Francisco, CA; Kapaa, Kona, Lahaina, HI; Virginia City, NV

WASHINGTON BUDDHIST VIHARA
5017 16th Street N.W., Washington, DC 20011

Ven. D. Piyananda Mahathera, President
Ven. H. Gunaratana Mahathera, Secretary General
The vihara is open daily and holds a Sunday service.
Meditations: Sunday—3:30 p.m.; Tuesday—7:30 p.m.; Wednesday—7:30 p.m.; Saturday—2:00 p.m. (for children).
Numerous Buddhist books available. Write for catalog.

WELL-SPRINGS
11667 Alba Road, Ben Lomond, CA 95005

Teaches relaxation techniques combined with movement-to-music and creative activities as means to self-discovery and growth. Day, week workshops; leadership training courses and private counseling sessions.
* The Well-Springs Series is available on records and cassettes. *Reminders from Well-Springs*, a booklet, is also for sale.

Aptos, Del Mar, Los Altos, San Diego, San Jose, CA; Santa Fe, NM; Seattle, WA.

WILSHIRE BOOK COMPANY
8721 Sunset Blvd., Los Angeles, CA 90069

Sells books and records on self hypnosis and numerous other subjects.

WORLD PLAN EXECUTIVE COUNCIL
1015 Gayley Avenue, Los Angeles, CA 90024

Provides instruction in Transcendental Meditation (TM) and the Science of Creative Intelligence (SCI). Includes International Meditation Society (IMS), Students International Meditational Society (SIMS), American Foundation for the Science of Creative Intelligence (AFCSI) and Spiritual Regeneration Movement (SRM). Maharishi International University is a separate corporation.

Regional centers: Berkeley, Los Angeles, San Francisco, CA; Denver, CO; New Haven, CT; Washington, DC; Miami, FL; Atlanta, GA; Honolulu, HI; Chicago, IL; Des Moines, IA; Cambridge, MA; Detroit, MI; Minneapolis, MN; Kansas City, St. Louis, MO; New York, NY; Columbus, OH; Philadelphia, PA; Houston, TX; Seattle, WA.

Over 330 additional centers throughout the U.S. and Canada.

YASODHARA ASHRAM
Kootenay Bay, B.C. VOB1X0

This "Community of Light" has a core group of 15 permanent residents. Includes farm, print shop, recording studio, bookstore, workshops in Yoga and contemporary growth techniques; 3-month intensive Yoga Teachers Course. Also 6-week work-study program. Spiritual leader is Swami Radha.

Spiritual bookstore. Tapes & records by Swami Radha. Mail order catalog.

YOGA CENTER OF ST. LOUIS
1502 Big Bend Blvd., Richmond Heights, MO 63117

Hatha yoga, meditation, Yamis study groups, Tai Chi Ch'uan, vegetarian dinners, nutrition classes, astrology.

Arnold, St. Louis, MO.

Affiliated with the Universal Great Brotherhood S.R.F.

YOGI GUPTA ASSOCIATION
127 East 56 Street, New York, NY 10022

Gives daily classes in Yoga postures, breathing, concentration, relaxation, and meditation in group and private lessons. Free introductory lesson offered. Public lectures are held weekly. Instruction is available for beginner, intermediate and advanced students.

* Instruction books and records available.

YOGA AND HEALTH CENTER
3212 Oaklawn, Dallas, TX 75219

Hatha yoga instruction. East Indian

grocery. Communal gathering and discussions once a month.

Occult and astrology books. Lending library.

YOGA ORGANIZATION FOR RESEARCH AND EDUCATION (YORE)
P.O. Box 417, Rutherford, NJ 07070

Teaches meditation, Hatha, Laya and Raja yogas. Also specializes in courses for people with psychological problems including those associated with alcoholism, drug abuse, retardation, and aging. Conducts and supports research in use of yoga. Gives retreats of one day and longer and holds monthly Sat-Sanga (informal gathering with speaker).

* By Katherine Da Silva: *Yoga–Ten Practical Lessons* (Vol. I & II) by mail. Record: *HATHA YOGA I*

Affiliated with Swami Kuvalyananda Yoga Foundation (SKY) 10 South Front Street, Philadelphia, PA

YOUNG LIFE
720 West Monument Blvd., Colorado Springs, CO 80901

Christian movement that conducts meetings on high school campuses and in private homes all over the U.S. and Canada.

See your local phone directory for the club nearest you.

YOUTH FOR CHRIST
P.O. Box 419, Wheaton, IL 60187

Program to bring Christianity to high-school-age people.

Meetings in private homes. Lectures, Bible study and rap sessions.

Campus Life magazine available by subscription. Books also available.

Over 300 local programs throughout

the United States and Canada. See your phone book.

ZEN

Japanese adaptation of Buddhist philosophy and techniques. Independent Zen Centers (listed alphabetically by state):

CALIFORNIA BOSATSUKAI
(Flower Sangha)
5632 Greek Oak Drive, Los Angeles, CA 90028

Affiliates: Los Gatos, San Diego, CA

CIMARRON ZEN CENTER OF RINZAI-JI
2505 Cimarron Street, Los Angeles, CA 90018

Daily meditation meetings open to the public. Instruction in Zen. Limited communal accommodations for regular members. Joshu Sasaki Roshi, director.

Tapes of chanting with lecture by Zen Master available, also new translation of Mumonkan.

Affiliates: Mt. Baldy, Redondo Beach, CA; Princeton, NJ; Jemez Springs, NM; Vancouver, B.C.

GENJO-JI
Wisteria Way and Almonte Blvd., Mill Valley, CA 94941

SAN FRANCISCO ZEN CENTER
300 Page Street, San Francisco, CA 94102

Resident participation at three main practice centers. Opportunity for varying degrees of participation by nonresident members and nonmembers. Instruction in zazen meditation at San Francisco. Guest dormitory space sometimes available.

Centers: San Francisco, Green Gulch Farm (Marin County), Zen Mountain Center (Tassajara), CA

Affiliates: Berkeley, Los Altos, CA

SANTA BARBARA ZEN GROUP
333 East Anapamu Street, Santa Barbara, CA 93105

ZEN MISSION SOCIETY
RR 1, Box 577, Mount Shasta, CA 96067

DIAMOND SANGHA
R.R. 1, Box 702, Haiku, HI 96708

Group and individual training in zazen, following the Harada-Yasutani line of Zen Buddhism, with koan study and a schedule of work and retreats. Residential and community memberships; visitors welcomed.

* Brochure, semi-annual journal, and instruction by mail are available.

Haiku (Maui), and Honolulu, HI

MINNEAPOLIS ZEN MEDITATION CENTER
419 5th Street S.E., Minneapolis, MN 55414

FIRST ZEN INSTITUTE OF AMERICA
113 East 30th Street, New York, NY 10016

NEW YORK ZEN CENTER
440 West End Avenue, New York, NY 10024

NEW YORK ZENDO OF THE ZEN STUDIES SOCIETY, INC.
223 East 67th Street, New York, NY 10021

Zen meditation in the Rinzai tradition, with daily practice by members under the guidance of Eido Shimano Roshi. Open public meeting on Thursday evenings with beginning instruction—6:15 to 9:00 p.m.

Affiliates: Chestnut Hill, MA; Livingston Manor, NY; Philadelphia, PA; Delaplane, VA

THE ZEN CENTER
7 Arnold Park, Rochester, NY 14607

Weekend instruction in Zen for nonmembers at intensive workshops. Residential and nonresidential practice for members.

Books available.

Affiliates: Englewood (Denver), CO; Jacksonville, St. Petersburg, FL; Atlanta, GA; Chicago, IL; Arlington (Boston), MA; Kingston, Toronto, ONT.; Montreal, QUE.

GREEN MOUNTAIN ZEN CENTER
Wardsboro, VT 05355

ZEN CENTER OF VANCOUVER
139 Water Street, Vancouver 3 B.C.

THE ZEN CENTRE
569 Christie Street, Toronto, ONT.

Additional source material about psycho-spiritual organizations:

A List of Organizations for the Practice of Zen Buddhism in the United States by Ronald W. Hadley

The most complete directory of Zen groups in the U.S. with details on practices, schedules, etc. Write c/o Alexander Levin—Chinese Dept. Dartmouth College, Hanover, NH 03755. Priced over $5.00

SPIRITUAL COMMUNITY GUIDE
P.O. Box 1080—San Rafael, CA 94902

Excellent up-to-date index to many psycho-spiritual organizations in the United States and Canada. It is updated every year. Contains hundreds of names and addresses of centers, ashrams, schools, bookstores, organic restaurants and food stores. Available in many bookstores.

Appendix B

CORRESPONDENCE INSTRUCTION

ALTORA SOUL SCIENCE ACADEMY
Guidance letters in traditions of the Quakertown Rosicrucians

ARCANA WORKSHOPS
Meditation training

ARICA INSTITUTE
2-record set on meditation and mantra

ASTARA
Course includes organized plan of esoteric study

BUILDERS OF THE ADYTUM
Course in Kabbala, Tarot, alchemy and esoteric astrology

CENTER FOR SPIRITUAL AWARENESS
Course in meditation and occult sciences

CHAKPORI-LING FOUNDATION SANGHA, INC.
Future course in acupuncture

DIAMOND SANGHA
Zen instruction

ECKINKAR
Course in Soul Travel

ESP LABORATORY
Courses in occultism, mysticism, Tarot, I Ching and magic

GLOBAL YOUTH EVANGELISM
Course in the Bible

HOLY ORDER OF MANS
Course in lay Christian discipleship and in Tarot

INSTITUTE OF ABILITY
30 lessons in self-awareness

INSTITUTE OF HUMAN ENGINEERING
48 lessons in the Science of Man

INSTITUTE OF MENTALPHYSICS
Courses in breathing, meditation and Tibetan philosophy

LIGHT OF YOGA SOCIETY
Light of Yoga Society Beginners Manual

LUCIS TRUST
Course on esoteric wisdom

MARK-AGE METACENTER, INC.
University of Life courses

THE ROSICRUCIAN FELLOW-SHIP
Courses in philosophy, astrology and the Bible

ROSICRUCIAN ORDER—A.M.O.R.C.
Courses in ancient secrets of creation and control of cosmic forces

SELF REALIZATION FELLOW-SHIP
Course in Raja yoga and other teachings of Yogananda

SUFI ORDER
Instruction manual on meditation techniques

UNITED CHURCH OF RELIGIOUS SCIENCE
48 lessons in mental control of your destiny through metaphysics

UNIVERSITY OF THE TREES
Three-year correspondence course in Direct Enlightenment

URANTIA FOUNDATION
Urantia Book of cosmological truths

WAILUA UNIVERSITY OF CONTEMPLATIVE ARTS
Tape cassette course in meditation and Hindu mysticism

WELL SPRINGS
Series of relaxation and creative techniques on tape and records

YOGA ORGANIZATION FOR RESEARCH AND EDUCATION
10 lessons in yogic techniques

YOGI GUPTA ASSOCIATION
Yoga instruction in books and on records